STAN MACK'S OUT-TAKES

STAN MACK'S OUT-TAKES*

*Guarantee: All Dialogue Overheard

Foreword by Bob Giraldi

THE OVERLOOK PRESS • Woodstock • New York

For my mother

First published in 1984 by

The Overlook Press
Lewis Hollow Road
Woodstock, New York 12498

Copyright © 1976–1984 by Stan Mack
Foreword © 1984 by The Overlook Press
Portions of this book first appeared in *Adweek*, *The Village Voice*, and *Channels*

Library of Congress Cataloging in Publication Data

Mack, Stan
  Stan Mack's Outtakes.

  I. Title. II. Title: Outtakes.
  PN6728.093M3 1984   741.5′973   84-42756
ISBN 0-87951-986-X (cloth)
ISBN 0-87951-997-5 (paper)

Book design by Bernard Schleifer

FOREWORD

IF WE ALL LOOKED in the mirror the way Stan Mack looks at the world, then there's a good possibility we would soon cure ourselves of all our self-importance, egomania, insecurity, bashfulness and guilt. But since someone's going to get paid to point out the egg all over our faces, I'm just glad it's Stan, because he is a gentleman who always executes his craft with charm, good-naturedness and only the gentlest of prodding. As we take our pratfalls in the slapstick routines of life, Stan Mack chronicles them with an unerring eye and ear, and yet never, ever personally offends any of us. That, I think, is a true sign of a classy humorist.

In this book, the creative community of New York is Stan's microcosm, and the glaring conceits and inconceivable absurdities encountered there are only small examples of more universal ironies. In professions such as advertising, publishing and (God forbid) film—all known havens for the neurotic—Stan, with his usual relentless honesty, uncovers and mentions all the embarrassing unmentionables of the human condition, and always with the unjudgmental and easy grace of a benevolent outside observer. In fact, Stan's objectivity is one of his greatest strengths. He never makes an assumption or claim, never levys blame, never attempts to tell us what to see or think. Stan's work is like *cinema verite* in a syndicated strip. He just turns on the camera and lets the film roll—the world puts its foot in its mouth well enough without direction.

In many of Stan Mack's strips, you will recognize in the wings self-portraits of the humorist, a short, ever-curious, note-jotting Stan with shaggy mustache and slouchy wardrobe, usually darting a whimsical smile or knowing glance, often the brunt of the joke himself. It's the fact that Stan the cartoonist can also mock Stan the man that makes me admire him so much. For when a person laughs at himself and his own foolishness, you also see the humor in yourself, and anyone who shows us something about ourselves deserves our highest accolades, to my way of thinking.

It seems that the feeling you come away with most in these illustrations—besides the blushing—is the complicity and understanding of the cartoonist. Stan leaves you with the feeling that he has been there before, that he has suffered all the same humiliations and anxieties as the people he draws. When Stan sketches a character, he gives everyone in the world a soulmate, someone to sympathize with. When he outlines a situation, he steps into some past moment of our lives and relives it with us. Suffice it to say, when you look at these "outtakes" by Stan, you won't just read cartoons in the ordinary sense; you'll take a gander at yourself, human interaction, society, and all the experiences and lessons of life.

Stan Mack is no less than a sort of pop-psychologist for the comic book set, a Freud of the Funnies. As a victim of his wit, and represented in these pages, I can say without hesitation that I consider it a kind of honor to have been publicly "shrunk" by him and still not feel like a nerd.

BOB GIRALDI

New York City, 1984

INTRODUCTION

AT FIRST GLANCE this book looks like a collection of comic strips about the media business. Certainly they look like comic strips. There's a row of boxes, funny looking people running around inside the boxes, and word balloons popping up over everyone's head. And there are lots of words inside the balloons. But there's something different about the words. You see, other cartoonists make up words and put them in fictional characters' mouths. My words are real. I take real words out of the mouths of real people.

Other comic strip artists work out of their own heads. They stare out of windows. They read the newspaper. They go for coffee with other cartoonists. They think! A lot. Eventually a light bulb clicks on over their heads, and they copy down the words illuminated by the light. I don't do that. I go to where people are busy at work. I try to hang around where advertising strategies are being planned, where commercials are being shot, where workers are complaining about their lot. I hear words I couldn't make up. I think, "That's something I would never have tought of. I'll just write it down." I work out of other peoples' heads.

The problem is getting to where the busy people are. The problem is being invited into the workplace, to the advertising agencies, production houses, studios where they're saying what to whom about which. . . . I can't recognize it if I don't hear it. But that means I might hear a business secret—a new tactic, a new strategy, a new "new and improved." And that's a fair concern. The funny thing is, I probably wouldn't recognize a secret if I fell over one. And for me, secrets aren't funny; gossip is boring, and business news is ho-hum. Business talk in these strips is just jargon leading up to the punch line. What's funny to me is the trivial, the human, the universal, the PEOPLE in the workplace. So I make a promise—a promise not always easily kept—to name no names (unless the subject agrees) and to gossip no gossip. And so people who enjoy a smile invite me in.

I hang out, listening and scribbling in my pad. Is it funny? Who knows, just write it down and worry about it later. Eventually, before overstaying my welcome, I thank everybody and wander off. Later, I go through my pad, copying out bits and pieces of dialogue. I think about the people and who said what to whom. I arrange and rearrange the words. A story emerges. Imagine, an art director on an aluminum foil account, in the middle of a serious creative session, suddenly gets nostalgic. He remembers the days of his youth—before the miraculous protective qualities of aluminum foil—when the smells and oils of his lunch seeped through their wax paper covering to tantalize him for an hour before the lunch bell. "Hey," I think, "I remember how my tuna fish sandwiches smelled. I can almost taste them now!" THAT'S FUN-NY! I'm going with it!"

So the hanging around is over. The editing is over. And now comes the visual. I look at the words and I think about who spoke them. How were they dressed? How did they look? How did they act. I sketch out the room, rough in the words, and take pen in hand. I draw a line. I draw a circle. It's a nose! I draw a face. It's the face of the art director in my story. But with a funny nose. I draw another face. It's the copywriter. He looks funny, too. Maybe it's what he's saying. I keep drawing. The characters move. They speak. Time rushes forward from box to box. . . . All of this is to the beat of the words. Magically, the media busness comes to life. It's real dialogue with a lot of exclamation marks, cartoonish pratfalls and rubbery faces. After all, I guarantee the accuracy of the words. I never guarantee the accuracy of the noses.

S.M.

STAN MACK'S OUT-TAKES

Applying for a Snow Job

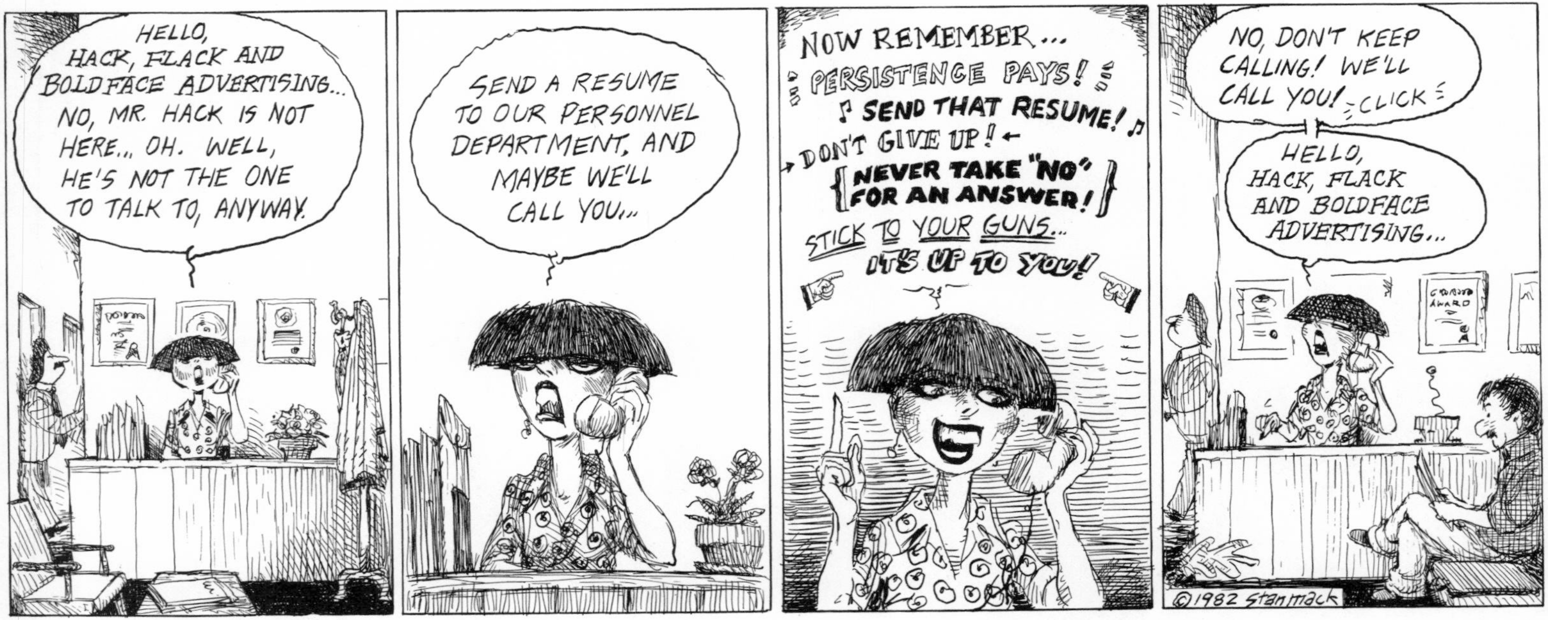
HELLO, HACK, FLACK AND BOLDFACE ADVERTISING... NO, MR. HACK IS NOT HERE... OH. WELL, HE'S NOT THE ONE TO TALK TO, ANYWAY.
SEND A RESUME TO OUR PERSONNEL DEPARTMENT, AND MAYBE WE'LL CALL YOU...
NOW REMEMBER...
PERSISTENCE PAYS!
SEND THAT RESUME!
DON'T GIVE UP!
NEVER TAKE "NO" FOR AN ANSWER!
STICK TO YOUR GUNS...
IT'S UP TO YOU!
NO, DON'T KEEP CALLING! WE'LL CALL YOU!
CLICK
HELLO, HACK, FLACK AND BOLDFACE ADVERTISING...
©1982 Stan Mack

Soapy Sales

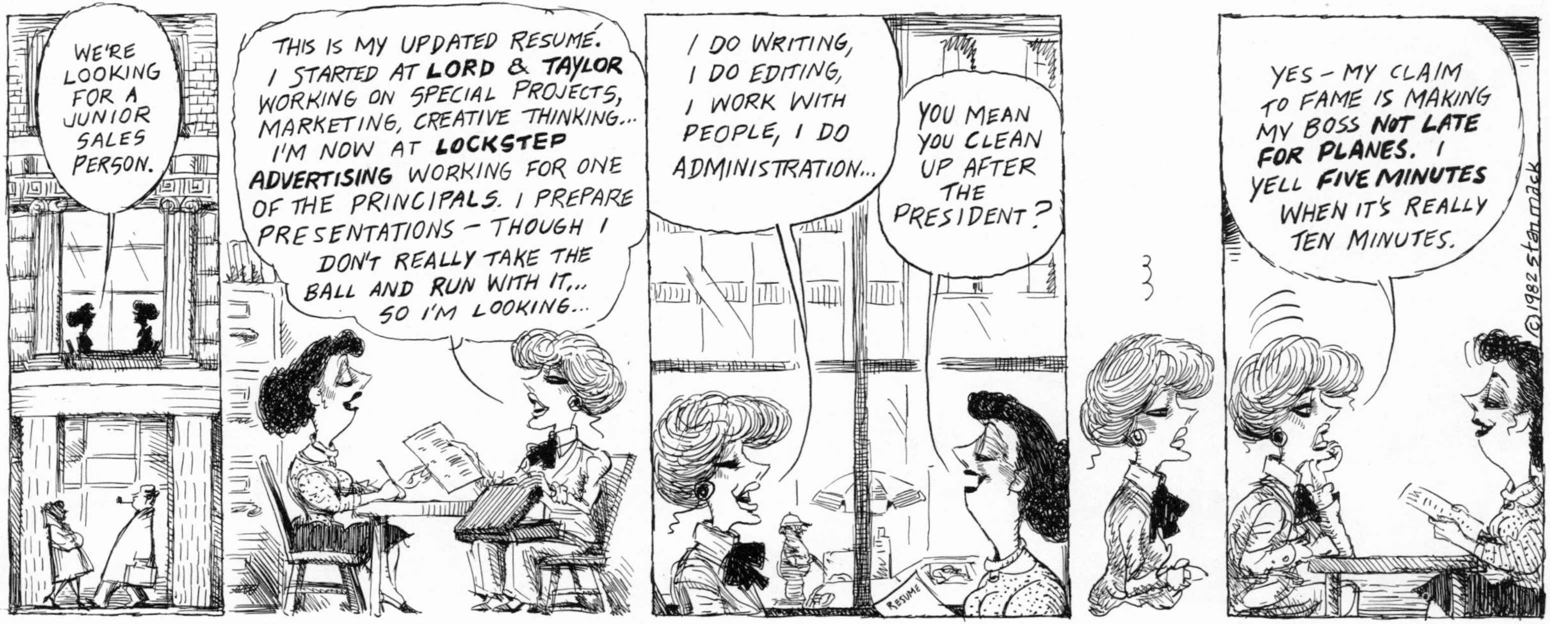
WE'RE LOOKING FOR A JUNIOR SALES PERSON.
THIS IS MY UPDATED RESUMÉ. I STARTED AT LORD & TAYLOR WORKING ON SPECIAL PROJECTS, MARKETING, CREATIVE THINKING... I'M NOW AT LOCKSTEP ADVERTISING WORKING FOR ONE OF THE PRINCIPALS. I PREPARE PRESENTATIONS – THOUGH I DON'T REALLY TAKE THE BALL AND RUN WITH IT... SO I'M LOOKING...
I DO WRITING, I DO EDITING, I WORK WITH PEOPLE, I DO ADMINISTRATION...
YOU MEAN YOU CLEAN UP AFTER THE PRESIDENT?
RESUME
YES – MY CLAIM TO FAME IS MAKING MY BOSS NOT LATE FOR PLANES. I YELL FIVE MINUTES WHEN IT'S REALLY TEN MINUTES.
© 1982 stamack

The Loony Tune

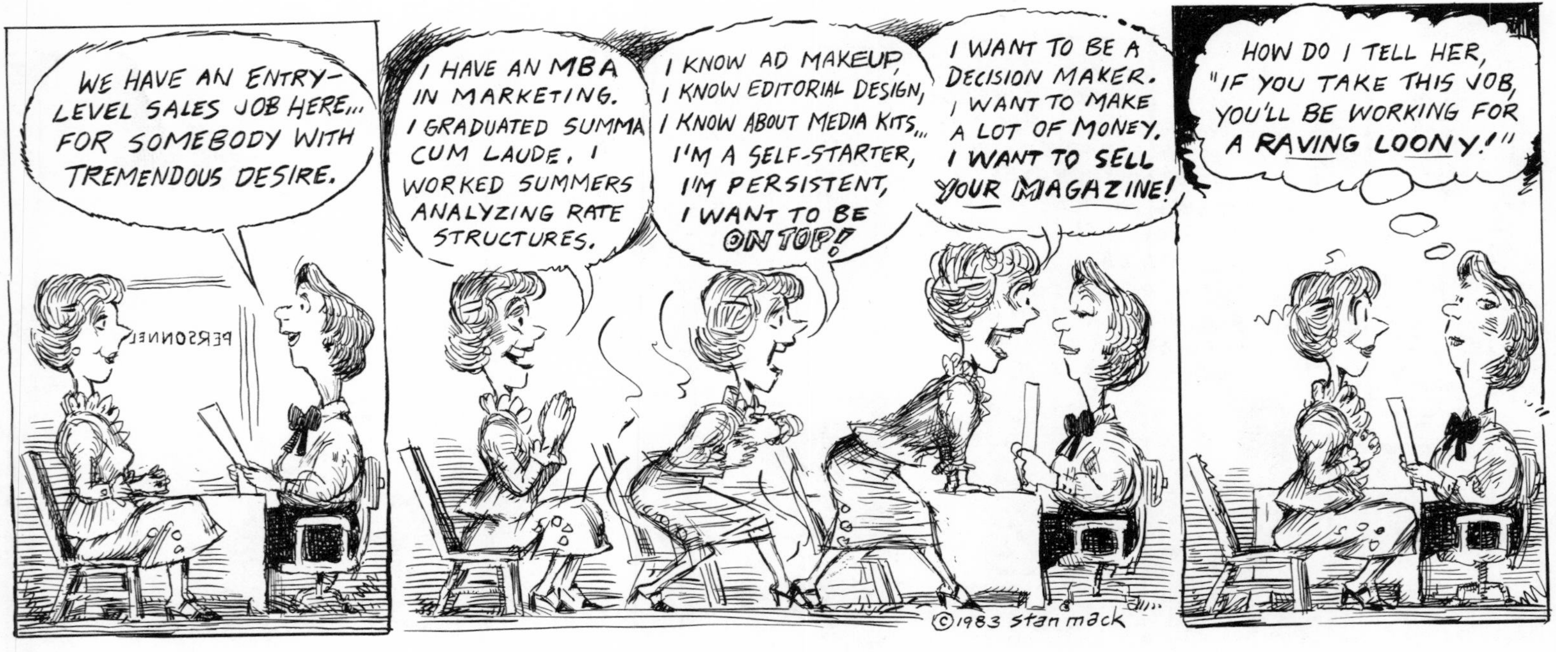
WE HAVE AN ENTRY-LEVEL SALES JOB HERE... FOR SOMEBODY WITH TREMENDOUS DESIRE.
PERSONNEL
I HAVE AN MBA IN MARKETING. I GRADUATED SUMMA CUM LAUDE. I WORKED SUMMERS ANALYZING RATE STRUCTURES.
I KNOW AD MAKEUP, I KNOW EDITORIAL DESIGN, I KNOW ABOUT MEDIA KITS... I'M A SELF-STARTER, I'M PERSISTENT, I WANT TO BE ON TOP!
I WANT TO BE A DECISION MAKER. I WANT TO MAKE A LOT OF MONEY. I WANT TO SELL YOUR MAGAZINE!
HOW DO I TELL HER, "IF YOU TAKE THIS JOB, YOU'LL BE WORKING FOR A RAVING LOONY!"
©1983 stan mack

No Shrinking Violets

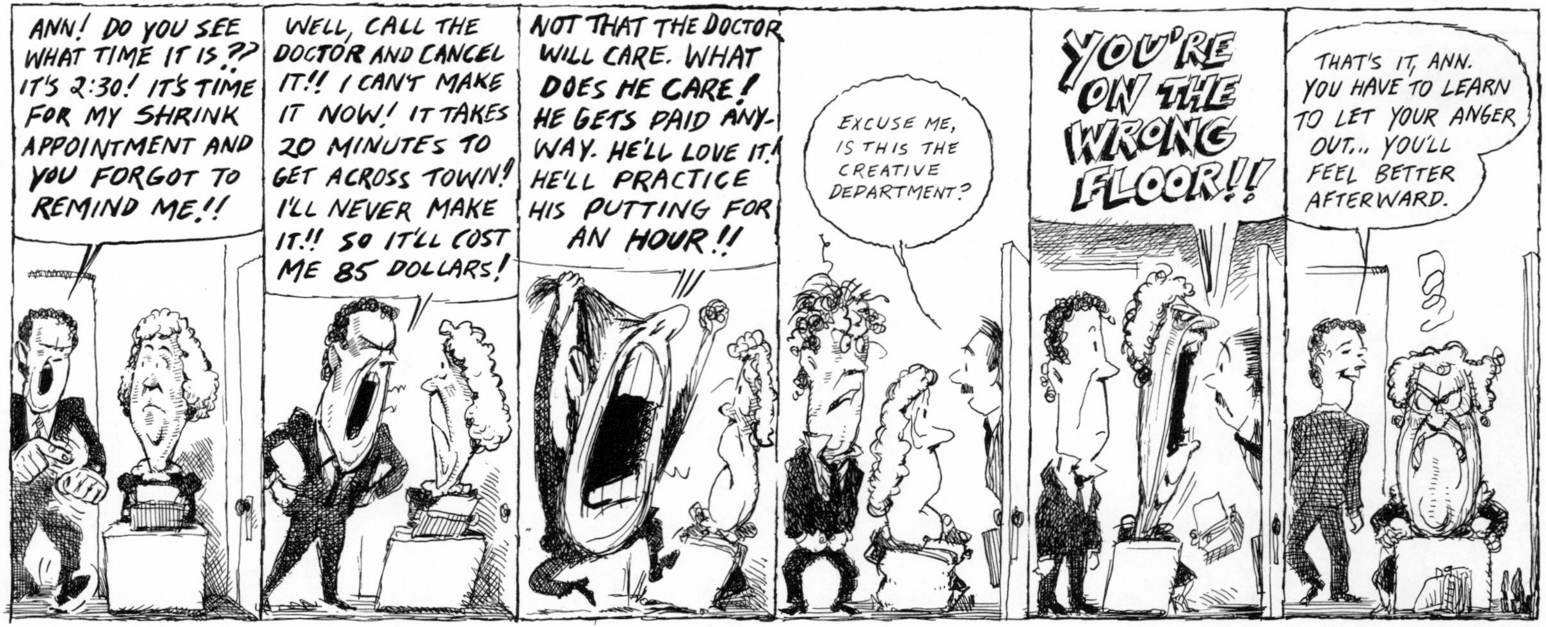
ANN! DO YOU SEE WHAT TIME IT IS?? IT'S 2:30! IT'S TIME FOR MY SHRINK APPOINTMENT AND YOU FORGOT TO REMIND ME!!
WELL, CALL THE DOCTOR AND CANCEL IT!! I CAN'T MAKE IT NOW! IT TAKES 20 MINUTES TO GET ACROSS TOWN! I'LL NEVER MAKE IT!! SO IT'LL COST ME 85 DOLLARS!
NOT THAT THE DOCTOR WILL CARE. WHAT DOES HE CARE! HE GETS PAID ANYWAY. HE'LL LOVE IT! HE'LL PRACTICE HIS PUTTING FOR AN HOUR!!
EXCUSE ME, IS THIS THE CREATIVE DEPARTMENT?
YOU'RE ON THE WRONG FLOOR!!
THAT'S IT, ANN. YOU HAVE TO LEARN TO LET YOUR ANGER OUT... YOU'LL FEEL BETTER AFTERWARD.

Moxie

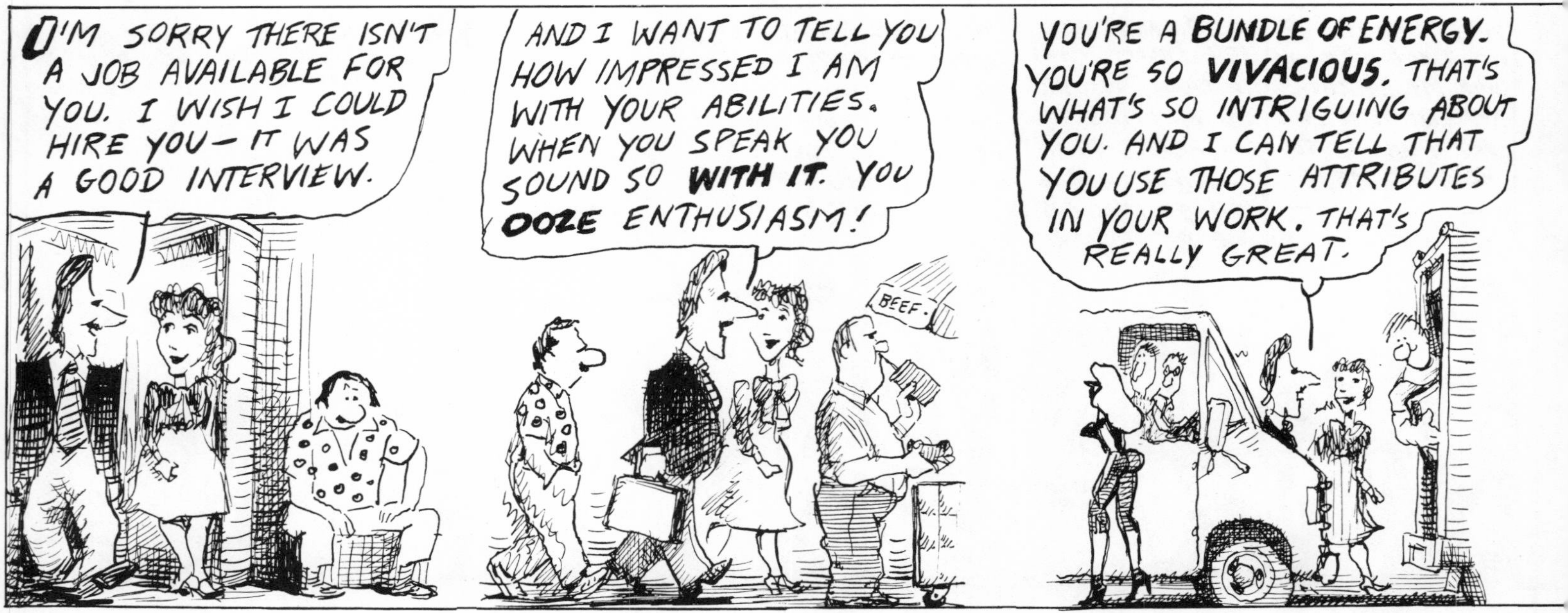
I'M SORRY THERE ISN'T A JOB AVAILABLE FOR YOU. I WISH I COULD HIRE YOU— IT WAS A GOOD INTERVIEW.
AND I WANT TO TELL YOU HOW IMPRESSED I AM WITH YOUR ABILITIES. WHEN YOU SPEAK YOU SOUND SO WITH IT. YOU OOZE ENTHUSIASM!
BEEF.
YOU'RE A BUNDLE OF ENERGY. YOU'RE SO VIVACIOUS. THAT'S WHAT'S SO INTRIGUING ABOUT YOU. AND I CAN TELL THAT YOU USE THOSE ATTRIBUTES IN YOUR WORK. THAT'S REALLY GREAT.

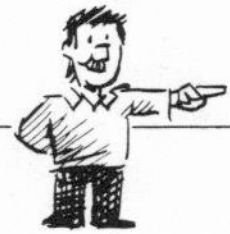

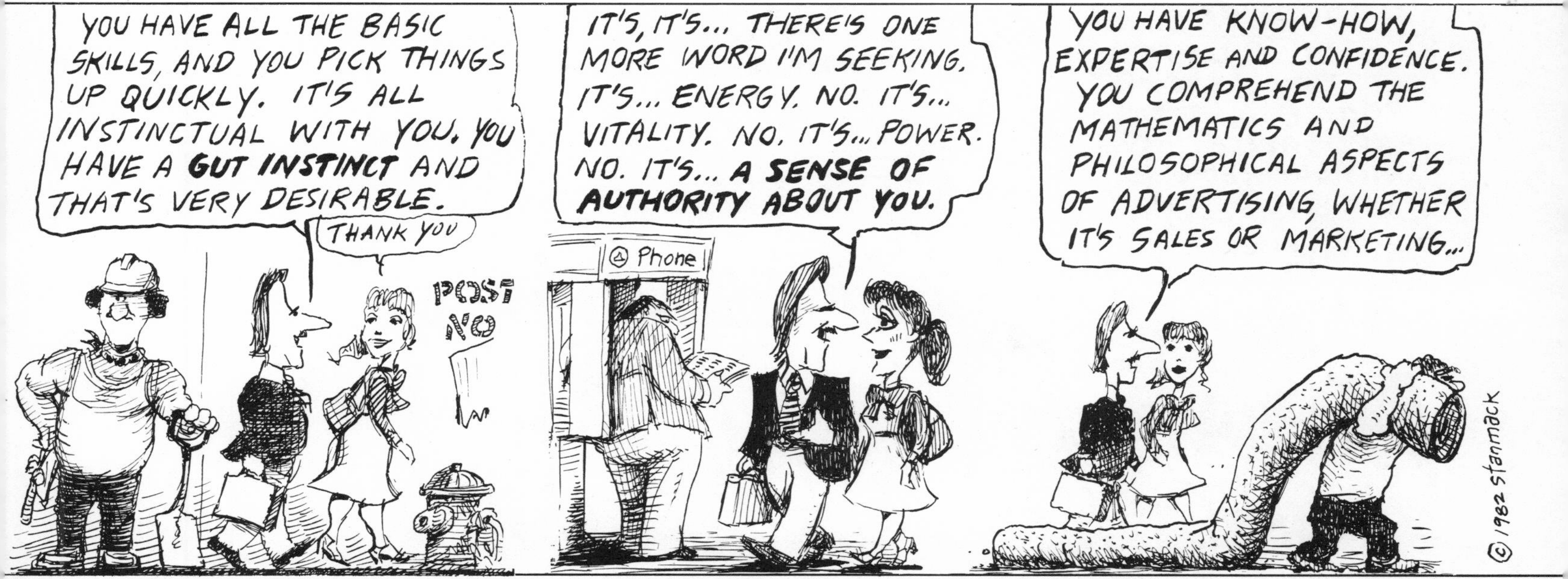
YOU HAVE ALL THE BASIC SKILLS, AND YOU PICK THINGS UP QUICKLY. IT'S ALL INSTINCTUAL WITH YOU. YOU HAVE A **GUT INSTINCT** AND THAT'S VERY DESIRABLE.
THANK YOU
POST NO
Phone
IT'S, IT'S... THERE'S ONE MORE WORD I'M SEEKING. IT'S... ENERGY. NO. IT'S... VITALITY. NO. IT'S... POWER. NO. IT'S... **A SENSE OF AUTHORITY ABOUT YOU.**
YOU HAVE KNOW-HOW, EXPERTISE AND CONFIDENCE. YOU COMPREHEND THE MATHEMATICS AND PHILOSOPHICAL ASPECTS OF ADVERTISING, WHETHER IT'S SALES OR MARKETING...
© 1982 stanmack

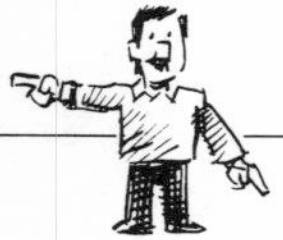

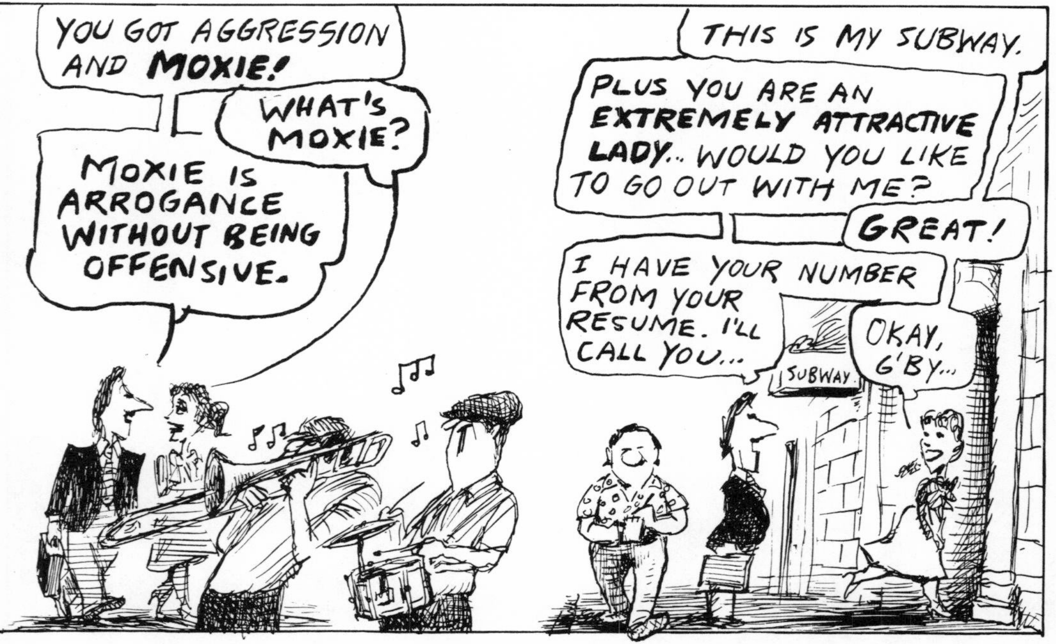
YOU GOT AGGRESSION AND MOXIE!
WHAT'S MOXIE?
MOXIE IS ARROGANCE WITHOUT BEING OFFENSIVE.
THIS IS MY SUBWAY.
PLUS YOU ARE AN EXTREMELY ATTRACTIVE LADY.. WOULD YOU LIKE TO GO OUT WITH ME?
GREAT!
I HAVE YOUR NUMBER FROM YOUR RESUME. I'LL CALL YOU...
OKAY, G'BY...
SUBWAY

The Sting

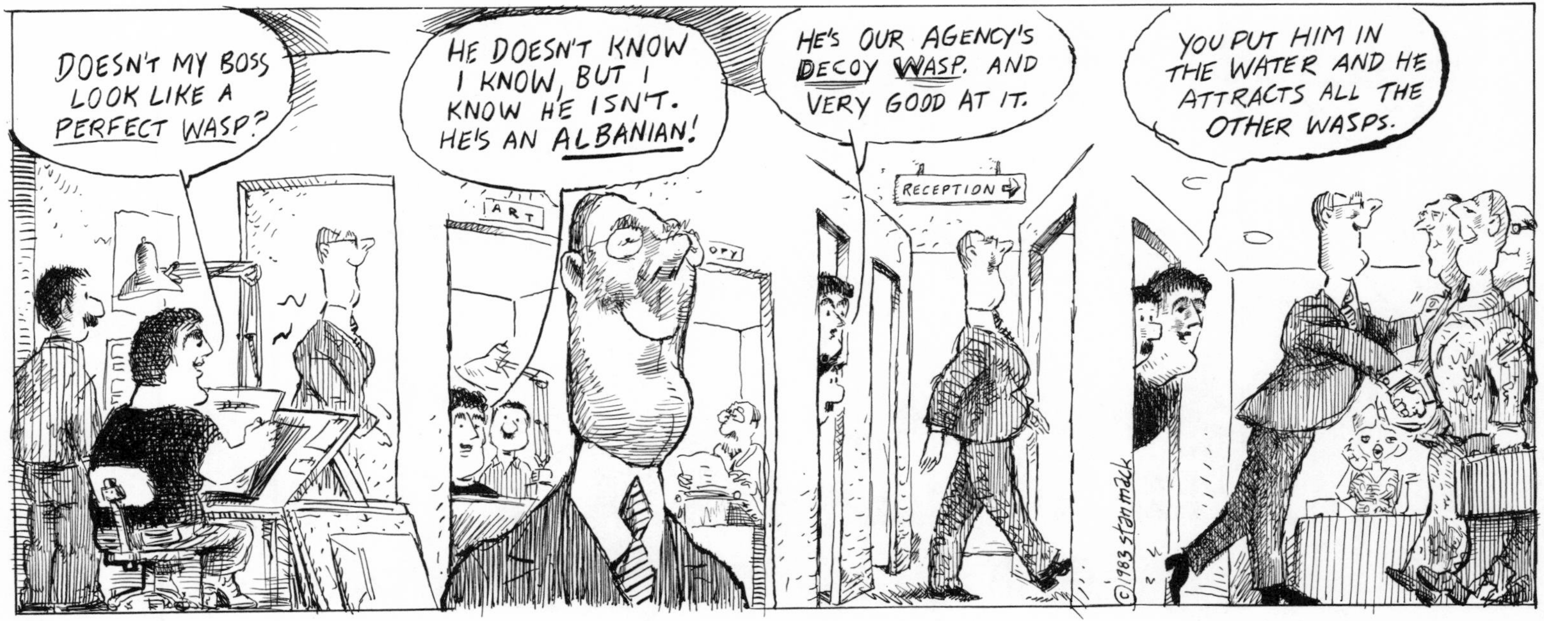
DOESN'T MY BOSS LOOK LIKE A PERFECT WASP?
HE DOESN'T KNOW I KNOW, BUT I KNOW HE ISN'T. HE'S AN ALBANIAN!
ART
HE'S OUR AGENCY'S DECOY WASP. AND VERY GOOD AT IT.
RECEPTION
©1983 stan mack
YOU PUT HIM IN THE WATER AND HE ATTRACTS ALL THE OTHER WASPS.

Central Caste-ing

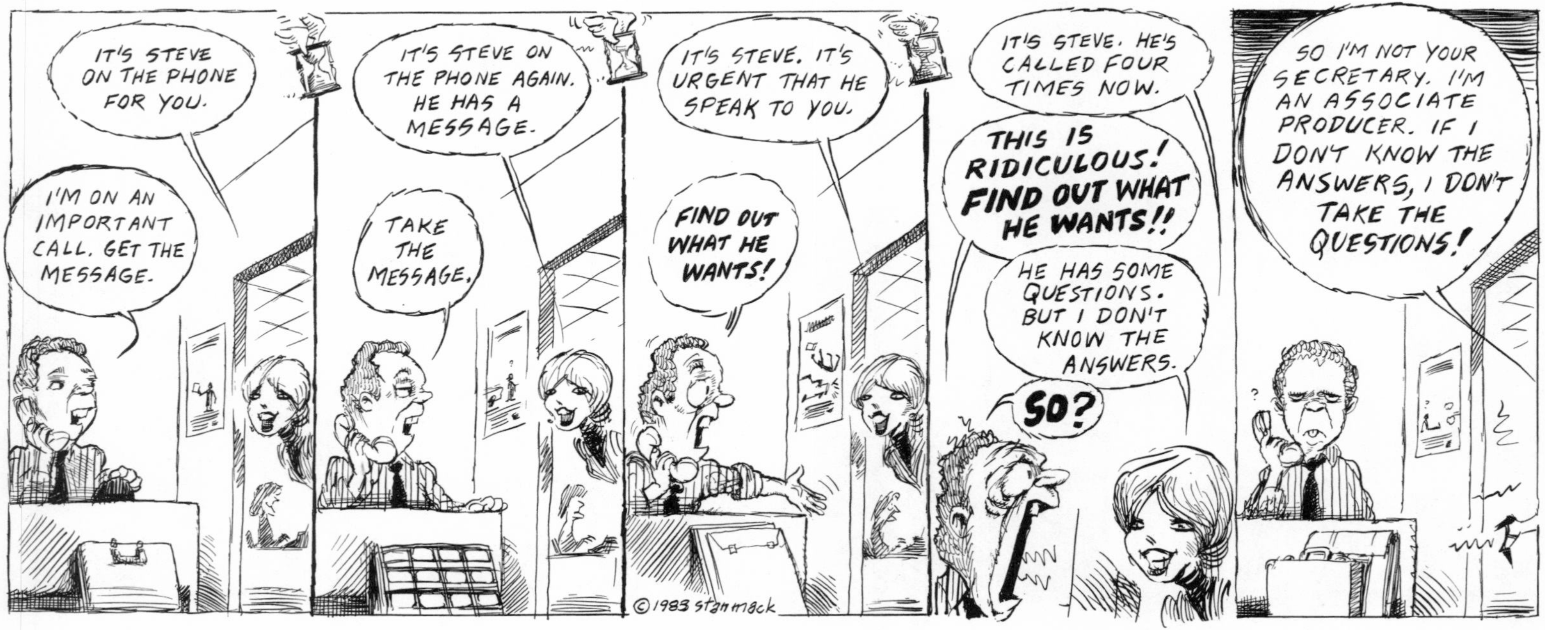
IT'S STEVE ON THE PHONE FOR YOU.
I'M ON AN IMPORTANT CALL. GET THE MESSAGE.
IT'S STEVE ON THE PHONE AGAIN. HE HAS A MESSAGE.
TAKE THE MESSAGE.
IT'S STEVE. IT'S URGENT THAT HE SPEAK TO YOU.
FIND OUT WHAT HE WANTS!
IT'S STEVE. HE'S CALLED FOUR TIMES NOW.
THIS IS RIDICULOUS! FIND OUT WHAT HE WANTS!!
HE HAS SOME QUESTIONS. BUT I DON'T KNOW THE ANSWERS.
SO?
SO I'M NOT YOUR SECRETARY. I'M AN ASSOCIATE PRODUCER. IF I DON'T KNOW THE ANSWERS, I DON'T TAKE THE QUESTIONS!
©1983 stan mack

What a Bummer

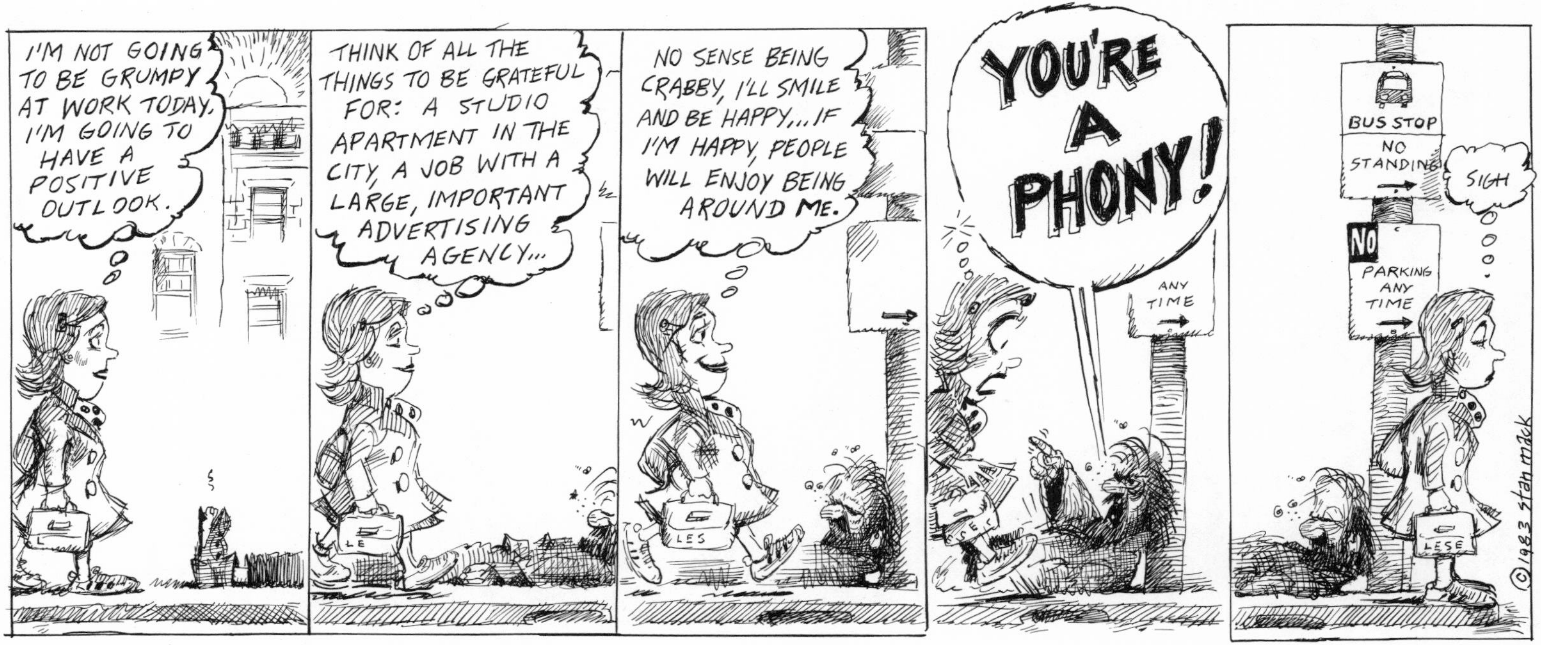
I'M NOT GOING TO BE GRUMPY AT WORK TODAY. I'M GOING TO HAVE A POSITIVE OUTLOOK.
THINK OF ALL THE THINGS TO BE GRATEFUL FOR: A STUDIO APARTMENT IN THE CITY, A JOB WITH A LARGE, IMPORTANT ADVERTISING AGENCY...
NO SENSE BEING CRABBY, I'LL SMILE AND BE HAPPY... IF I'M HAPPY, PEOPLE WILL ENJOY BEING AROUND ME.
YOU'RE A PHONY!
ANY TIME
BUS STOP
NO STANDING
NO
PARKING ANY TIME
SIGH
©1983 stan mack

Slick Talker

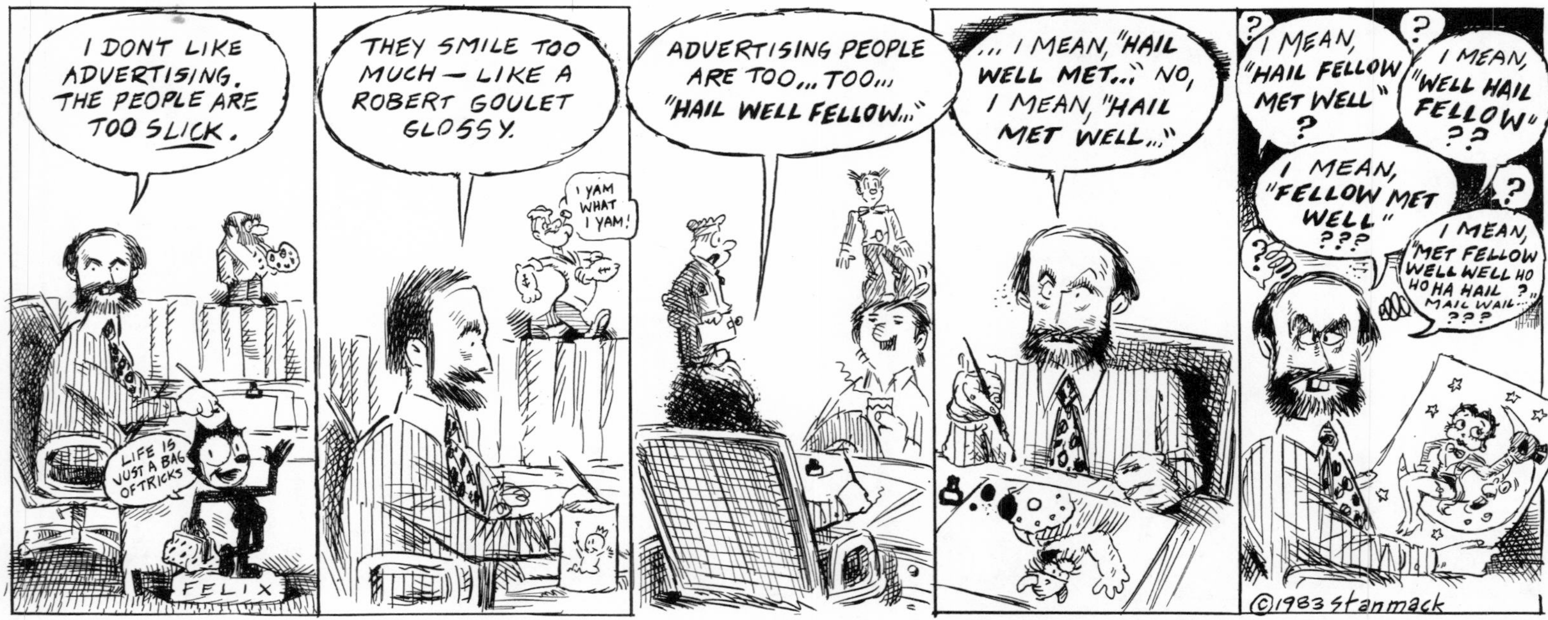
I DON'T LIKE ADVERTISING. THE PEOPLE ARE TOO SLICK.
LIFE IS VUST A BAG OF TRICKS
FELIX
THEY SMILE TOO MUCH — LIKE A ROBERT GOULET GLOSSY.
I YAM WHAT I YAM!
ADVERTISING PEOPLE ARE TOO... TOO... "HAIL WELL FELLOW..."
... I MEAN, "HAIL WELL MET..." NO, I MEAN, "HAIL MET WELL..."
I MEAN, "HAIL FELLOW MET WELL" ?
I MEAN, "WELL HAIL FELLOW" ??
I MEAN, "FELLOW MET WELL" ???
I MEAN, "MET FELLOW WELL WELL HO HO HA HAIL ? MAIL WAIL..." ???
©1983 stanmack

Ad Glib

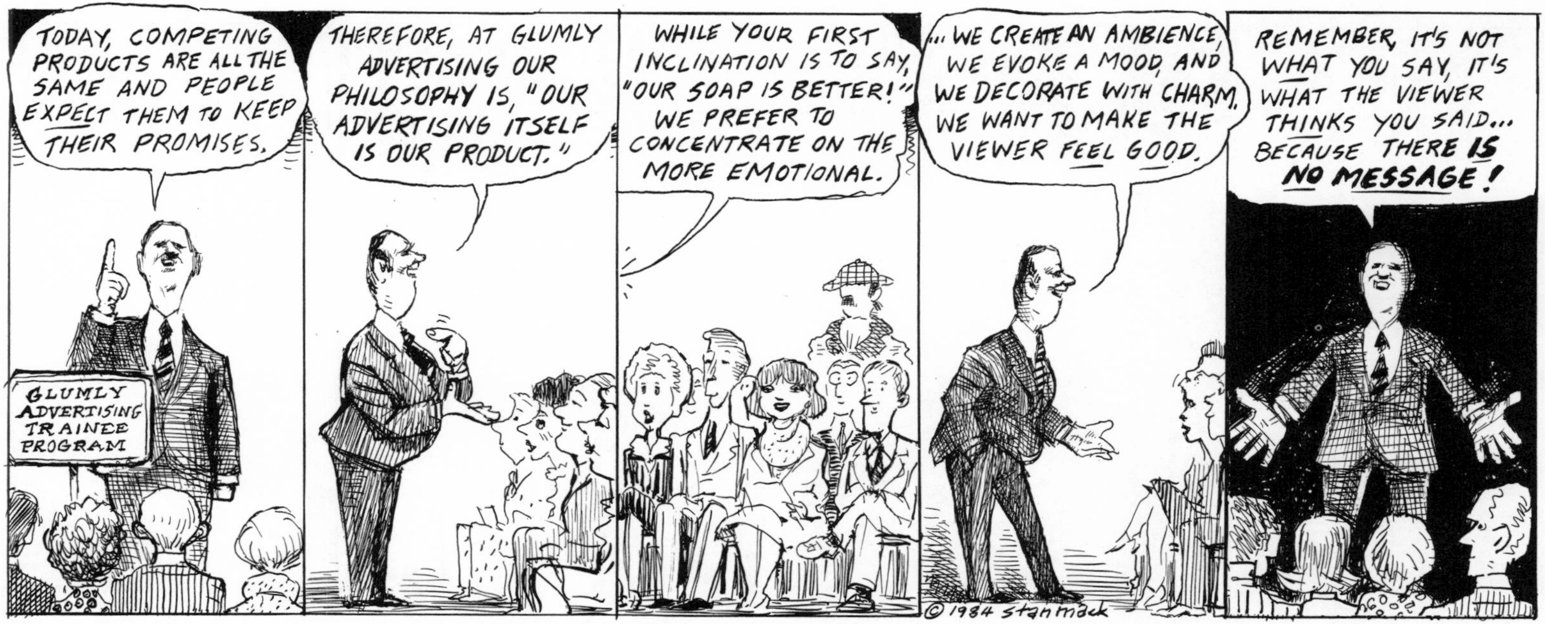

TODAY, COMPETING PRODUCTS ARE ALL THE SAME AND PEOPLE EXPECT THEM TO KEEP THEIR PROMISES.
GLUMLY ADVERTISING TRAINEE PROGRAM
THEREFORE, AT GLUMLY ADVERTISING OUR PHILOSOPHY IS, "OUR ADVERTISING ITSELF IS OUR PRODUCT."
WHILE YOUR FIRST INCLINATION IS TO SAY, "OUR SOAP IS BETTER!" WE PREFER TO CONCENTRATE ON THE MORE EMOTIONAL.
... WE CREATE AN AMBIENCE, WE EVOKE A MOOD, AND WE DECORATE WITH CHARM. WE WANT TO MAKE THE VIEWER FEEL GOOD.
REMEMBER, IT'S NOT WHAT YOU SAY, IT'S WHAT THE VIEWER THINKS YOU SAID... BECAUSE THERE IS NO MESSAGE!
© 1984 stan mack

A Cast of Thousands

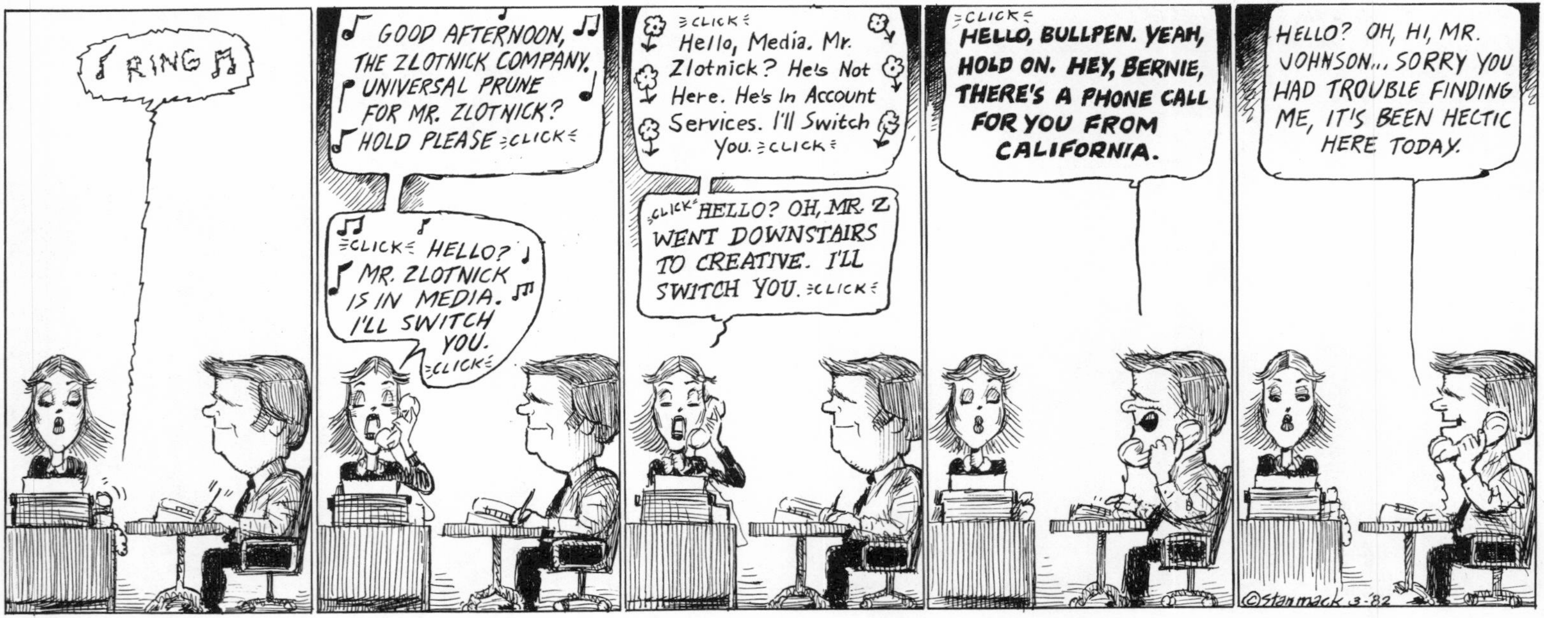
RING
GOOD AFTERNOON, THE ZLOTNICK COMPANY. UNIVERSAL PRUNE FOR MR. ZLOTNICK? HOLD PLEASE CLICK
CLICK HELLO? MR. ZLOTNICK IS IN MEDIA. I'LL SWITCH YOU. CLICK
CLICK Hello, Media. Mr. Zlotnick? He's Not Here. He's In Account Services. I'll Switch You. CLICK
CLICK HELLO? OH, MR. Z WENT DOWNSTAIRS TO CREATIVE. I'LL SWITCH YOU. CLICK
CLICK HELLO, BULLPEN. YEAH, HOLD ON. HEY, BERNIE, THERE'S A PHONE CALL FOR YOU FROM CALIFORNIA.
HELLO? OH, HI, MR. JOHNSON... SORRY YOU HAD TROUBLE FINDING ME, IT'S BEEN HECTIC HERE TODAY.
©Stanmack 3-'82

Truth in Selling

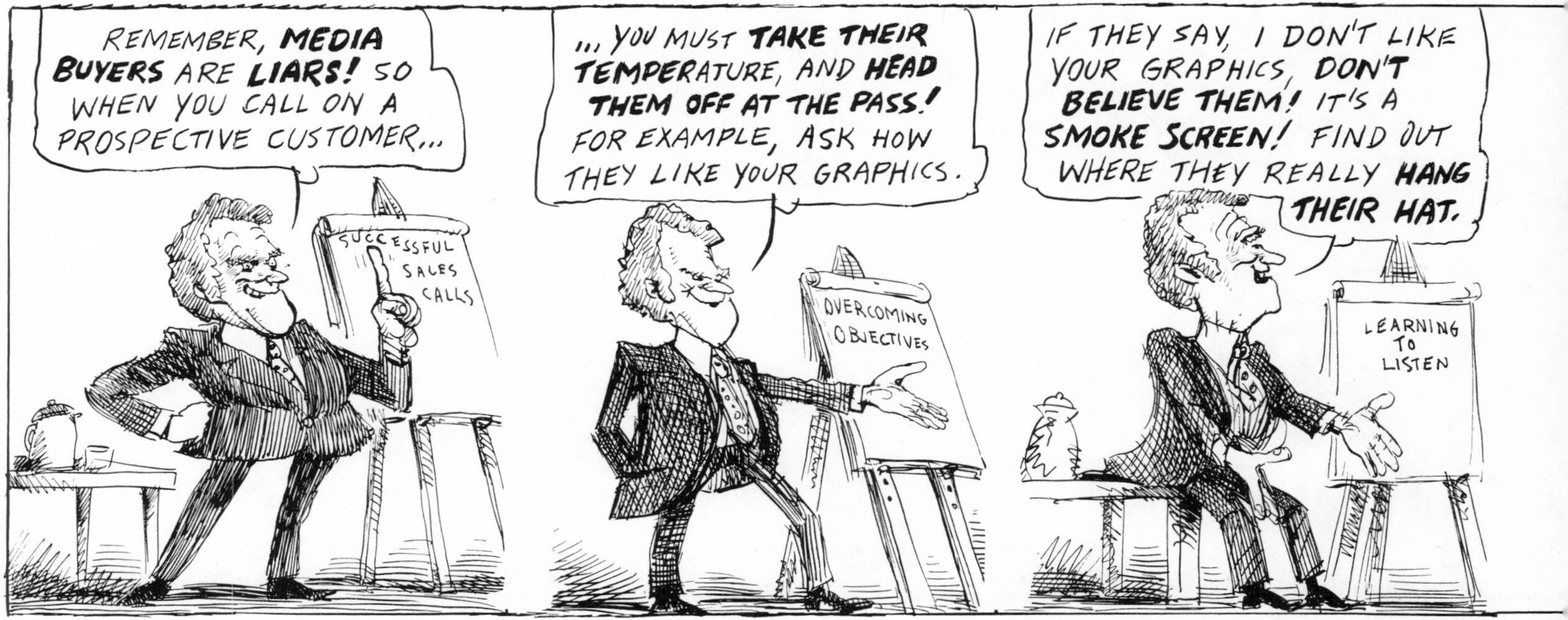

REMEMBER, MEDIA BUYERS ARE LIARS! SO WHEN YOU CALL ON A PROSPECTIVE CUSTOMER...
SUCCESSFUL SALES CALLS
..., YOU MUST TAKE THEIR TEMPERATURE, AND HEAD THEM OFF AT THE PASS! FOR EXAMPLE, ASK HOW THEY LIKE YOUR GRAPHICS.
OVERCOMING OBJECTIVES
IF THEY SAY, I DON'T LIKE YOUR GRAPHICS, DON'T BELIEVE THEM! IT'S A SMOKE SCREEN! FIND OUT WHERE THEY REALLY HANG THEIR HAT.
LEARNING TO LISTEN

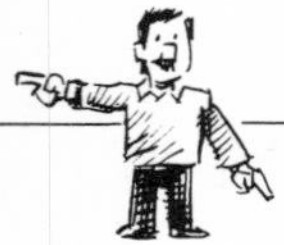

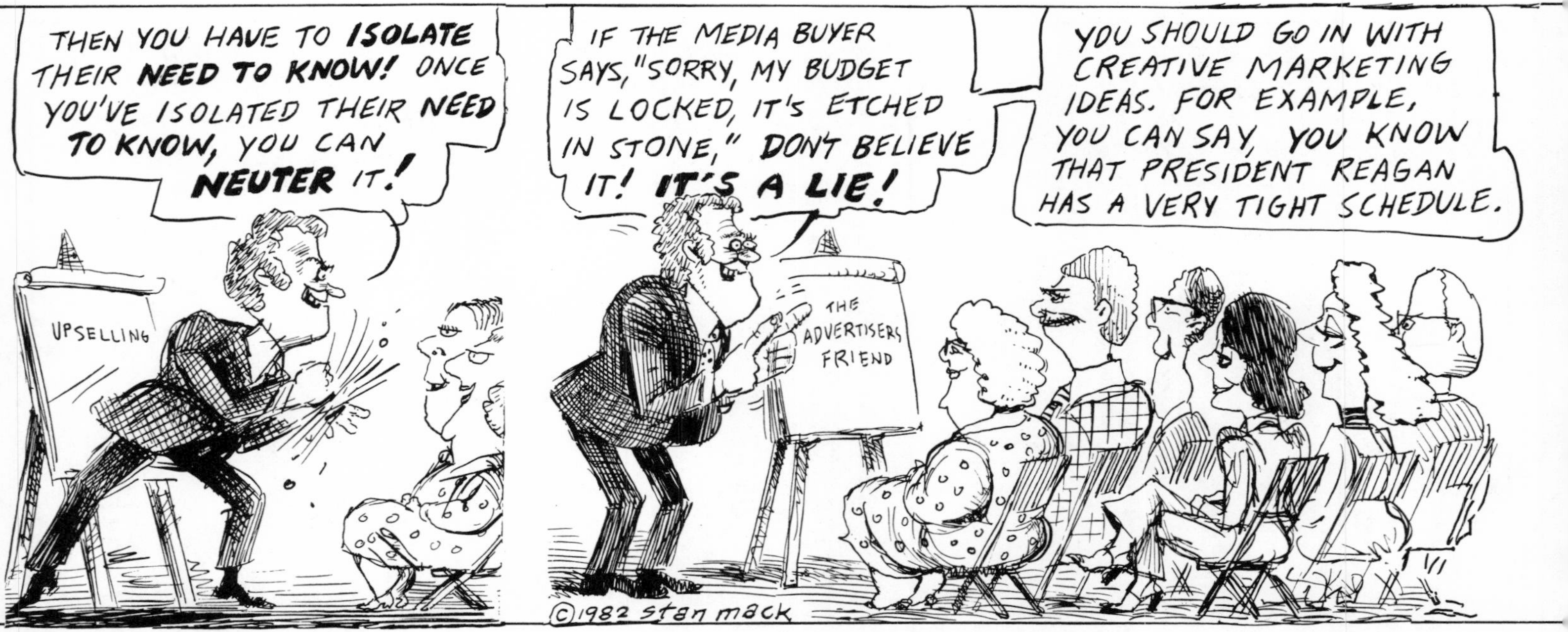
THEN YOU HAVE TO ISOLATE THEIR NEED TO KNOW! ONCE YOU'VE ISOLATED THEIR NEED TO KNOW, YOU CAN NEUTER IT!
UPSELLING
IF THE MEDIA BUYER SAYS, "SORRY, MY BUDGET IS LOCKED, IT'S ETCHED IN STONE," DON'T BELIEVE IT! IT'S A LIE!
THE ADVERTISERS FRIEND
YOU SHOULD GO IN WITH CREATIVE MARKETING IDEAS. FOR EXAMPLE, YOU CAN SAY, YOU KNOW THAT PRESIDENT REAGAN HAS A VERY TIGHT SCHEDULE.
©1982 stan mack

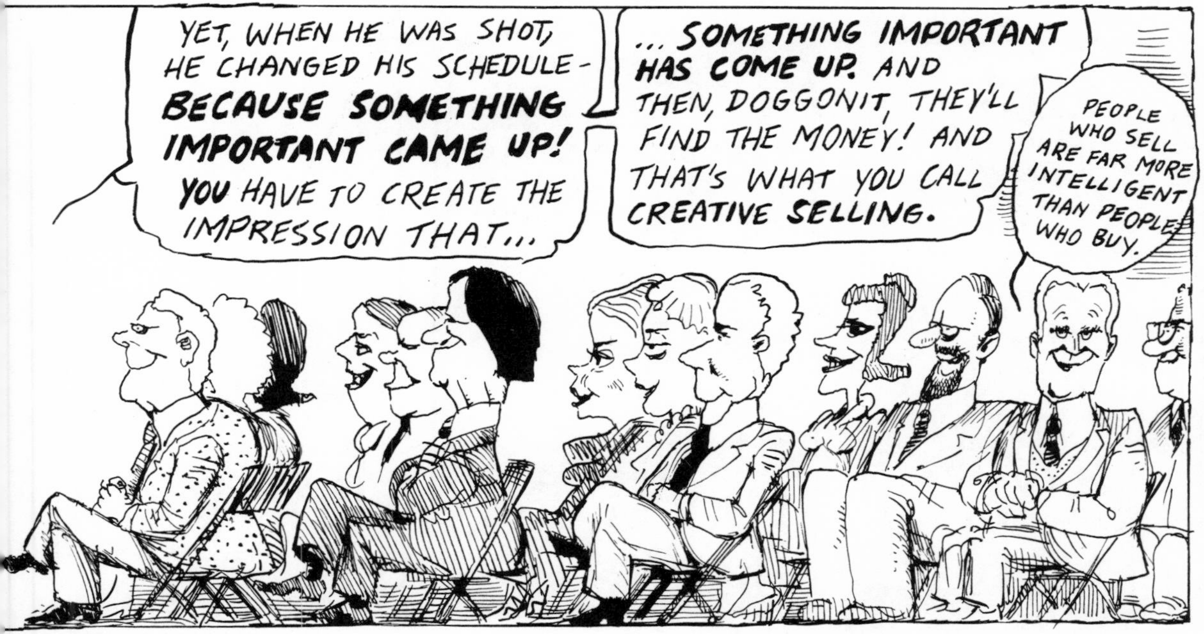
YET, WHEN HE WAS SHOT, HE CHANGED HIS SCHEDULE- BECAUSE SOMETHING IMPORTANT CAME UP! YOU HAVE TO CREATE THE IMPRESSION THAT...
... SOMETHING IMPORTANT HAS COME UP. AND THEN, DOGGONIT, THEY'LL FIND THE MONEY! AND THAT'S WHAT YOU CALL CREATIVE SELLING.
PEOPLE WHO SELL ARE FAR MORE INTELLIGENT THAN PEOPLE WHO BUY.

Ah, Grace Under Pressure

The Slick-Fielding Receptionist

Question of Ethics

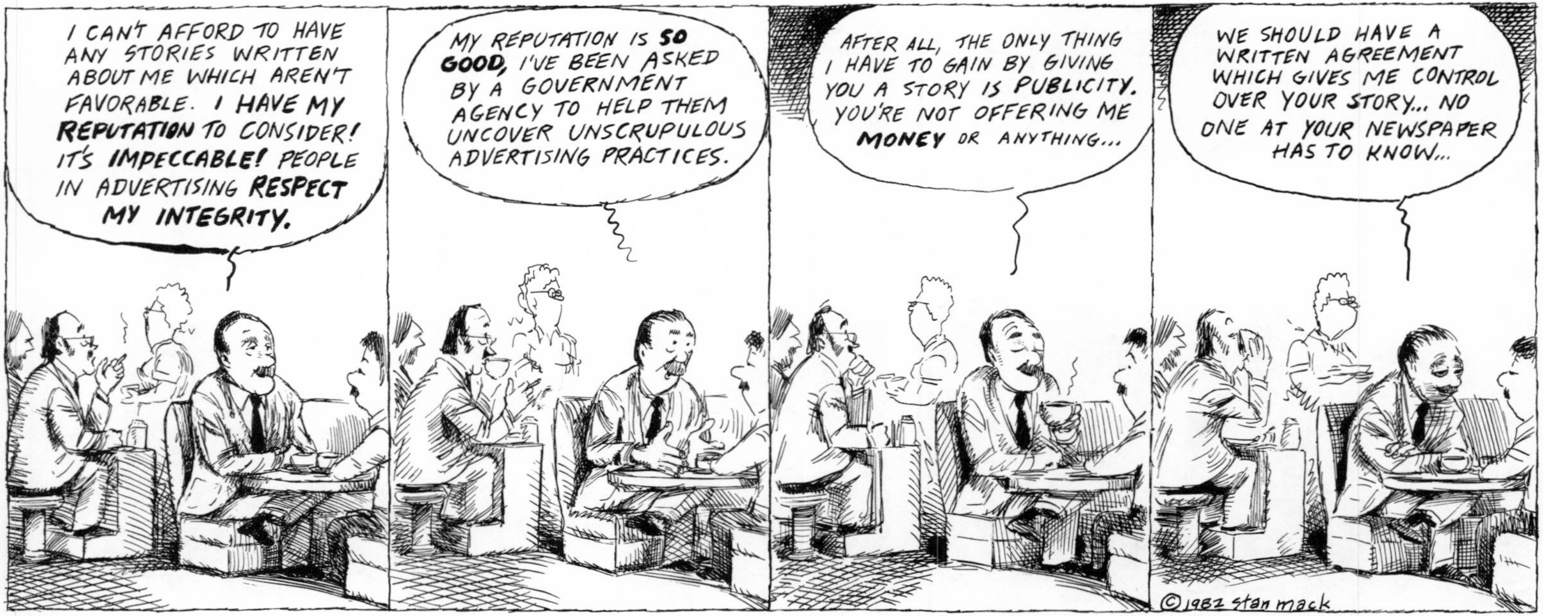

I CAN'T AFFORD TO HAVE ANY STORIES WRITTEN ABOUT ME WHICH AREN'T FAVORABLE. I HAVE MY REPUTATION TO CONSIDER! IT'S IMPECCABLE! PEOPLE IN ADVERTISING RESPECT MY INTEGRITY.
MY REPUTATION IS SO GOOD, I'VE BEEN ASKED BY A GOVERNMENT AGENCY TO HELP THEM UNCOVER UNSCRUPULOUS ADVERTISING PRACTICES.
AFTER ALL, THE ONLY THING I HAVE TO GAIN BY GIVING YOU A STORY IS PUBLICITY. YOU'RE NOT OFFERING ME MONEY OR ANYTHING...
WE SHOULD HAVE A WRITTEN AGREEMENT WHICH GIVES ME CONTROL OVER YOUR STORY... NO ONE AT YOUR NEWSPAPER HAS TO KNOW...
©1982 stan mack

No-Account Executive

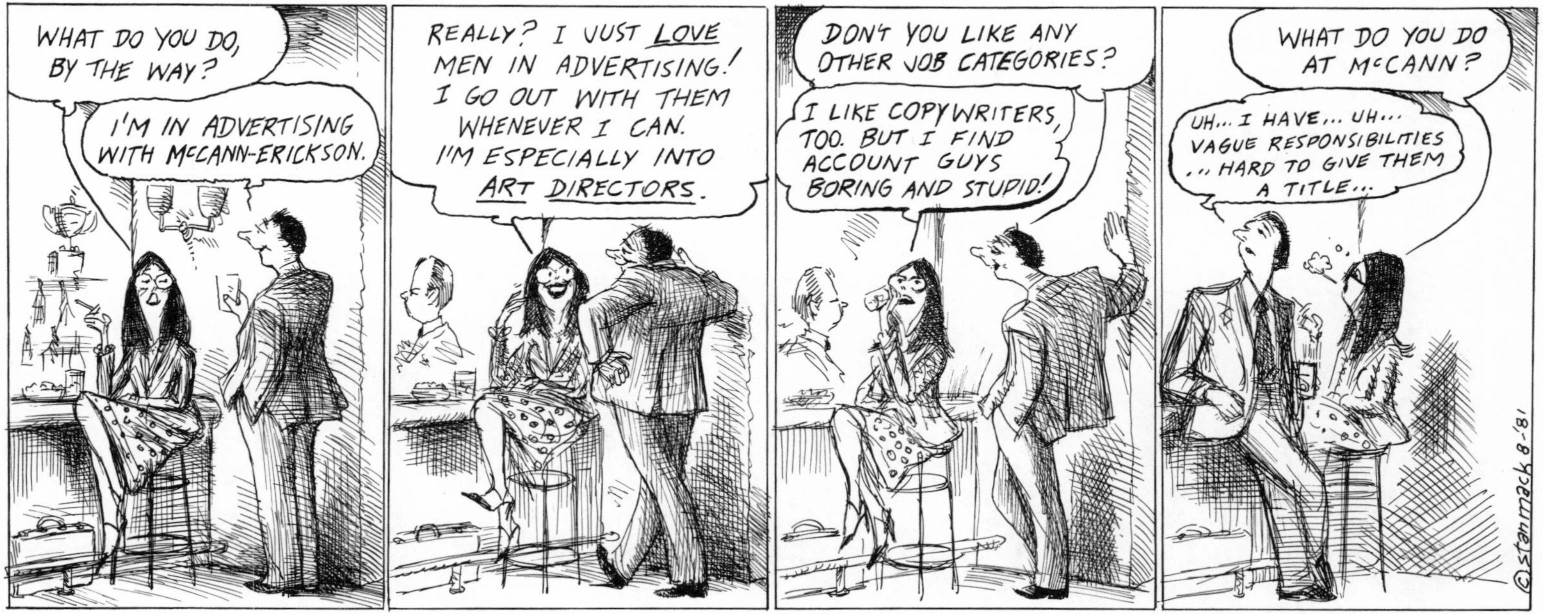
WHAT DO YOU DO, BY THE WAY?
I'M IN ADVERTISING WITH McCANN-ERICKSON.
REALLY? I JUST LOVE MEN IN ADVERTISING! I GO OUT WITH THEM WHENEVER I CAN. I'M ESPECIALLY INTO ART DIRECTORS.
DON'T YOU LIKE ANY OTHER JOB CATEGORIES?
I LIKE COPYWRITERS, TOO. BUT I FIND ACCOUNT GUYS BORING AND STUPID!
WHAT DO YOU DO AT McCANN?
UH... I HAVE... UH... VAGUE RESPONSIBILITIES ... HARD TO GIVE THEM A TITLE...
©stanmack 8-'81

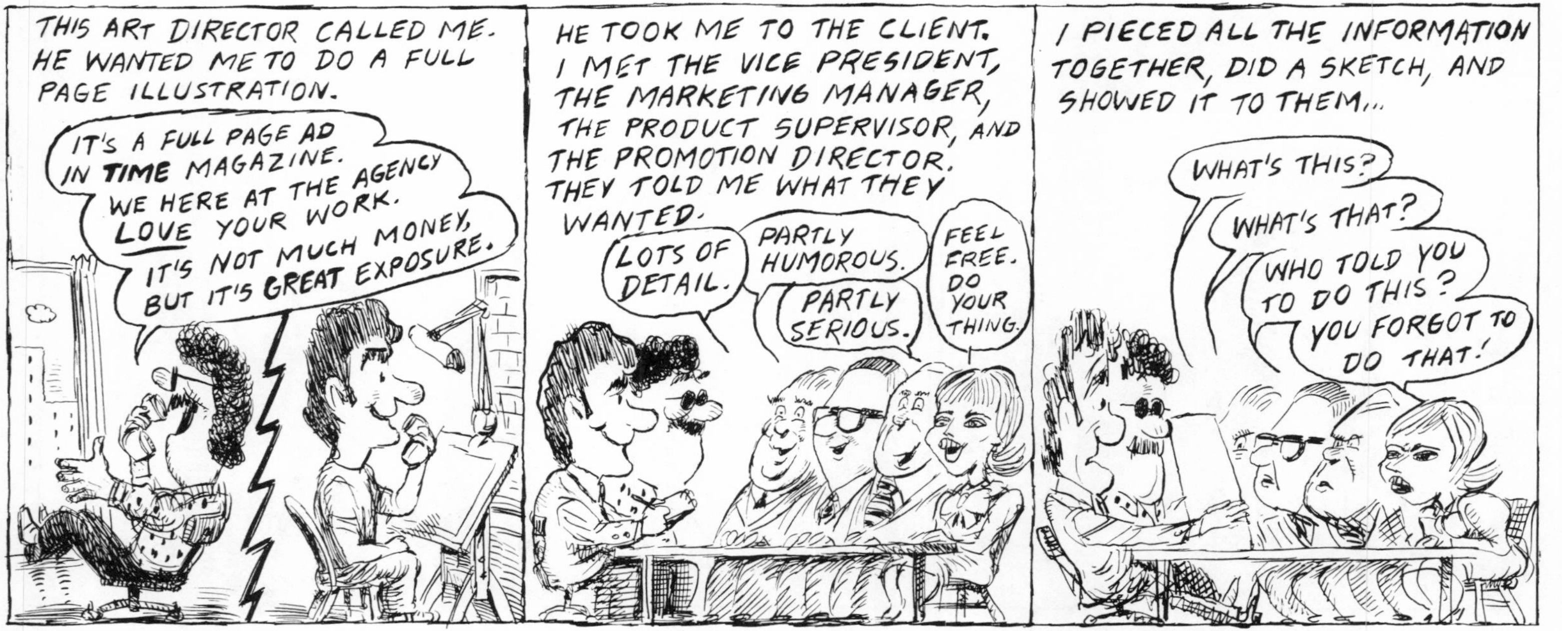
THIS ART DIRECTOR CALLED ME. HE WANTED ME TO DO A FULL PAGE ILLUSTRATION.
IT'S A FULL PAGE AD IN TIME MAGAZINE. WE HERE AT THE AGENCY LOVE YOUR WORK. IT'S NOT MUCH MONEY, BUT IT'S GREAT EXPOSURE.
HE TOOK ME TO THE CLIENT. I MET THE VICE PRESIDENT, THE MARKETING MANAGER, THE PRODUCT SUPERVISOR, AND THE PROMOTION DIRECTOR. THEY TOLD ME WHAT THEY WANTED.
LOTS OF DETAIL.
PARTLY HUMOROUS.
PARTLY SERIOUS.
FEEL FREE. DO YOUR THING.
I PIECED ALL THE INFORMATION TOGETHER, DID A SKETCH, AND SHOWED IT TO THEM...
WHAT'S THIS?
WHAT'S THAT?
WHO TOLD YOU TO DO THIS?
YOU FORGOT TO DO THAT!

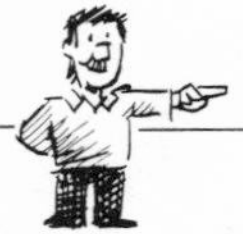

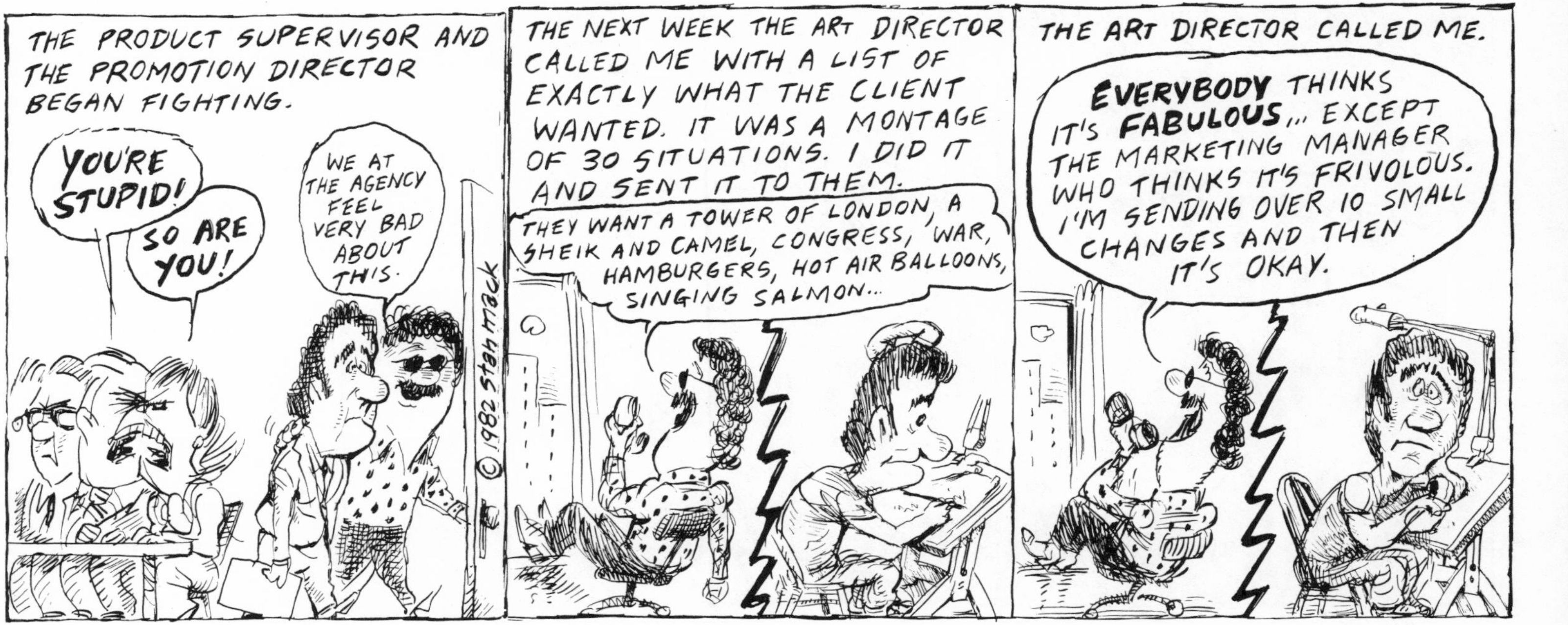

THE PRODUCT SUPERVISOR AND THE PROMOTION DIRECTOR BEGAN FIGHTING.
YOU'RE STUPID!
SO ARE YOU!
WE AT THE AGENCY FEEL VERY BAD ABOUT THIS.
© 1982 stan mack
THE NEXT WEEK THE ART DIRECTOR CALLED ME WITH A LIST OF EXACTLY WHAT THE CLIENT WANTED. IT WAS A MONTAGE OF 30 SITUATIONS. I DID IT AND SENT IT TO THEM.
THEY WANT A TOWER OF LONDON, A SHEIK AND CAMEL, CONGRESS, WAR, HAMBURGERS, HOT AIR BALLOONS, SINGING SALMON...
THE ART DIRECTOR CALLED ME.
EVERYBODY THINKS IT'S FABULOUS... EXCEPT THE MARKETING MANAGER WHO THINKS IT'S FRIVOLOUS. I'M SENDING OVER 10 SMALL CHANGES AND THEN IT'S OKAY.

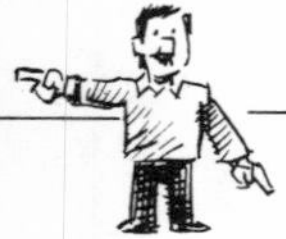

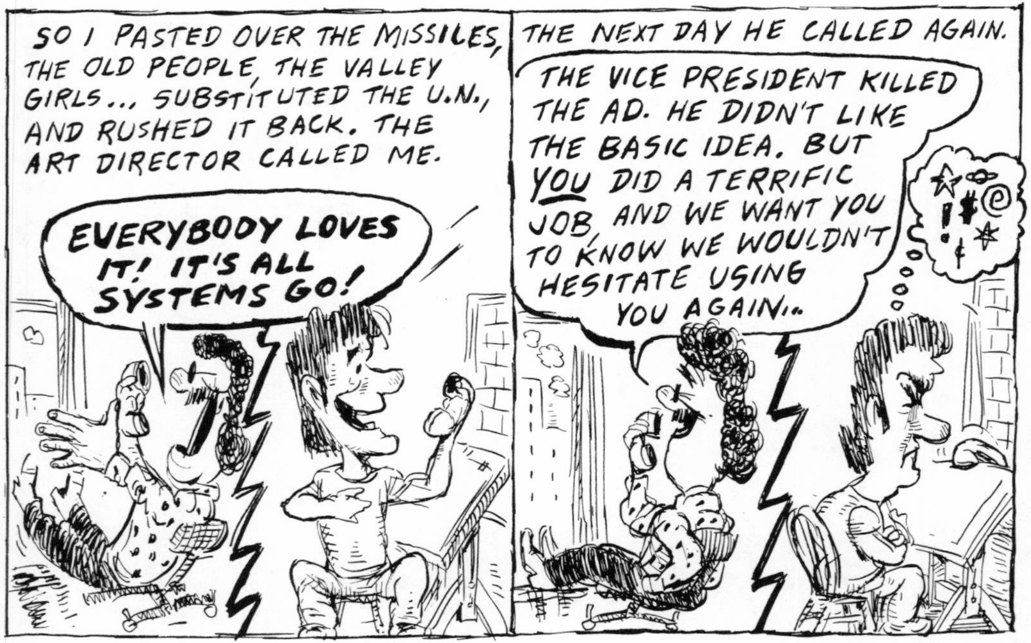
SO I PASTED OVER THE MISSILES, THE OLD PEOPLE, THE VALLEY GIRLS..., SUBSTITUTED THE U.N., AND RUSHED IT BACK. THE ART DIRECTOR CALLED ME.
EVERYBODY LOVES IT! IT'S ALL SYSTEMS GO!
THE NEXT DAY HE CALLED AGAIN.
THE VICE PRESIDENT KILLED THE AD. HE DIDN'T LIKE THE BASIC IDEA. BUT YOU DID A TERRIFIC JOB, AND WE WANT YOU TO KNOW WE WOULDN'T HESITATE USING YOU AGAIN..

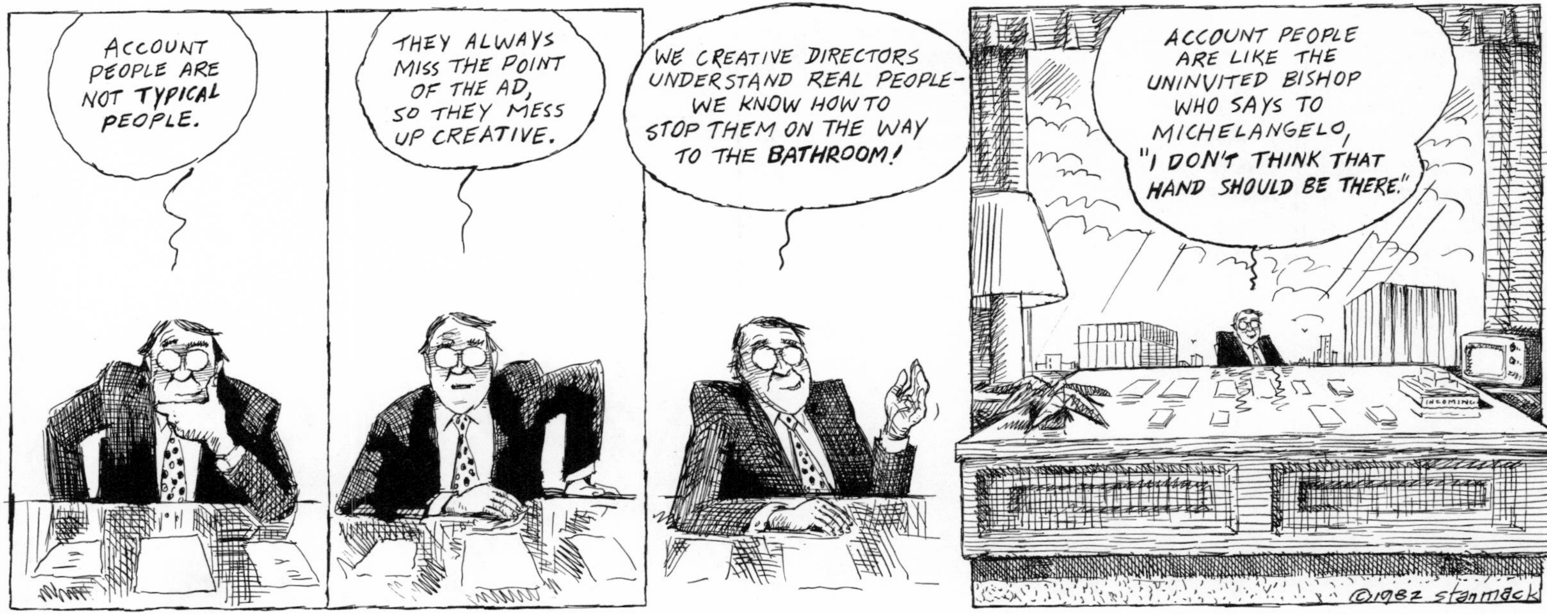
ACCOUNT PEOPLE ARE NOT TYPICAL PEOPLE.
THEY ALWAYS MISS THE POINT OF THE AD, SO THEY MESS UP CREATIVE.
WE CREATIVE DIRECTORS UNDERSTAND REAL PEOPLE- WE KNOW HOW TO STOP THEM ON THE WAY TO THE BATHROOM!
ACCOUNT PEOPLE ARE LIKE THE UNINVITED BISHOP WHO SAYS TO MICHELANGELO, "I DON'T THINK THAT HAND SHOULD BE THERE."
INCOMING
©1982 stanmack

Negotiated Piece

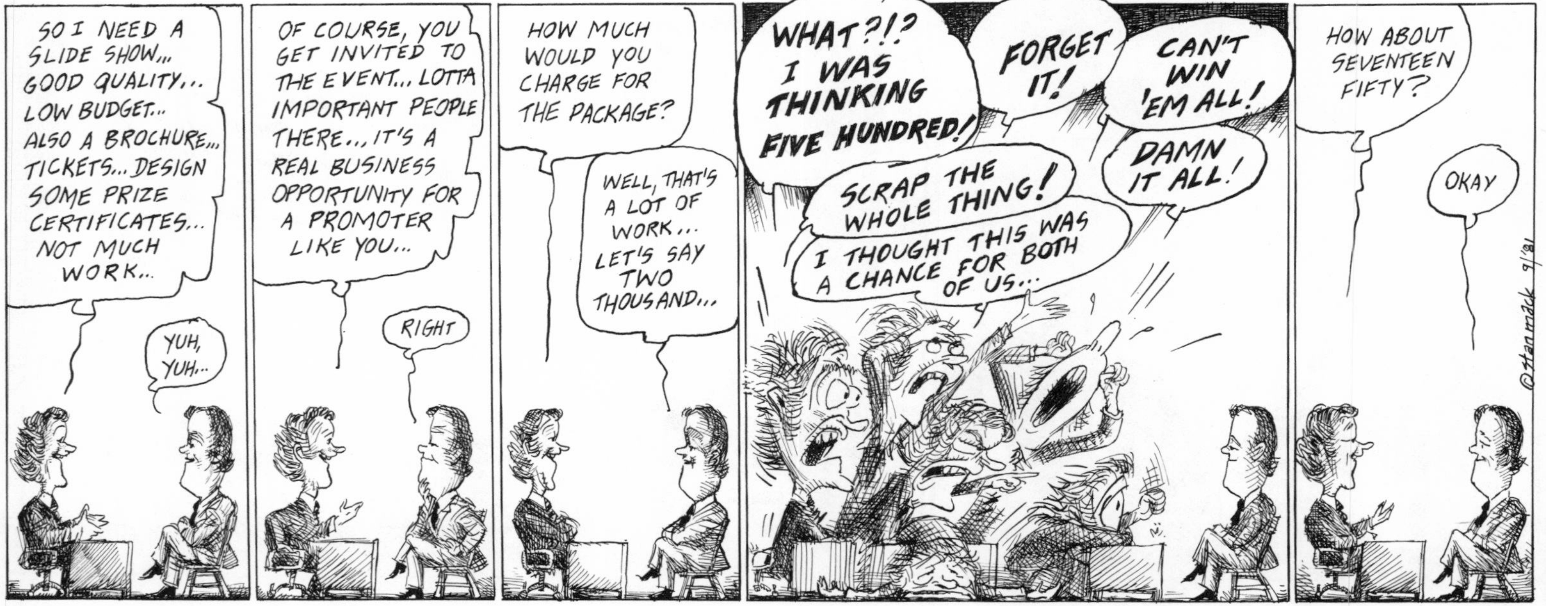
SO I NEED A SLIDE SHOW... GOOD QUALITY... LOW BUDGET... ALSO A BROCHURE... TICKETS... DESIGN SOME PRIZE CERTIFICATES... NOT MUCH WORK...
YUH, YUH...
OF COURSE, YOU GET INVITED TO THE EVENT... LOTTA IMPORTANT PEOPLE THERE... IT'S A REAL BUSINESS OPPORTUNITY FOR A PROMOTER LIKE YOU...
RIGHT
HOW MUCH WOULD YOU CHARGE FOR THE PACKAGE?
WELL, THAT'S A LOT OF WORK... LET'S SAY TWO THOUSAND...
WHAT?!? I WAS THINKING FIVE HUNDRED!
FORGET IT!
CAN'T WIN 'EM ALL!
SCRAP THE WHOLE THING!
DAMN IT ALL!
I THOUGHT THIS WAS A CHANCE FOR BOTH OF US...
HOW ABOUT SEVENTEEN FIFTY?
OKAY

A Vague to Stand On

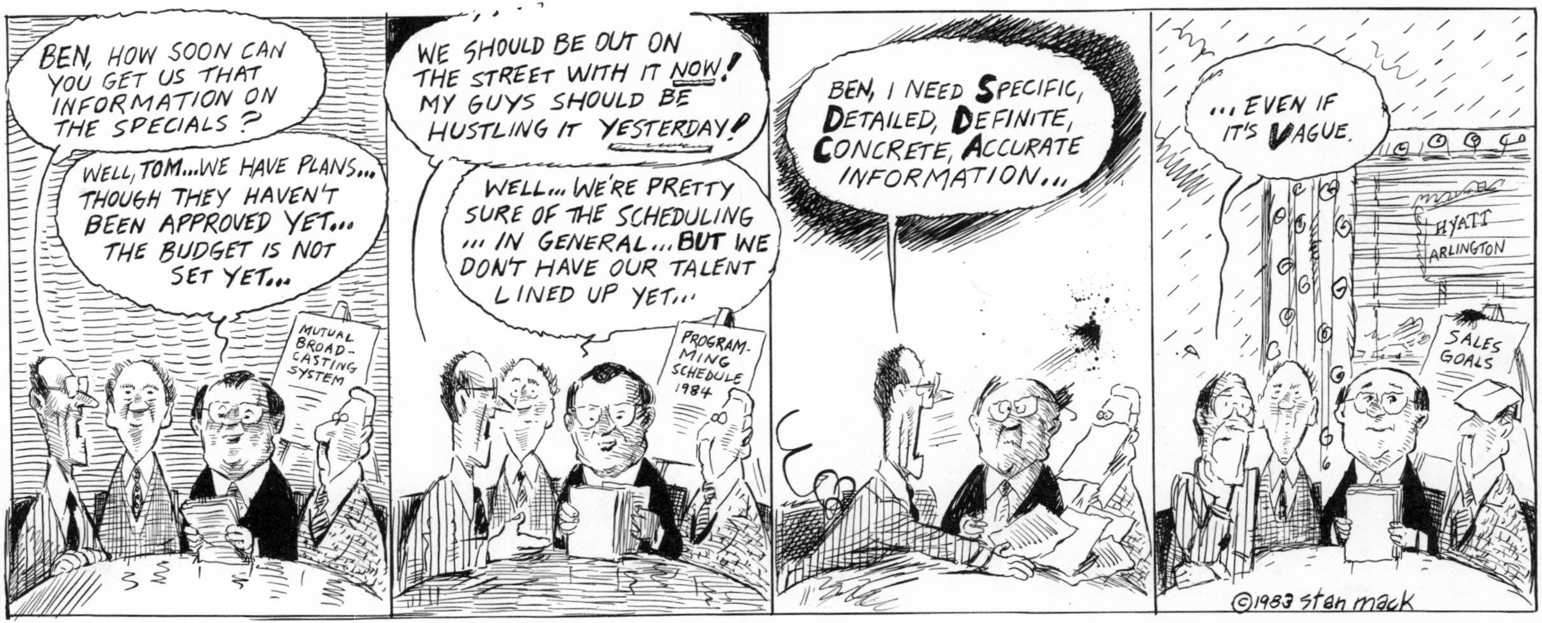

BEN, HOW SOON CAN YOU GET US THAT INFORMATION ON THE SPECIALS?
WELL, TOM...WE HAVE PLANS... THOUGH THEY HAVEN'T BEEN APPROVED YET... THE BUDGET IS NOT SET YET...
MUTUAL BROAD-CASTING SYSTEM
WE SHOULD BE OUT ON THE STREET WITH IT NOW! MY GUYS SHOULD BE HUSTLING IT YESTERDAY!
WELL... WE'RE PRETTY SURE OF THE SCHEDULING ... IN GENERAL... BUT WE DON'T HAVE OUR TALENT LINED UP YET...
PROGRAM-MING SCHEDULE 1984
BEN, I NEED SPECIFIC, DETAILED, DEFINITE, CONCRETE, ACCURATE INFORMATION...
...EVEN IF IT'S VAGUE.
HYATT ARLINGTON
SALES GOALS
©1983 stan mack

Promise Him Anything . . .

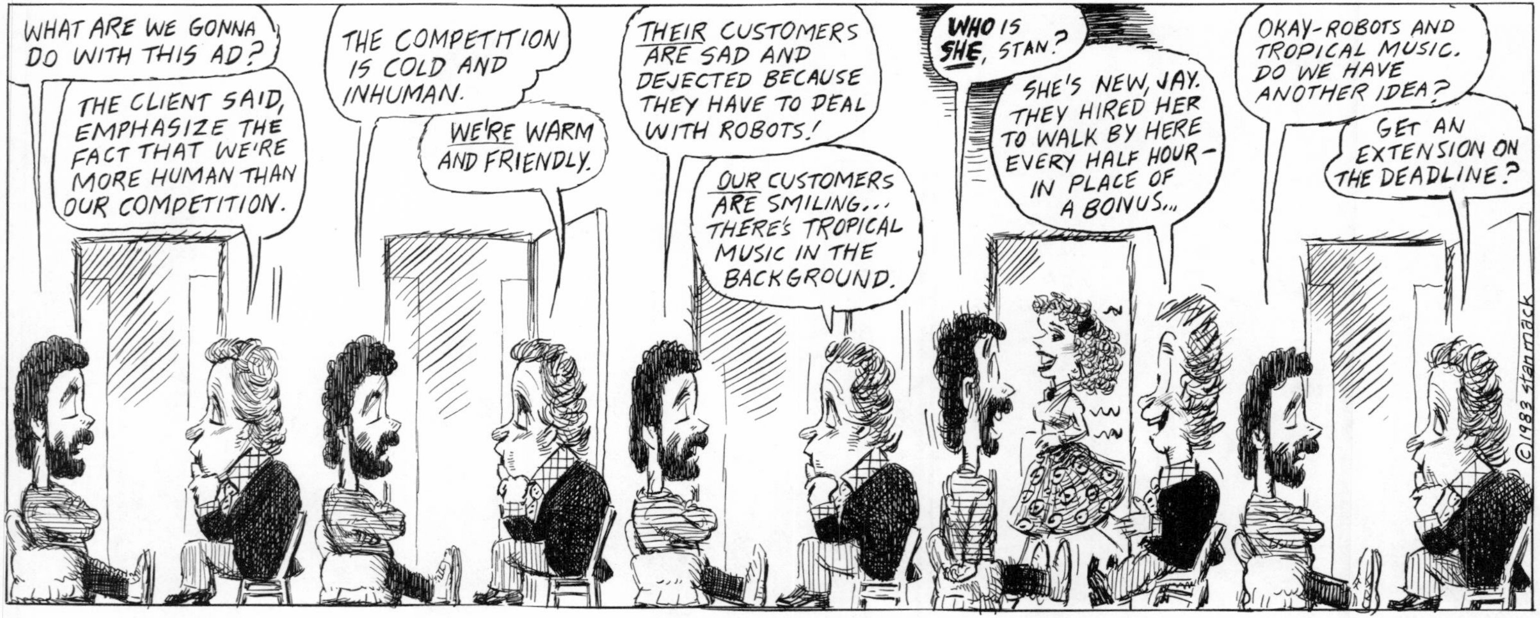
WHAT ARE WE GONNA DO WITH THIS AD?
THE CLIENT SAID, EMPHASIZE THE FACT THAT WE'RE MORE HUMAN THAN OUR COMPETITION.
THE COMPETITION IS COLD AND INHUMAN.
WE'RE WARM AND FRIENDLY.
THEIR CUSTOMERS ARE SAD AND DEJECTED BECAUSE THEY HAVE TO DEAL WITH ROBOTS!
OUR CUSTOMERS ARE SMILING... THERE'S TROPICAL MUSIC IN THE BACKGROUND.
WHO IS SHE, STAN?
SHE'S NEW, JAY. THEY HIRED HER TO WALK BY HERE EVERY HALF HOUR - IN PLACE OF A BONUS...
OKAY - ROBOTS AND TROPICAL MUSIC. DO WE HAVE ANOTHER IDEA?
GET AN EXTENSION ON THE DEADLINE?
©1983 stanmack

Perking up

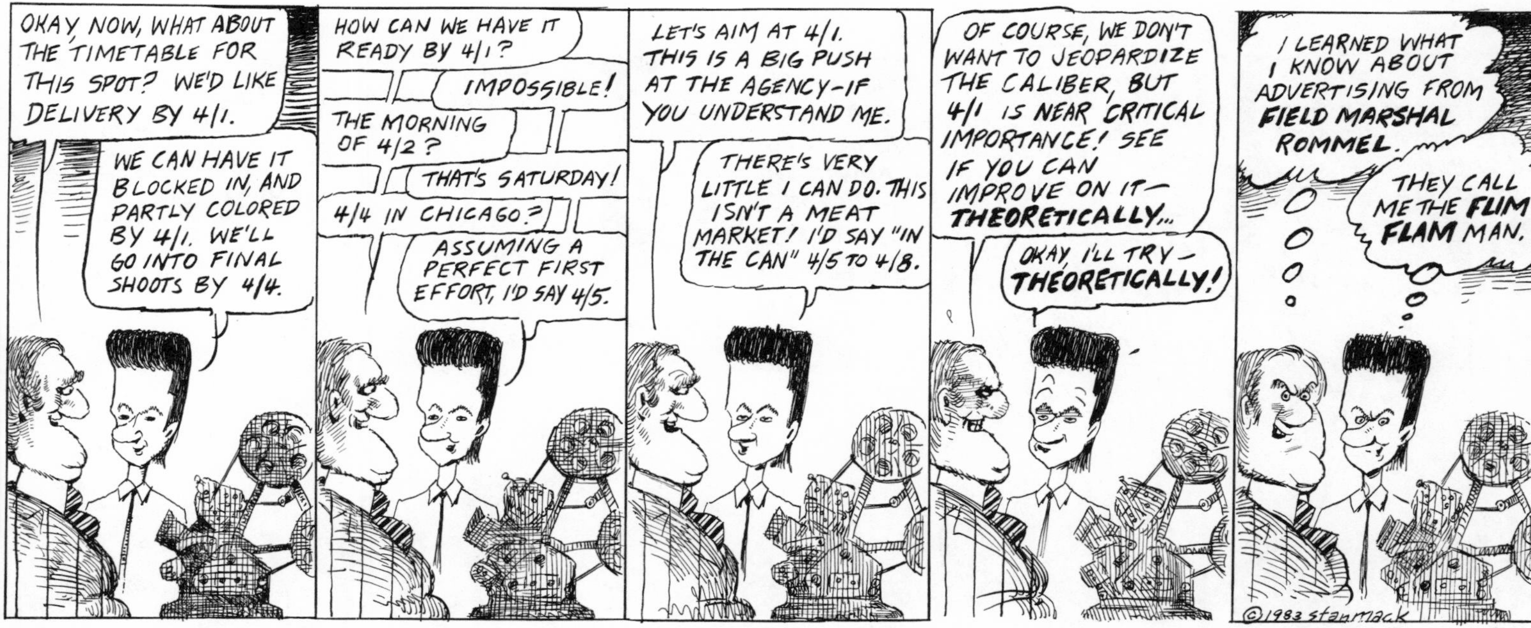

OKAY, NOW, WHAT ABOUT THE TIMETABLE FOR THIS SPOT? WE'D LIKE DELIVERY BY 4/1.
WE CAN HAVE IT BLOCKED IN, AND PARTLY COLORED BY 4/1. WE'LL GO INTO FINAL SHOOTS BY 4/4.
HOW CAN WE HAVE IT READY BY 4/1?
IMPOSSIBLE!
THE MORNING OF 4/2?
THAT'S SATURDAY!
4/4 IN CHICAGO?
ASSUMING A PERFECT FIRST EFFORT, I'D SAY 4/5.
LET'S AIM AT 4/1. THIS IS A BIG PUSH AT THE AGENCY—IF YOU UNDERSTAND ME.
THERE'S VERY LITTLE I CAN DO. THIS ISN'T A MEAT MARKET! I'D SAY "IN THE CAN" 4/5 TO 4/8.
OF COURSE, WE DON'T WANT TO JEOPARDIZE THE CALIBER, BUT 4/1 IS NEAR CRITICAL IMPORTANCE! SEE IF YOU CAN IMPROVE ON IT—THEORETICALLY...
OKAY, I'LL TRY—THEORETICALLY!
I LEARNED WHAT I KNOW ABOUT ADVERTISING FROM FIELD MARSHAL ROMMEL.
THEY CALL ME THE FLIM-FLAM MAN.
©1983 stanmack

Flushed With Success

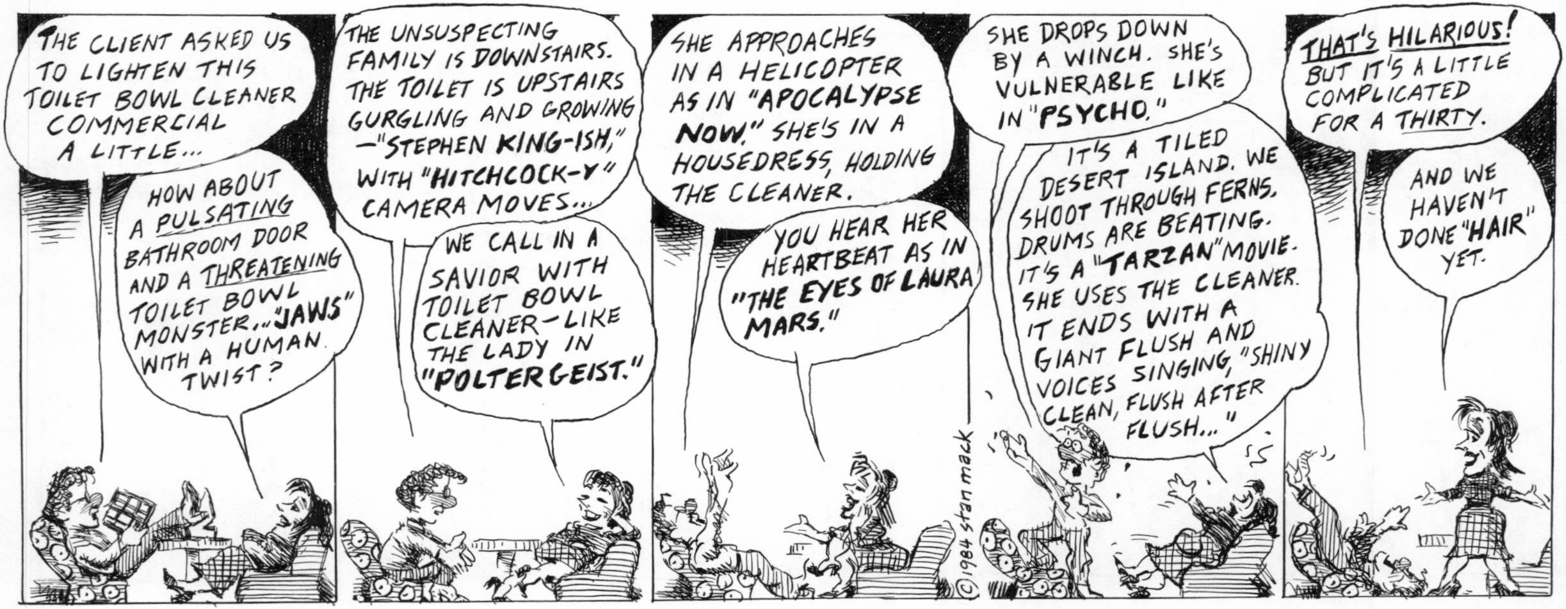

THE CLIENT ASKED US TO LIGHTEN THIS TOILET BOWL CLEANER COMMERCIAL A LITTLE...
HOW ABOUT A PULSATING BATHROOM DOOR AND A THREATENING TOILET BOWL MONSTER... "JAWS" WITH A HUMAN TWIST?
THE UNSUSPECTING FAMILY IS DOWNSTAIRS. THE TOILET IS UPSTAIRS GURGLING AND GROWING —"STEPHEN KING-ISH," WITH "HITCHCOCK-Y" CAMERA MOVES...
WE CALL IN A SAVIOR WITH TOILET BOWL CLEANER—LIKE THE LADY IN "POLTERGEIST."
SHE APPROACHES IN A HELICOPTER AS IN "APOCALYPSE NOW." SHE'S IN A HOUSEDRESS, HOLDING THE CLEANER.
YOU HEAR HER HEARTBEAT AS IN "THE EYES OF LAURA MARS."
©1984 stan mack
SHE DROPS DOWN BY A WINCH. SHE'S VULNERABLE LIKE IN "PSYCHO."
IT'S A TILED DESERT ISLAND. WE SHOOT THROUGH FERNS. DRUMS ARE BEATING. IT'S A "TARZAN" MOVIE. SHE USES THE CLEANER. IT ENDS WITH A GIANT FLUSH AND VOICES SINGING, "SHINY CLEAN, FLUSH AFTER FLUSH..."
THAT'S HILARIOUS! BUT IT'S A LITTLE COMPLICATED FOR A THIRTY.
AND WE HAVEN'T DONE "HAIR" YET.

Esprit de Corpse

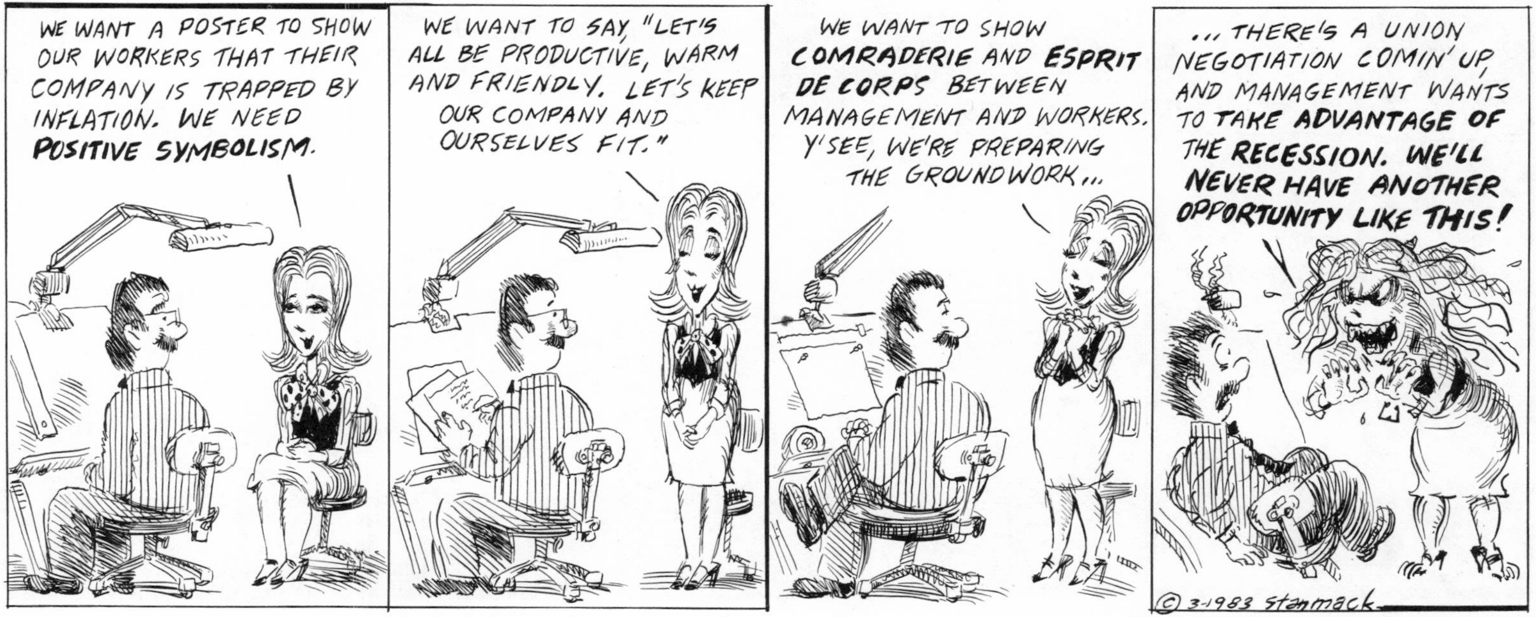
WE WANT A POSTER TO SHOW OUR WORKERS THAT THEIR COMPANY IS TRAPPED BY INFLATION. WE NEED POSITIVE SYMBOLISM.
WE WANT TO SAY, "LET'S ALL BE PRODUCTIVE, WARM AND FRIENDLY. LET'S KEEP OUR COMPANY AND OURSELVES FIT."
WE WANT TO SHOW COMRADERIE AND ESPRIT DE CORPS BETWEEN MANAGEMENT AND WORKERS. Y'SEE, WE'RE PREPARING THE GROUNDWORK...
... THERE'S A UNION NEGOTIATION COMIN' UP, AND MANAGEMENT WANTS TO TAKE ADVANTAGE OF THE RECESSION. WE'LL NEVER HAVE ANOTHER OPPORTUNITY LIKE THIS!
© 3-1983 stanmack

Copy Cat

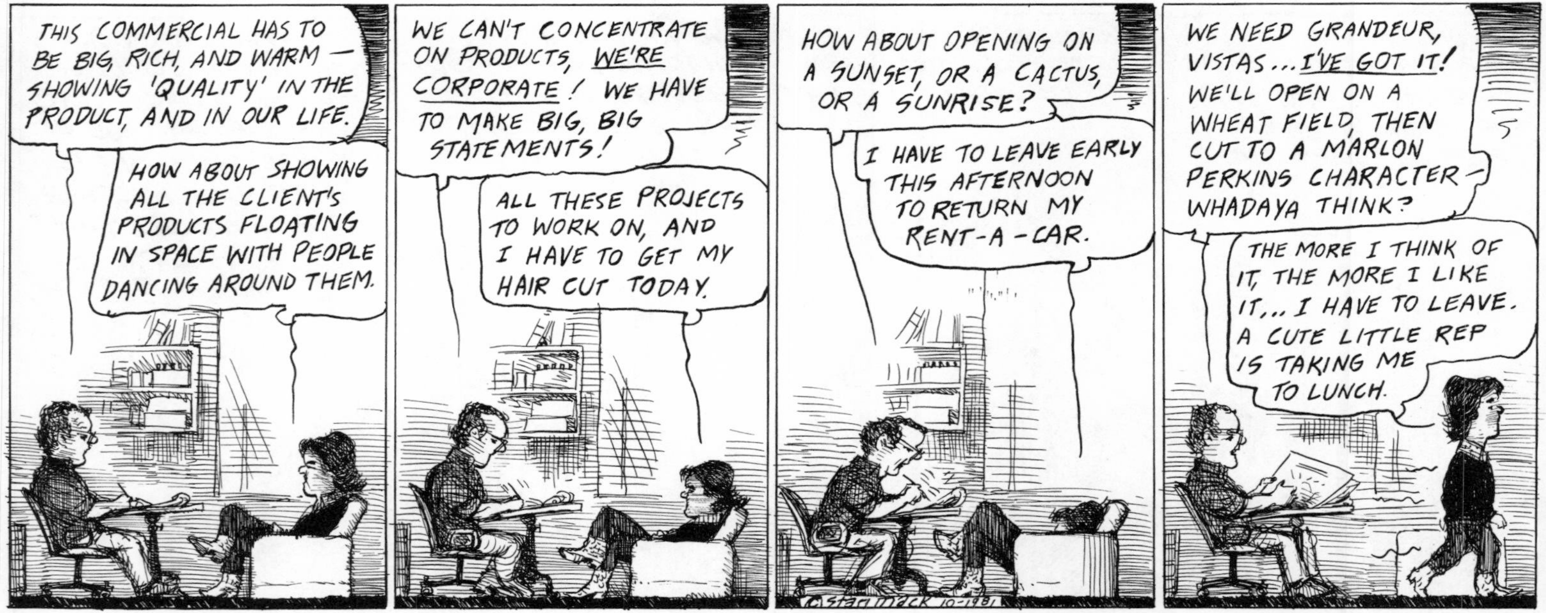
THIS COMMERCIAL HAS TO BE BIG, RICH, AND WARM — SHOWING 'QUALITY' IN THE PRODUCT, AND IN OUR LIFE.
HOW ABOUT SHOWING ALL THE CLIENT'S PRODUCTS FLOATING IN SPACE WITH PEOPLE DANCING AROUND THEM.
WE CAN'T CONCENTRATE ON PRODUCTS, WE'RE CORPORATE! WE HAVE TO MAKE BIG, BIG STATEMENTS!
ALL THESE PROJECTS TO WORK ON, AND I HAVE TO GET MY HAIR CUT TODAY.
HOW ABOUT OPENING ON A SUNSET, OR A CACTUS, OR A SUNRISE?
I HAVE TO LEAVE EARLY THIS AFTERNOON TO RETURN MY RENT-A-CAR.
WE NEED GRANDEUR, VISTAS... I'VE GOT IT! WE'LL OPEN ON A WHEAT FIELD, THEN CUT TO A MARLON PERKINS CHARACTER — WHADAYA THINK?
THE MORE I THINK OF IT, THE MORE I LIKE IT... I HAVE TO LEAVE. A CUTE LITTLE REP IS TAKING ME TO LUNCH.
© STAN MACK 10-1981

But Mostly, He's Modest

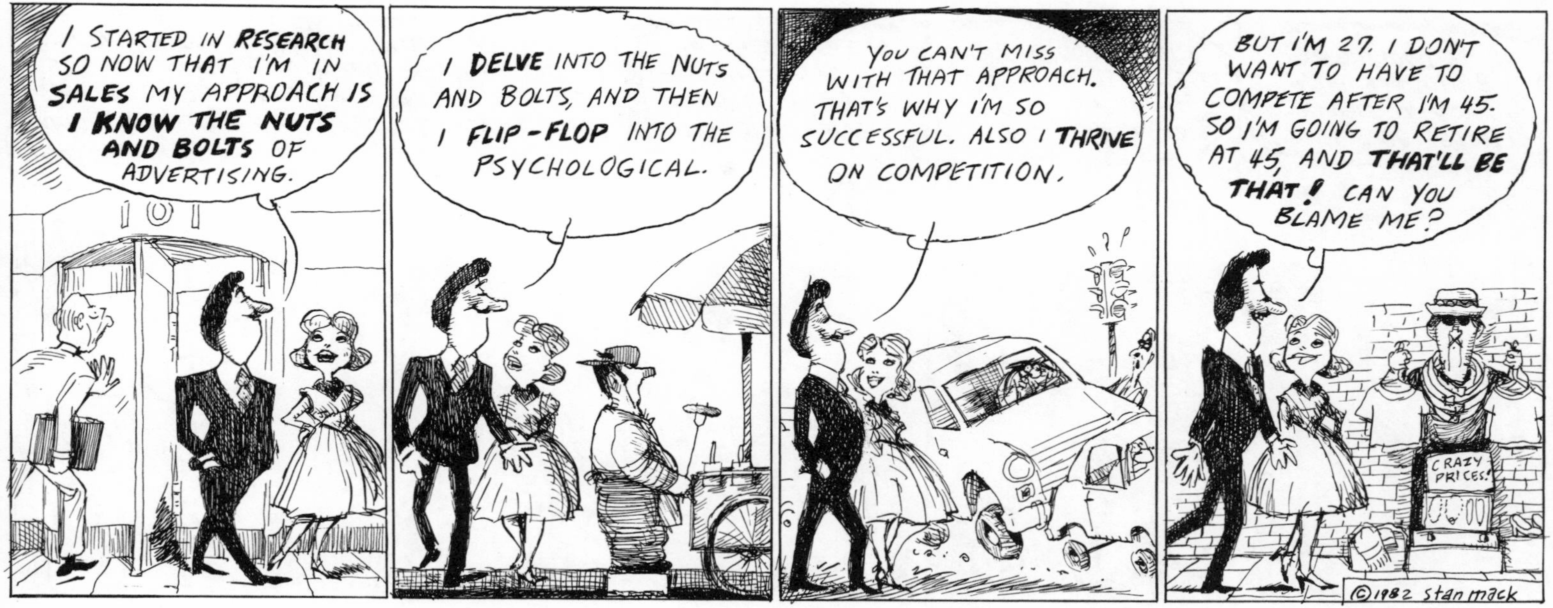
I STARTED IN RESEARCH SO NOW THAT I'M IN SALES MY APPROACH IS I KNOW THE NUTS AND BOLTS OF ADVERTISING.
101
I DELVE INTO THE NUTS AND BOLTS, AND THEN I FLIP-FLOP INTO THE PSYCHOLOGICAL.
YOU CAN'T MISS WITH THAT APPROACH. THAT'S WHY I'M SO SUCCESSFUL. ALSO I THRIVE ON COMPETITION.
BUT I'M 27. I DON'T WANT TO HAVE TO COMPETE AFTER I'M 45. SO I'M GOING TO RETIRE AT 45, AND THAT'LL BE THAT! CAN YOU BLAME ME?
CRAZY PRICES!
©1982 stan mack

Connecticut Ethnic in P & G's Court

One of Life's More Graphic Lessons

Coiffuror

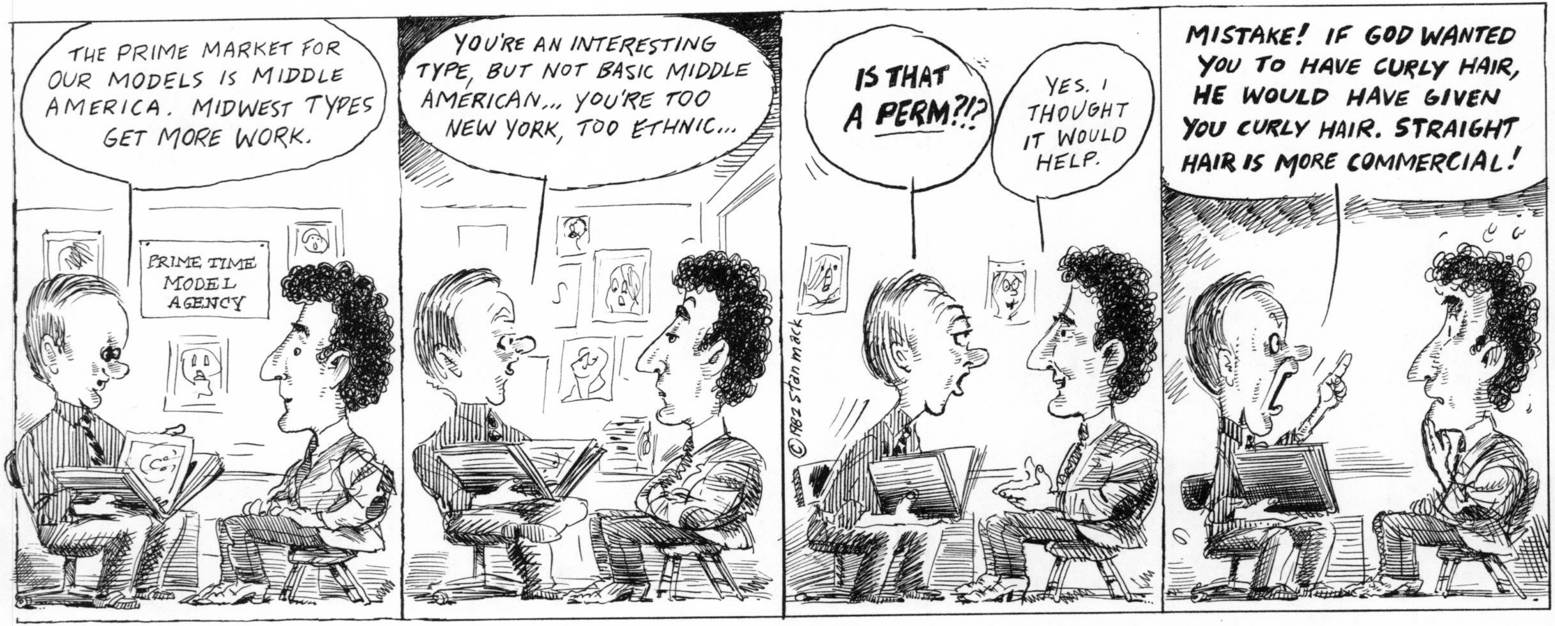
THE PRIME MARKET FOR OUR MODELS IS MIDDLE AMERICA. MIDWEST TYPES GET MORE WORK.
PRIME TIME MODEL AGENCY
YOU'RE AN INTERESTING TYPE, BUT NOT BASIC MIDDLE AMERICAN... YOU'RE TOO NEW YORK, TOO ETHNIC...
©1982 stan mack
IS THAT A PERM?!?
YES. I THOUGHT IT WOULD HELP.
MISTAKE! IF GOD WANTED YOU TO HAVE CURLY HAIR, HE WOULD HAVE GIVEN YOU CURLY HAIR. STRAIGHT HAIR IS MORE COMMERCIAL!

Soap Stud

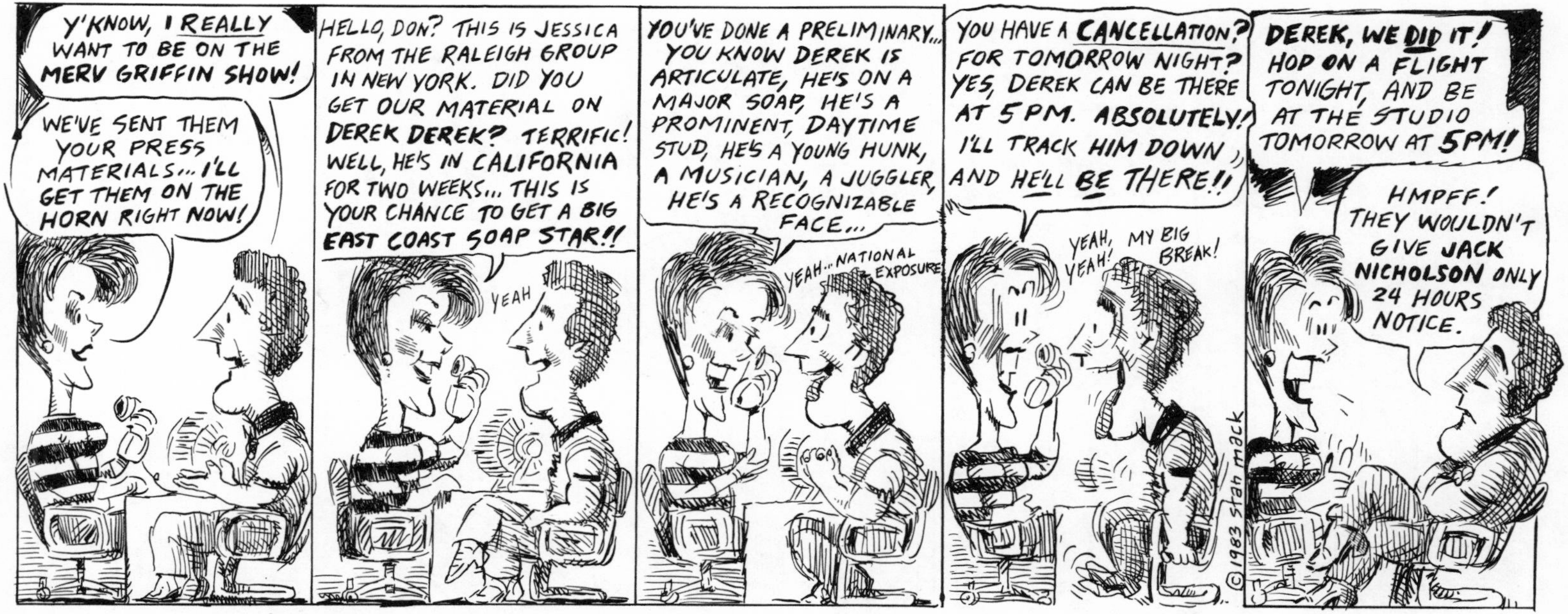
Y'KNOW, I REALLY WANT TO BE ON THE MERV GRIFFIN SHOW!
WE'VE SENT THEM YOUR PRESS MATERIALS... I'LL GET THEM ON THE HORN RIGHT NOW!
HELLO, DON? THIS IS JESSICA FROM THE RALEIGH GROUP IN NEW YORK. DID YOU GET OUR MATERIAL ON DEREK DEREK? TERRIFIC! WELL, HE'S IN CALIFORNIA FOR TWO WEEKS... THIS IS YOUR CHANCE TO GET A BIG EAST COAST SOAP STAR!!
YEAH
YOU'VE DONE A PRELIMINARY... YOU KNOW DEREK IS ARTICULATE, HE'S ON A MAJOR SOAP, HE'S A PROMINENT, DAYTIME STUD, HE'S A YOUNG HUNK, A MUSICIAN, A JUGGLER, HE'S A RECOGNIZABLE FACE...
YEAH... NATIONAL EXPOSURE
YOU HAVE A CANCELLATION? FOR TOMORROW NIGHT? YES, DEREK CAN BE THERE AT 5PM. ABSOLUTELY! I'LL TRACK HIM DOWN AND HE'LL BE THERE!!
YEAH, YEAH!
MY BIG BREAK!
©1983 stan mack
DEREK, WE DID IT! HOP ON A FLIGHT TONIGHT, AND BE AT THE STUDIO TOMORROW AT 5PM!
HMPFF! THEY WOULDN'T GIVE JACK NICHOLSON ONLY 24 HOURS NOTICE.

Fertile Fields

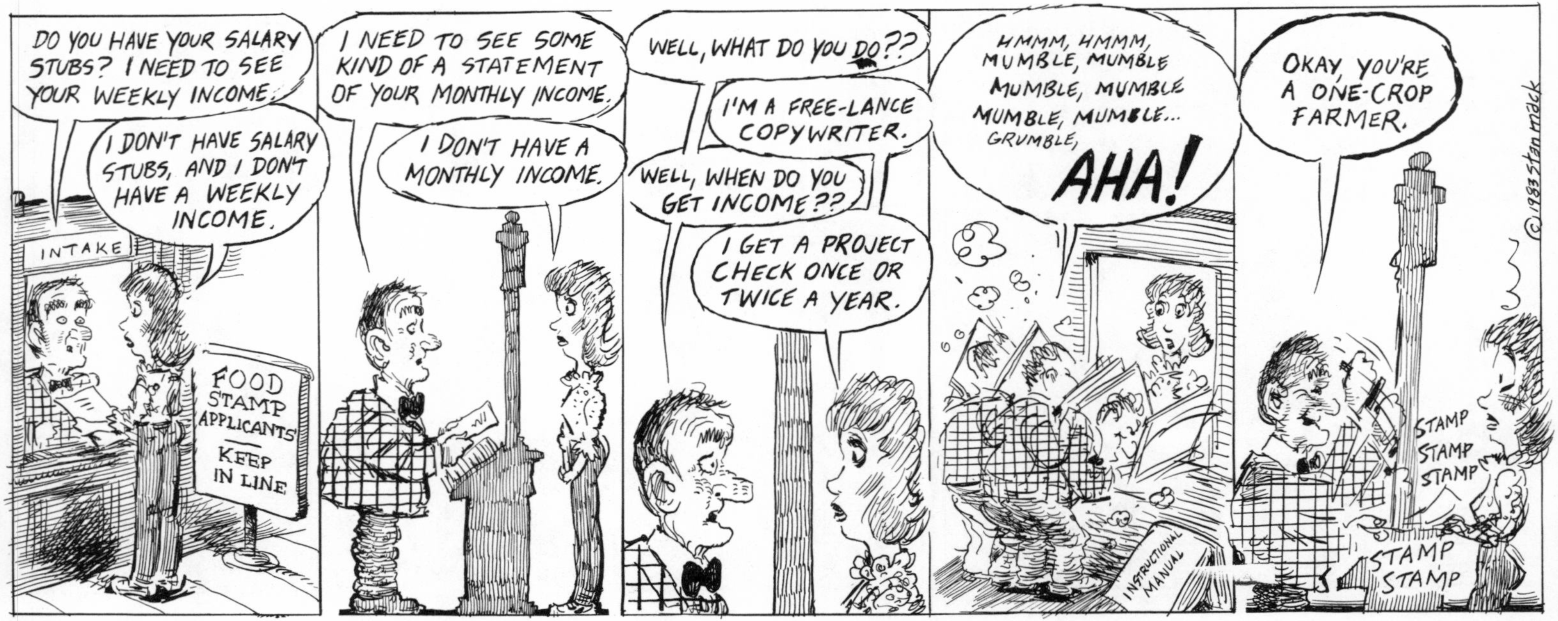
DO YOU HAVE YOUR SALARY STUBS? I NEED TO SEE YOUR WEEKLY INCOME.
I DON'T HAVE SALARY STUBS, AND I DON'T HAVE A WEEKLY INCOME.
INTAKE
FOOD STAMP APPLICANTS' KEEP IN LINE
I NEED TO SEE SOME KIND OF A STATEMENT OF YOUR MONTHLY INCOME.
I DON'T HAVE A MONTHLY INCOME.
WELL, WHAT DO YOU DO??
I'M A FREE-LANCE COPYWRITER.
WELL, WHEN DO YOU GET INCOME??
I GET A PROJECT CHECK ONCE OR TWICE A YEAR.
HMMM, HMMM, MUMBLE, MUMBLE MUMBLE, MUMBLE MUMBLE, MUMBLE... GRUMBLE,
AHA!
INSTRUCTIONAL MANUAL
OKAY, YOU'RE A ONE-CROP FARMER.
STAMP STAMP STAMP
STAMP STAMP
© 1983 Stan Mack

A Pale Imitation

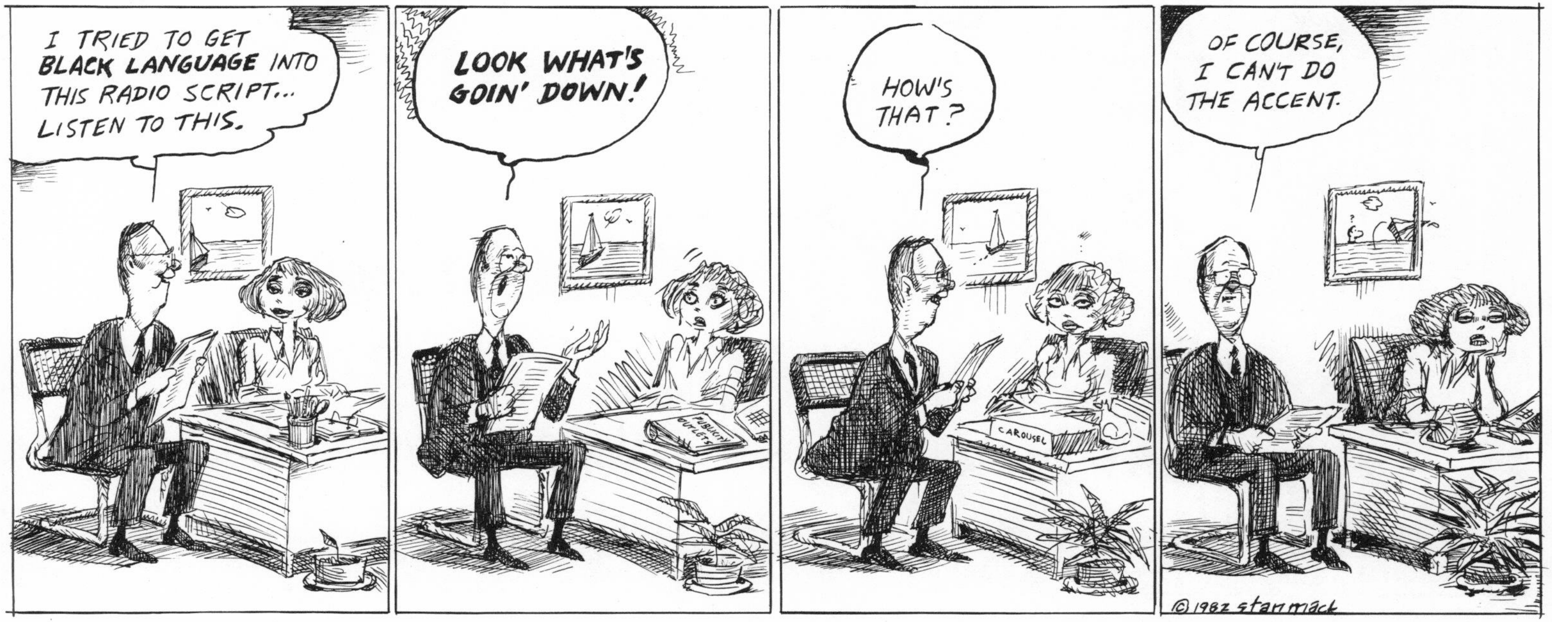
I TRIED TO GET BLACK LANGUAGE INTO THIS RADIO SCRIPT... LISTEN TO THIS.
LOOK WHAT'S GOIN' DOWN!
PUBLICITY OUTLETS
HOW'S THAT?
CAROUSEL
OF COURSE, I CAN'T DO THE ACCENT.
© 1982 stan mack

The Master's Voice

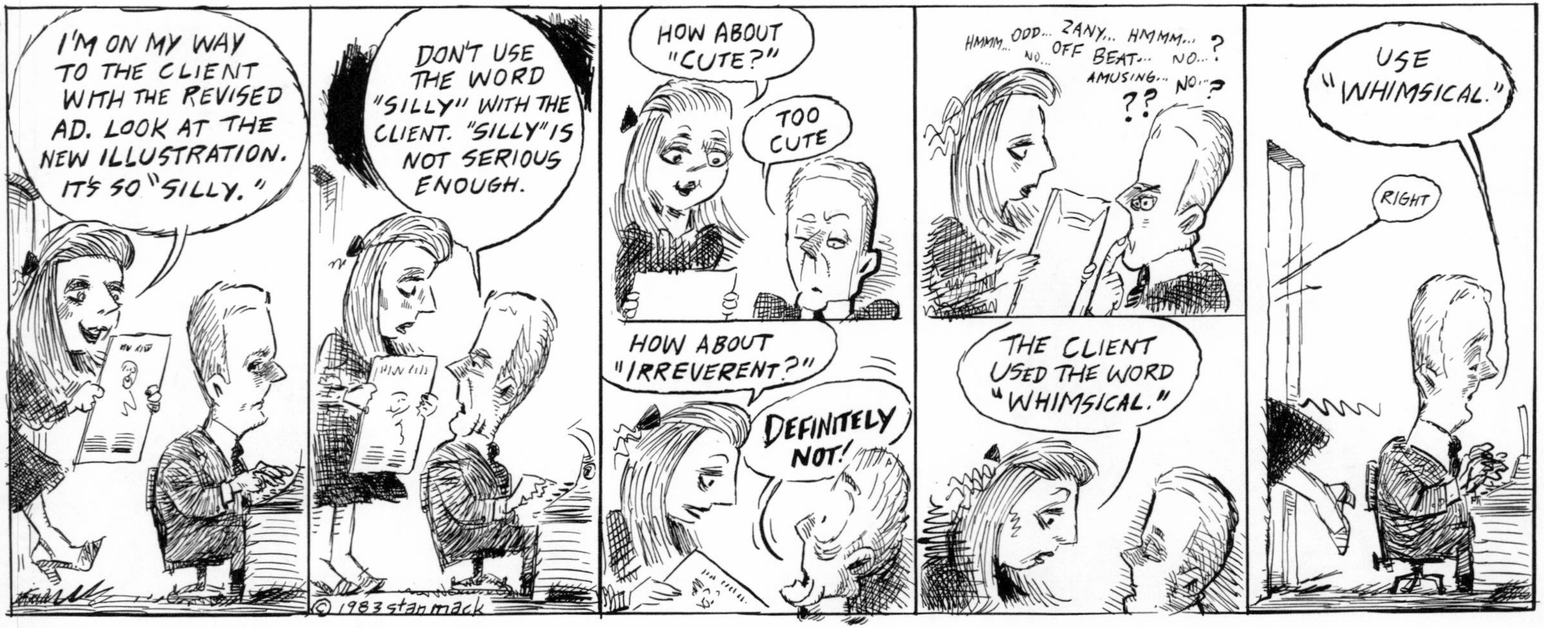

I'M ON MY WAY TO THE CLIENT WITH THE REVISED AD. LOOK AT THE NEW ILLUSTRATION. IT'S SO "SILLY."
DON'T USE THE WORD "SILLY" WITH THE CLIENT. "SILLY" IS NOT SERIOUS ENOUGH.
© 1983 stan mack
HOW ABOUT "CUTE?"
TOO CUTE
HOW ABOUT "IRREVERENT?"
DEFINITELY NOT!
HMMM... ODD... ZANY... HMMM... ?
NO... OFF BEAT... NO...?
AMUSING... NO...?
??
THE CLIENT USED THE WORD "WHIMSICAL."
USE "WHIMSICAL."
RIGHT

Animated Conversation

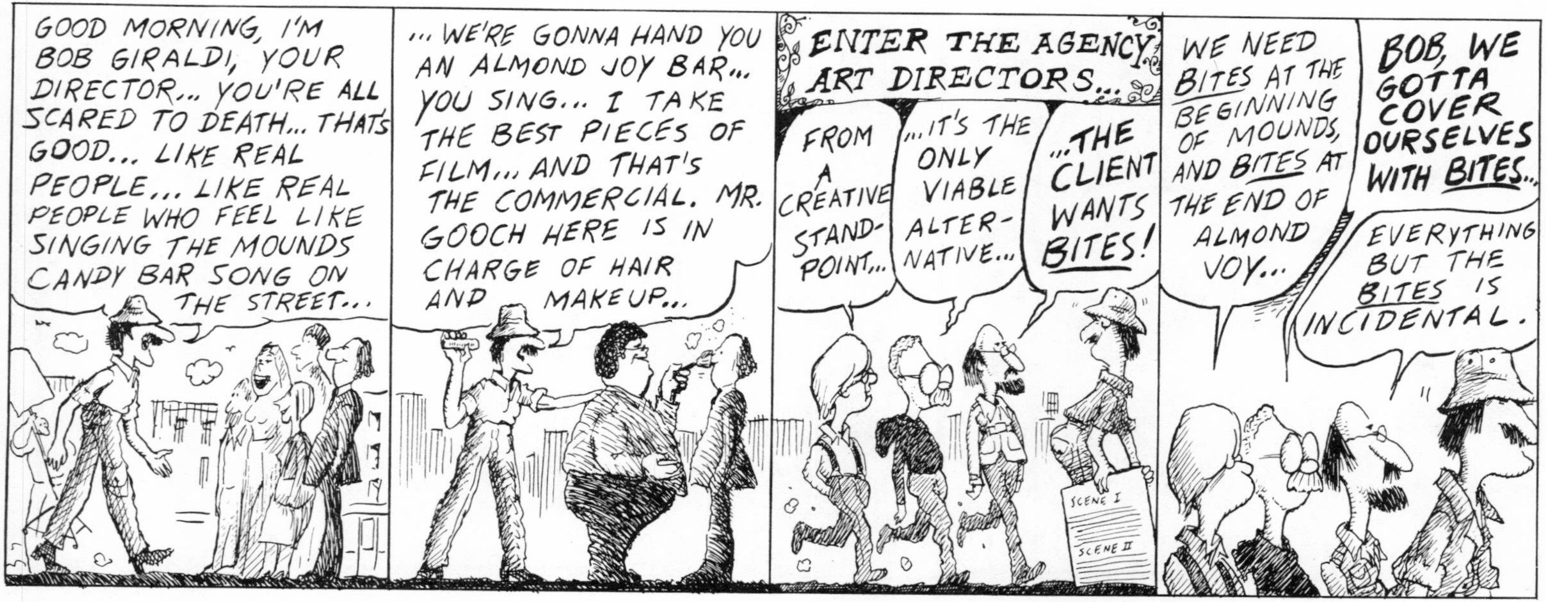
GOOD MORNING, I'M BOB GIRALDI, YOUR DIRECTOR... YOU'RE ALL SCARED TO DEATH... THAT'S GOOD... LIKE REAL PEOPLE... LIKE REAL PEOPLE WHO FEEL LIKE SINGING THE MOUNDS CANDY BAR SONG ON THE STREET...
... WE'RE GONNA HAND YOU AN ALMOND JOY BAR... YOU SING... I TAKE THE BEST PIECES OF FILM... AND THAT'S THE COMMERCIAL. MR. GOOCH HERE IS IN CHARGE OF HAIR AND MAKEUP...
ENTER THE AGENCY ART DIRECTORS...
FROM A CREATIVE STAND-POINT...
...IT'S THE ONLY VIABLE ALTER-NATIVE...
...THE CLIENT WANTS BITES!
SCENE I
SCENE II
WE NEED BITES AT THE BEGINNING OF MOUNDS, AND BITES AT THE END OF ALMOND JOY...
BOB, WE GOTTA COVER OURSELVES WITH BITES...
EVERYTHING BUT THE BITES IS INCIDENTAL.

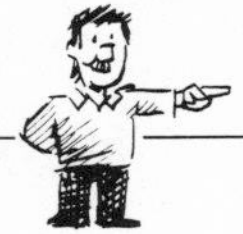

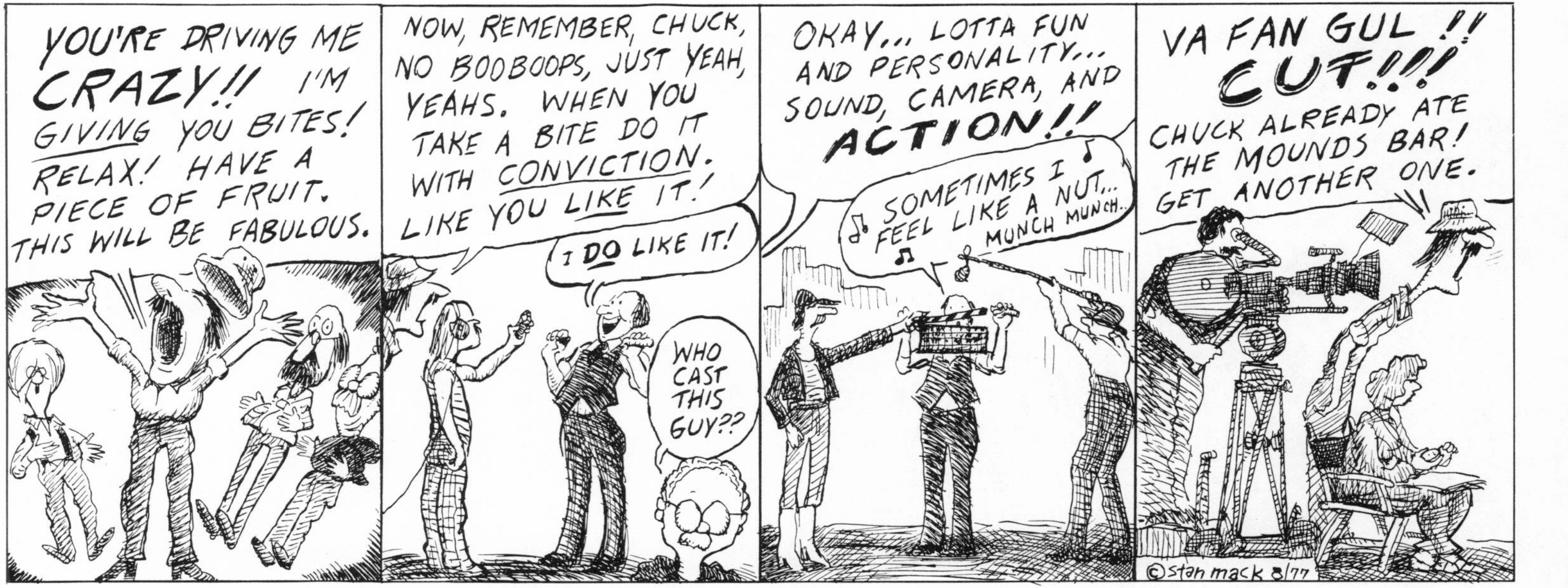
YOU'RE DRIVING ME CRAZY!! I'M GIVING YOU BITES! RELAX! HAVE A PIECE OF FRUIT. THIS WILL BE FABULOUS.
NOW, REMEMBER, CHUCK, NO BOOBOOPS, JUST YEAH, YEAHS. WHEN YOU TAKE A BITE DO IT WITH CONVICTION. LIKE YOU LIKE IT!
I DO LIKE IT!
WHO CAST THIS GUY??
OKAY... LOTTA FUN AND PERSONALITY... SOUND, CAMERA, AND ACTION!!
SOMETIMES I FEEL LIKE A NUT... MUNCH MUNCH...
VA FAN GUL !! CUT!!!! CHUCK ALREADY ATE THE MOUNDS BAR! GET ANOTHER ONE.
©stan mack 8/77

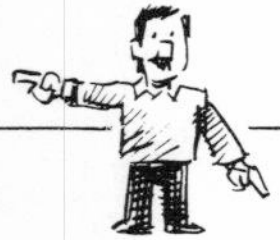

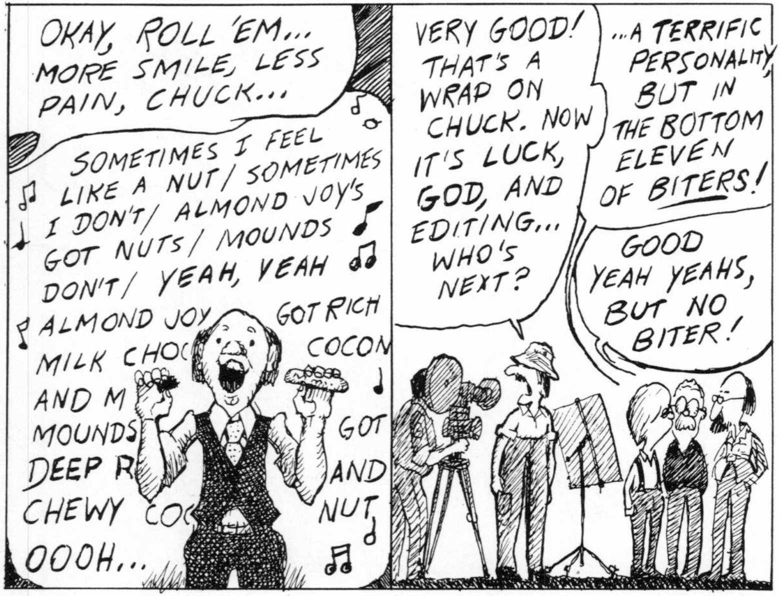
OKAY, ROLL 'EM... MORE SMILE, LESS PAIN, CHUCK...
SOMETIMES I FEEL LIKE A NUT/ SOMETIMES I DON'T/ ALMOND JOY'S GOT NUTS/ MOUNDS DON'T/ YEAH, YEAH
ALMOND JOY
GOT RICH
MILK CHO
COCON
AND M
MOUNDS
GOT
DEEP R
AND
CHEWY
COC
NUT
OOOH...
VERY GOOD! THAT'S A WRAP ON CHUCK. NOW IT'S LUCK, GOD, AND EDITING... WHO'S NEXT?
...A TERRIFIC PERSONALITY, BUT IN THE BOTTOM ELEVEN OF BITERS!
GOOD YEAH YEAHS, BUT NO BITER!

As You Leica

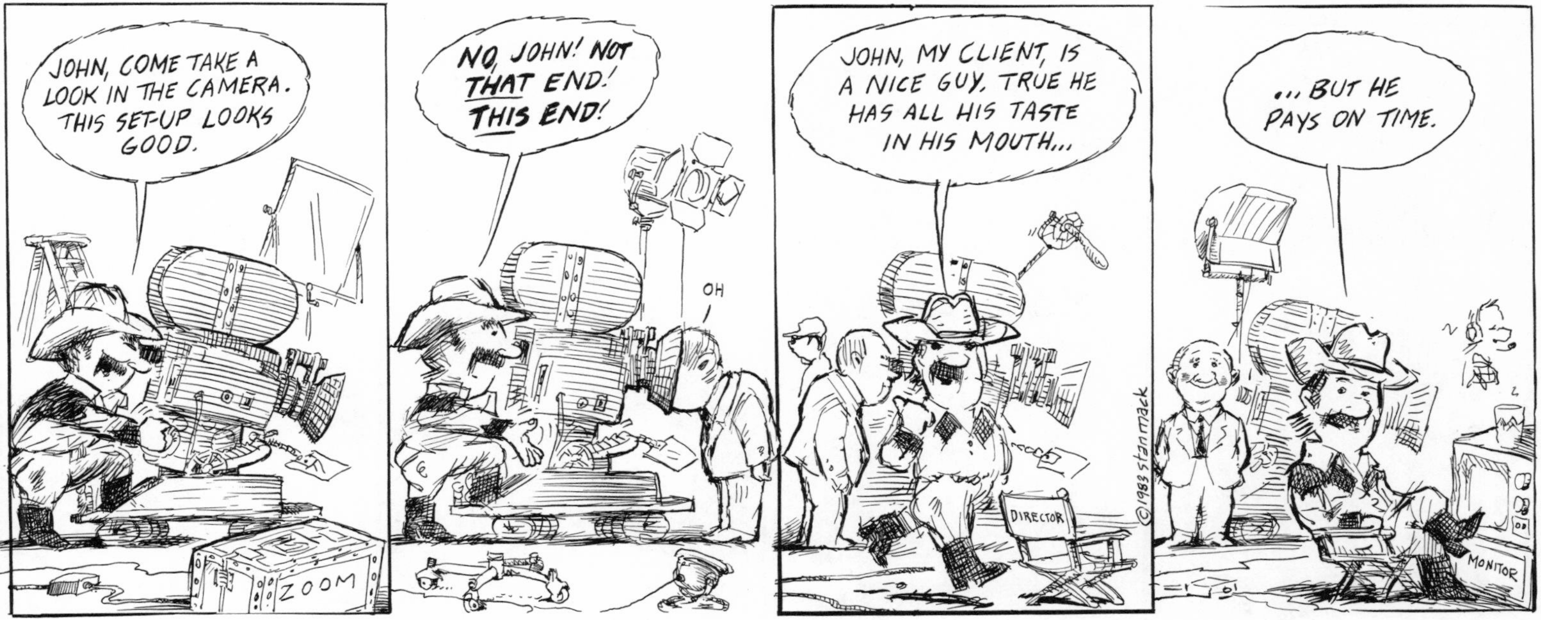

JOHN, COME TAKE A LOOK IN THE CAMERA. THIS SET-UP LOOKS GOOD.
ZOOM
NO, JOHN! NOT THAT END! THIS END!
OH
JOHN, MY CLIENT, IS A NICE GUY. TRUE HE HAS ALL HIS TASTE IN HIS MOUTH...
DIRECTOR
©1983 stanmack
...BUT HE PAYS ON TIME.
MONITOR

Thanks a Little

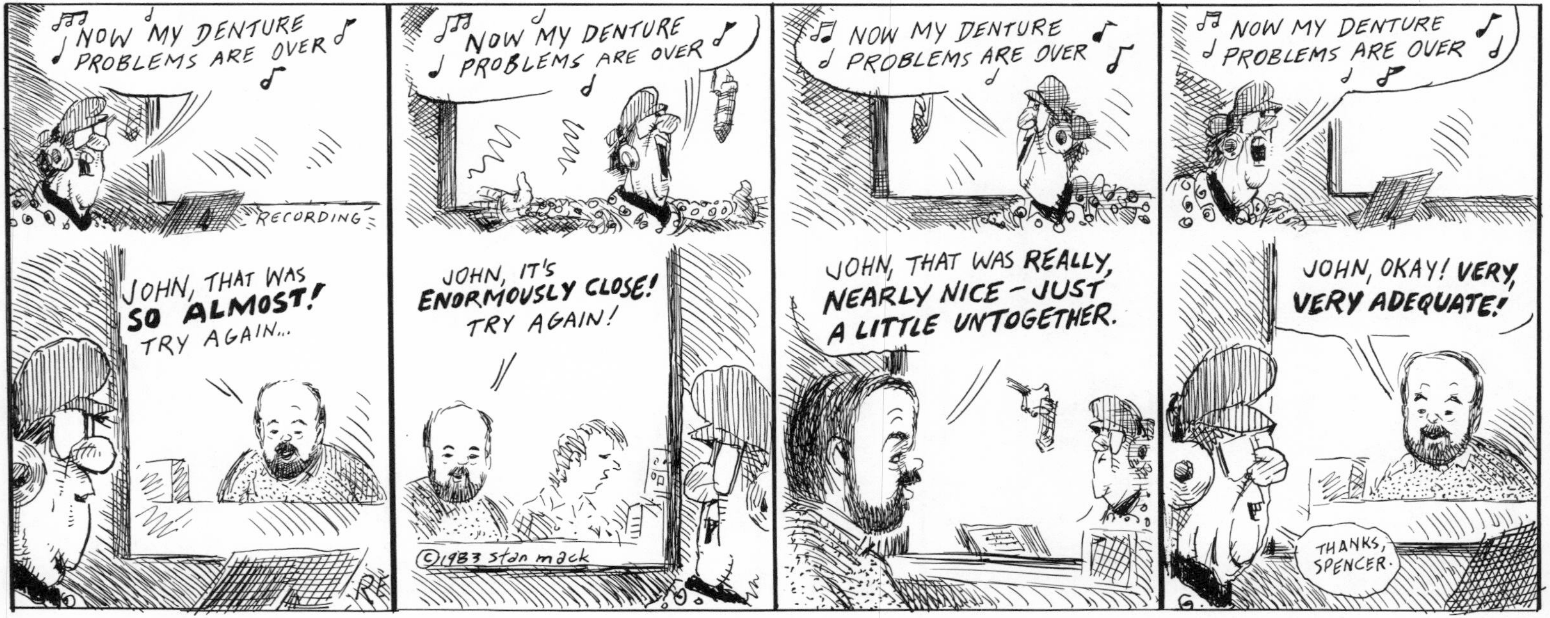
NOW MY DENTURE PROBLEMS ARE OVER
RECORDING
JOHN, THAT WAS SO ALMOST! TRY AGAIN...
NOW MY DENTURE PROBLEMS ARE OVER
JOHN, IT'S ENORMOUSLY CLOSE! TRY AGAIN!
©1983 stan mack
NOW MY DENTURE PROBLEMS ARE OVER
JOHN, THAT WAS REALLY, NEARLY NICE - JUST A LITTLE UNTOGETHER.
NOW MY DENTURE PROBLEMS ARE OVER
JOHN, OKAY! VERY, VERY ADEQUATE!
THANKS, SPENCER.

What's Your Beef?

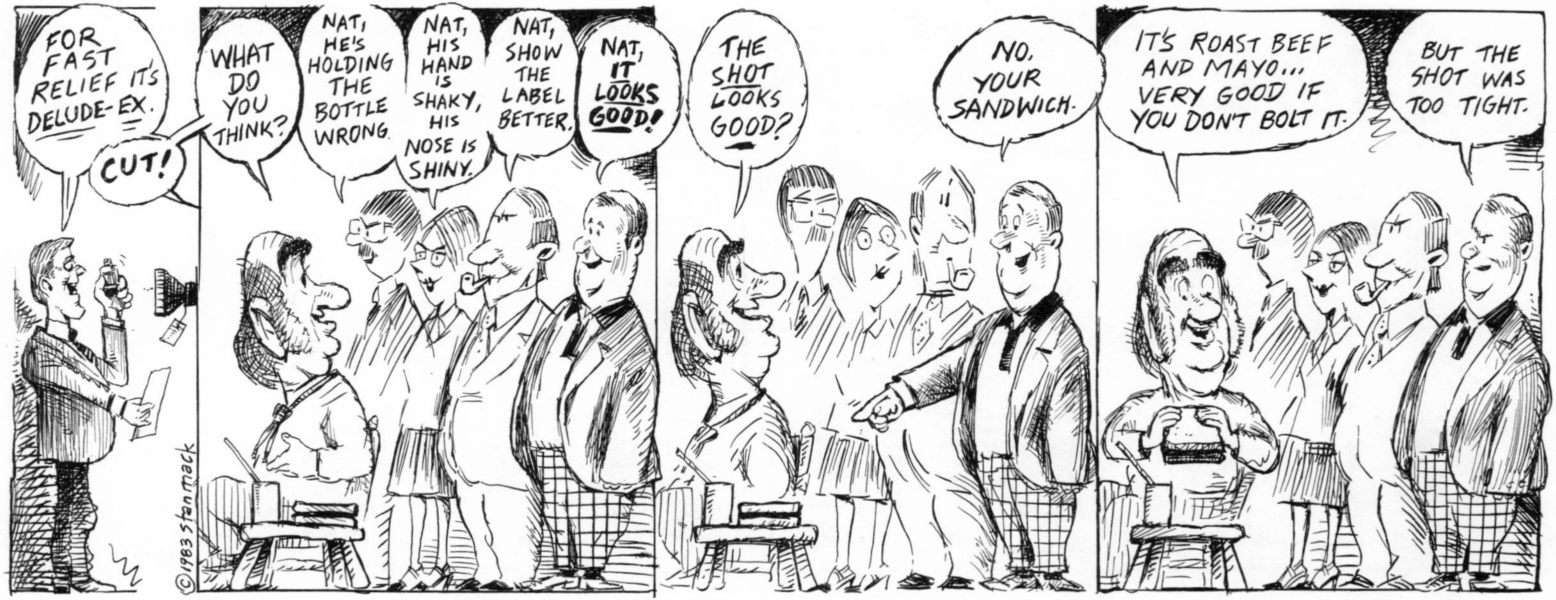
FOR FAST RELIEF IT'S DELUDE-EX.
CUT!
WHAT DO YOU THINK?
NAT, HE'S HOLDING THE BOTTLE WRONG.
NAT, HIS HAND IS SHAKY, HIS NOSE IS SHINY.
NAT, SHOW THE LABEL BETTER.
NAT, IT LOOKS GOOD!
THE SHOT LOOKS GOOD?
NO, YOUR SANDWICH.
IT'S ROAST BEEF AND MAYO... VERY GOOD IF YOU DON'T BOLT IT.
BUT THE SHOT WAS TOO TIGHT.
©1983 stan mack

Pulling Punches

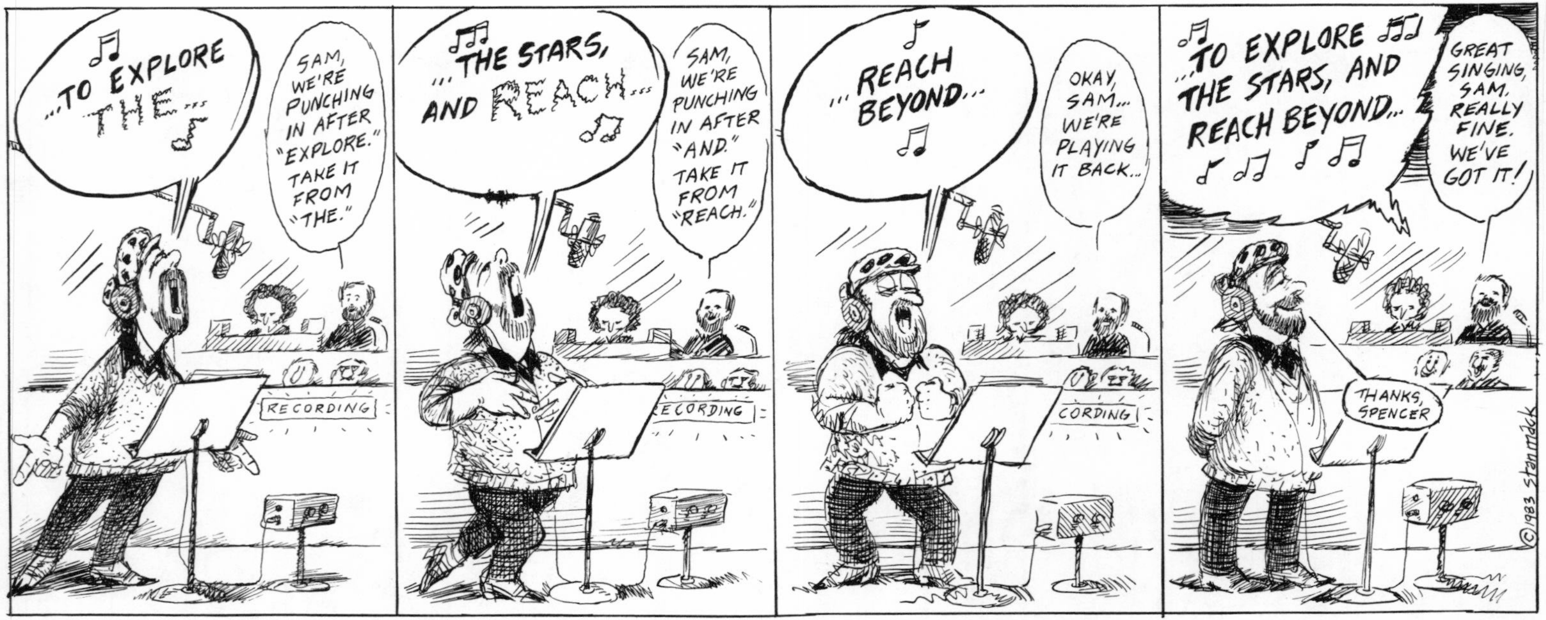

...TO EXPLORE THE...
SAM, WE'RE PUNCHING IN AFTER "EXPLORE." TAKE IT FROM "THE."
RECORDING
...THE STARS, AND REACH...
SAM, WE'RE PUNCHING IN AFTER "AND." TAKE IT FROM "REACH."
ECORDING
...REACH BEYOND...
OKAY, SAM... WE'RE PLAYING IT BACK...
CORDING
...TO EXPLORE THE STARS, AND REACH BEYOND...
GREAT SINGING, SAM, REALLY FINE. WE'VE GOT IT!
THANKS, SPENCER
©1983 stanmack

Reality Testing

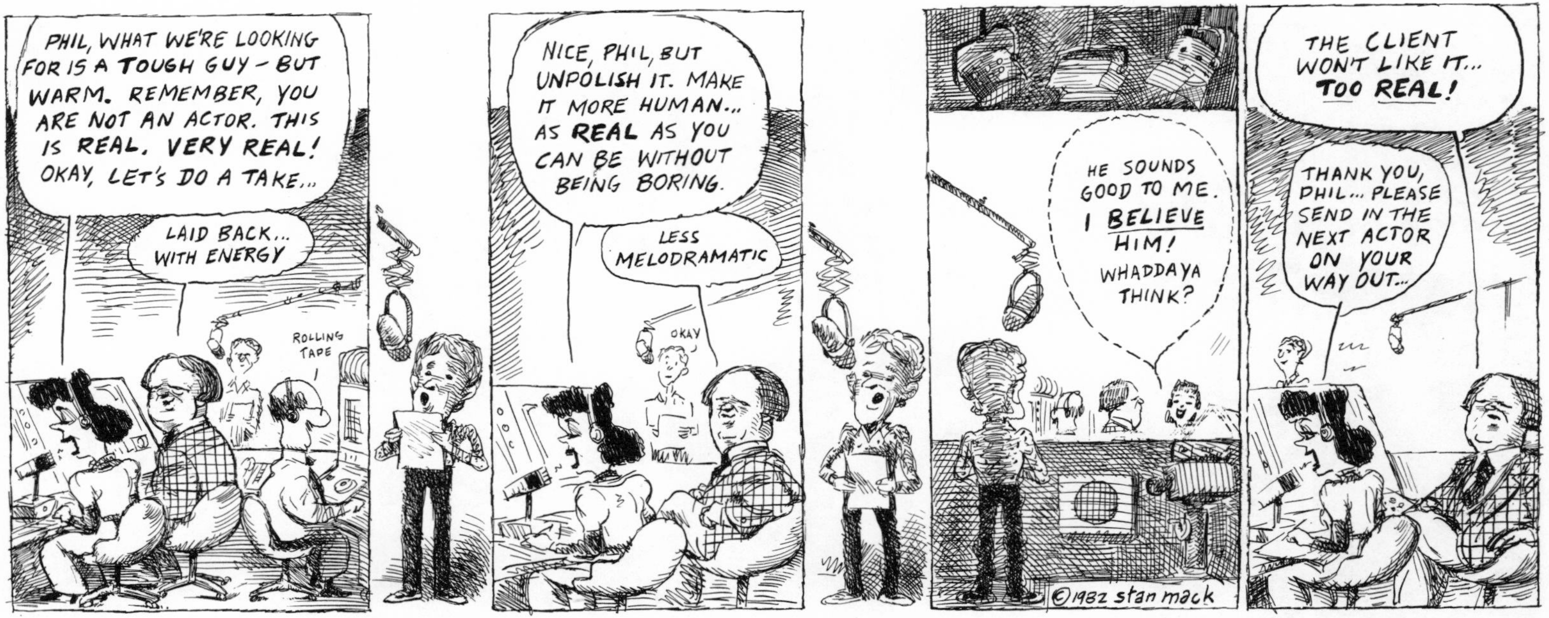
PHIL, WHAT WE'RE LOOKING FOR IS A TOUGH GUY - BUT WARM. REMEMBER, YOU ARE NOT AN ACTOR. THIS IS REAL. VERY REAL! OKAY, LET'S DO A TAKE...
LAID BACK... WITH ENERGY
ROLLING TAPE
NICE, PHIL, BUT UNPOLISH IT. MAKE IT MORE HUMAN... AS REAL AS YOU CAN BE WITHOUT BEING BORING.
LESS MELODRAMATIC
OKAY
HE SOUNDS GOOD TO ME. I BELIEVE HIM! WHADDAYA THINK?
©1982 stan mack
THE CLIENT WON'T LIKE IT... TOO REAL!
THANK YOU, PHIL... PLEASE SEND IN THE NEXT ACTOR ON YOUR WAY OUT...

Once More, With Feeling

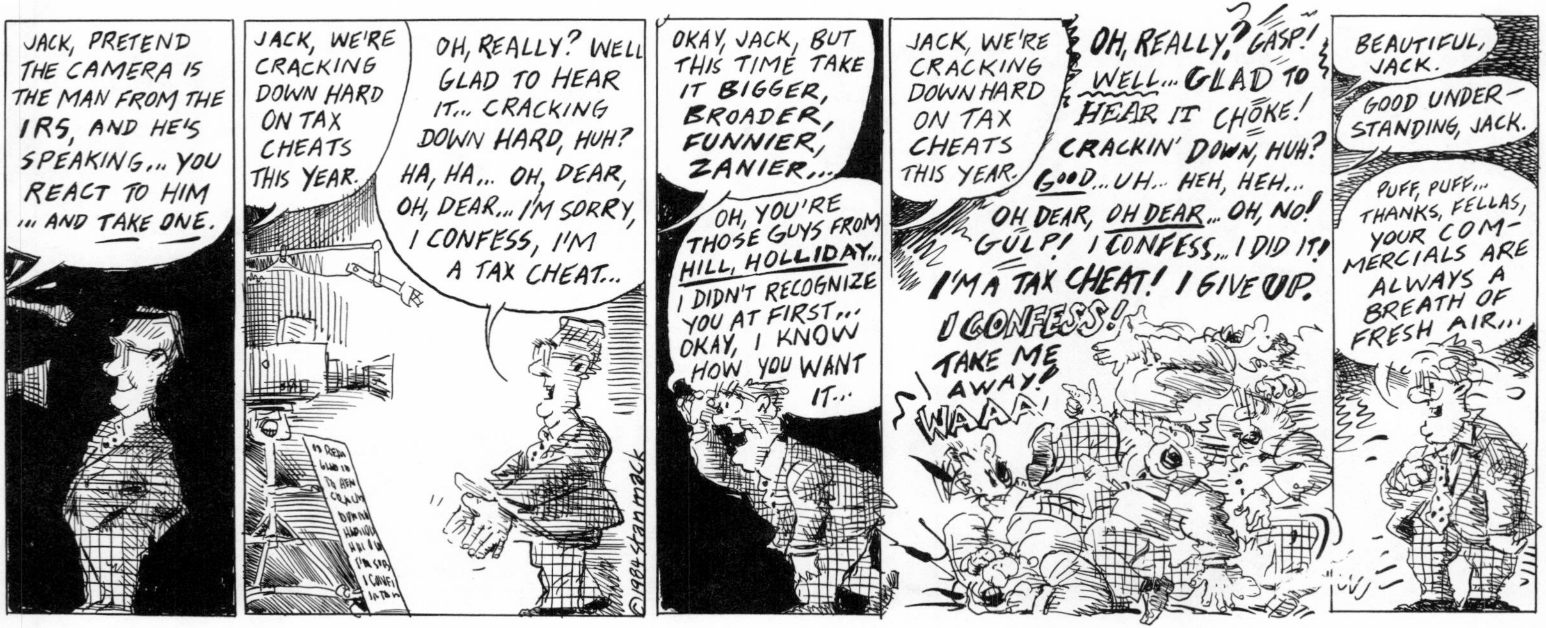
JACK, PRETEND THE CAMERA IS THE MAN FROM THE IRS, AND HE'S SPEAKING... YOU REACT TO HIM ... AND TAKE ONE.
JACK, WE'RE CRACKING DOWN HARD ON TAX CHEATS THIS YEAR.
OH, REALLY? WELL GLAD TO HEAR IT... CRACKING DOWN HARD, HUH? HA, HA... OH, DEAR, OH, DEAR... I'M SORRY, I CONFESS, I'M A TAX CHEAT...
©1984 stan mack
OKAY, JACK, BUT THIS TIME TAKE IT BIGGER, BROADER, FUNNIER, ZANIER...
OH, YOU'RE THOSE GUYS FROM HILL, HOLLIDAY... I DIDN'T RECOGNIZE YOU AT FIRST... OKAY, I KNOW HOW YOU WANT IT...
JACK, WE'RE CRACKING DOWN HARD ON TAX CHEATS THIS YEAR.
OH, REALLY? GASP! WELL... GLAD TO HEAR IT CHOKE! CRACKIN' DOWN, HUH? GOOD... UH... HEH, HEH... OH DEAR, OH DEAR... OH, NO! GULP! I CONFESS... I DID IT! I'M A TAX CHEAT! I GIVE UP. I CONFESS! TAKE ME AWAY!
WAAA!
BEAUTIFUL, JACK.
GOOD UNDERSTANDING, JACK.
PUFF, PUFF... THANKS, FELLAS, YOUR COMMERCIALS ARE ALWAYS A BREATH OF FRESH AIR...

Disorganized Labor

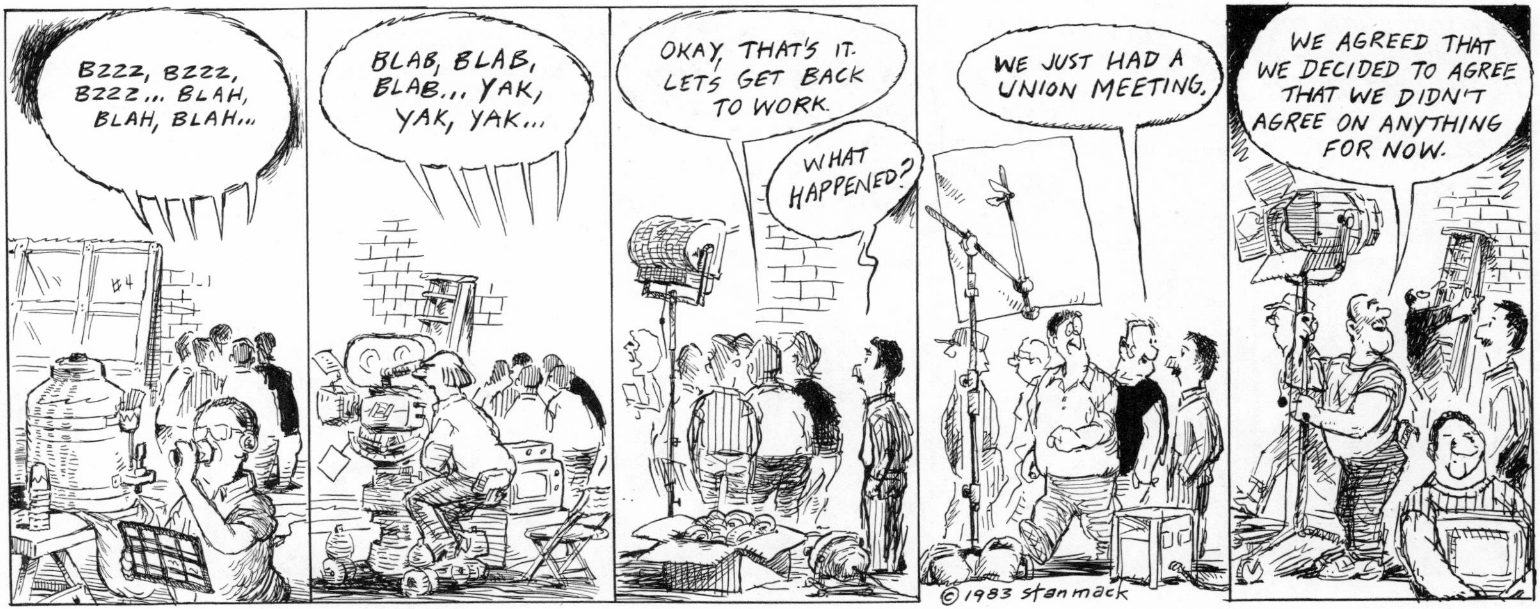
BZZZ, BZZZ, BZZZ... BLAH, BLAH, BLAH, BLAH...
#4
BLAB, BLAB, BLAB... YAK, YAK, YAK...
OKAY, THAT'S IT. LETS GET BACK TO WORK.
WHAT HAPPENED?
WE JUST HAD A UNION MEETING.
WE AGREED THAT WE DECIDED TO AGREE THAT WE DIDN'T AGREE ON ANYTHING FOR NOW.
© 1983 stanmack

Jingle Jingoism

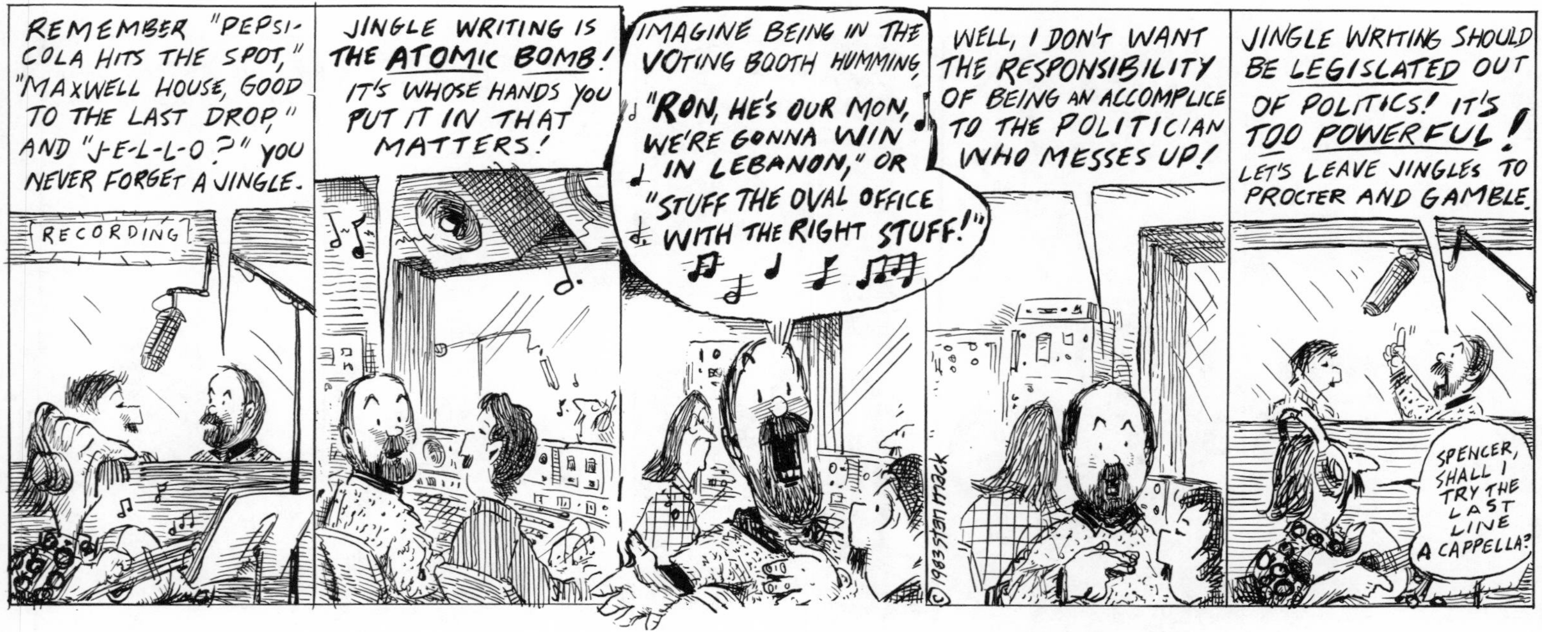
REMEMBER "PEPSI-COLA HITS THE SPOT," "MAXWELL HOUSE, GOOD TO THE LAST DROP," AND "J-E-L-L-O?" YOU NEVER FORGET A JINGLE.
RECORDING
JINGLE WRITING IS THE ATOMIC BOMB! IT'S WHOSE HANDS YOU PUT IT IN THAT MATTERS!
IMAGINE BEING IN THE VOTING BOOTH HUMMING, "RON, HE'S OUR MON, WE'RE GONNA WIN IN LEBANON," OR "STUFF THE OVAL OFFICE WITH THE RIGHT STUFF!"
© 1983 STAN MACK
WELL, I DON'T WANT THE RESPONSIBILITY OF BEING AN ACCOMPLICE TO THE POLITICIAN WHO MESSES UP!
JINGLE WRITING SHOULD BE LEGISLATED OUT OF POLITICS! IT'S TOO POWERFUL! LET'S LEAVE JINGLES TO PROCTER AND GAMBLE.
SPENCER, SHALL I TRY THE LAST LINE A CAPPELLA?

Vox Popular

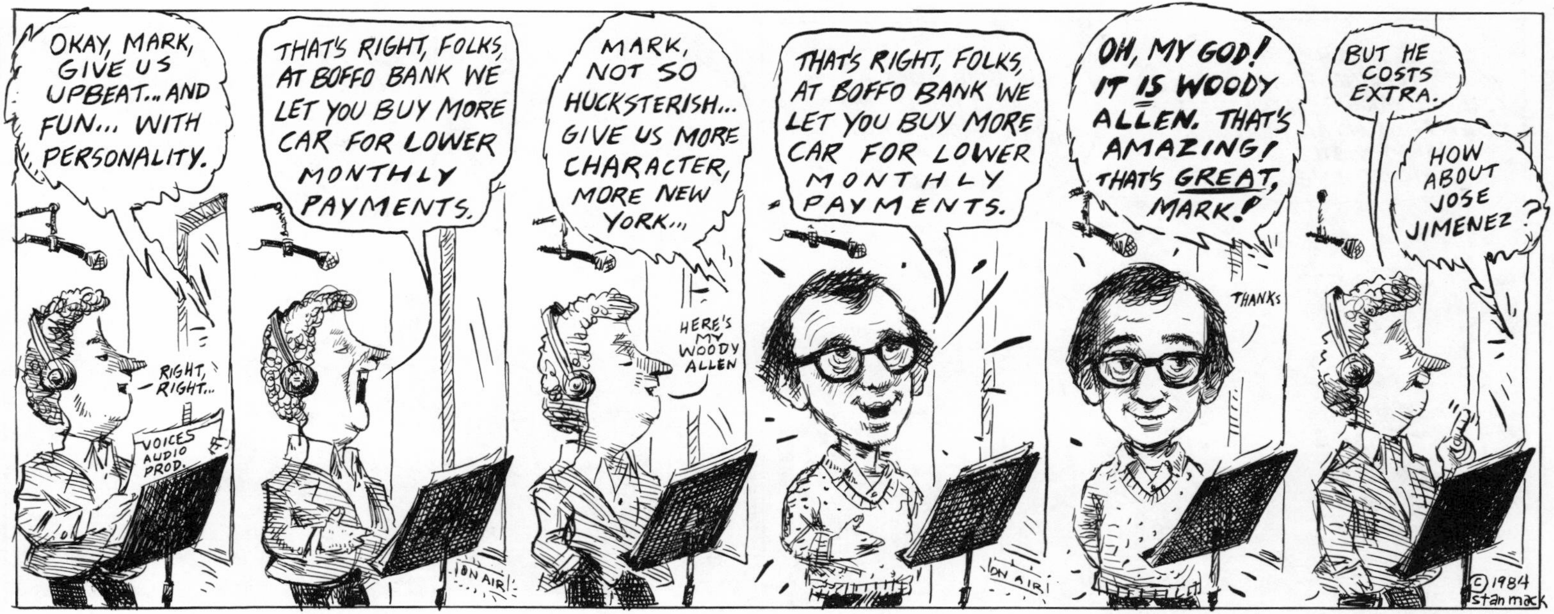

OKAY, MARK, GIVE US UPBEAT... AND FUN... WITH PERSONALITY.
RIGHT, RIGHT...
VOICES AUDIO PROD.
THAT'S RIGHT, FOLKS, AT BOFFO BANK WE LET YOU BUY MORE CAR FOR LOWER MONTHLY PAYMENTS.
ON AIR
MARK, NOT SO HUCKSTERISH... GIVE US MORE CHARACTER, MORE NEW YORK...
HERE'S MY WOODY ALLEN
THAT'S RIGHT, FOLKS, AT BOFFO BANK WE LET YOU BUY MORE CAR FOR LOWER MONTHLY PAYMENTS.
ON AIR
OH, MY GOD! IT IS WOODY ALLEN. THAT'S AMAZING! THAT'S GREAT, MARK!
THANKS
BUT HE COSTS EXTRA.
HOW ABOUT JOSE JIMENEZ?
© 1984 stan mack

Sob Sister

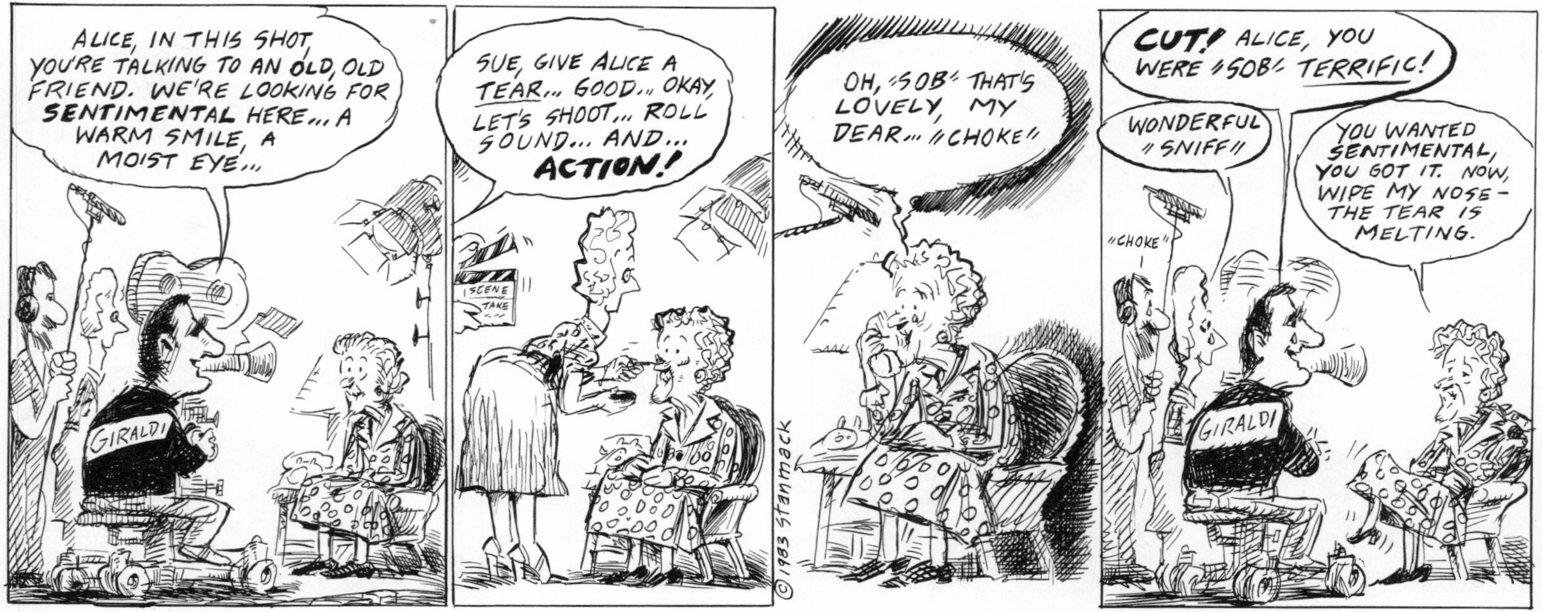
ALICE, IN THIS SHOT, YOU'RE TALKING TO AN OLD, OLD FRIEND. WE'RE LOOKING FOR SENTIMENTAL HERE... A WARM SMILE, A MOIST EYE...
GIRALDI
SUE, GIVE ALICE A TEAR... GOOD... OKAY, LET'S SHOOT... ROLL SOUND... AND... ACTION!
SCENE
TAKE
OH, "SOB" THAT'S LOVELY, MY DEAR... "CHOKE"
© 1983 stanmack
CUT! ALICE, YOU WERE "SOB" TERRIFIC!
WONDERFUL "SNIFF"
"CHOKE"
YOU WANTED SENTIMENTAL, YOU GOT IT. NOW, WIPE MY NOSE— THE TEAR IS MELTING.
GIRALDI

Zoo Story

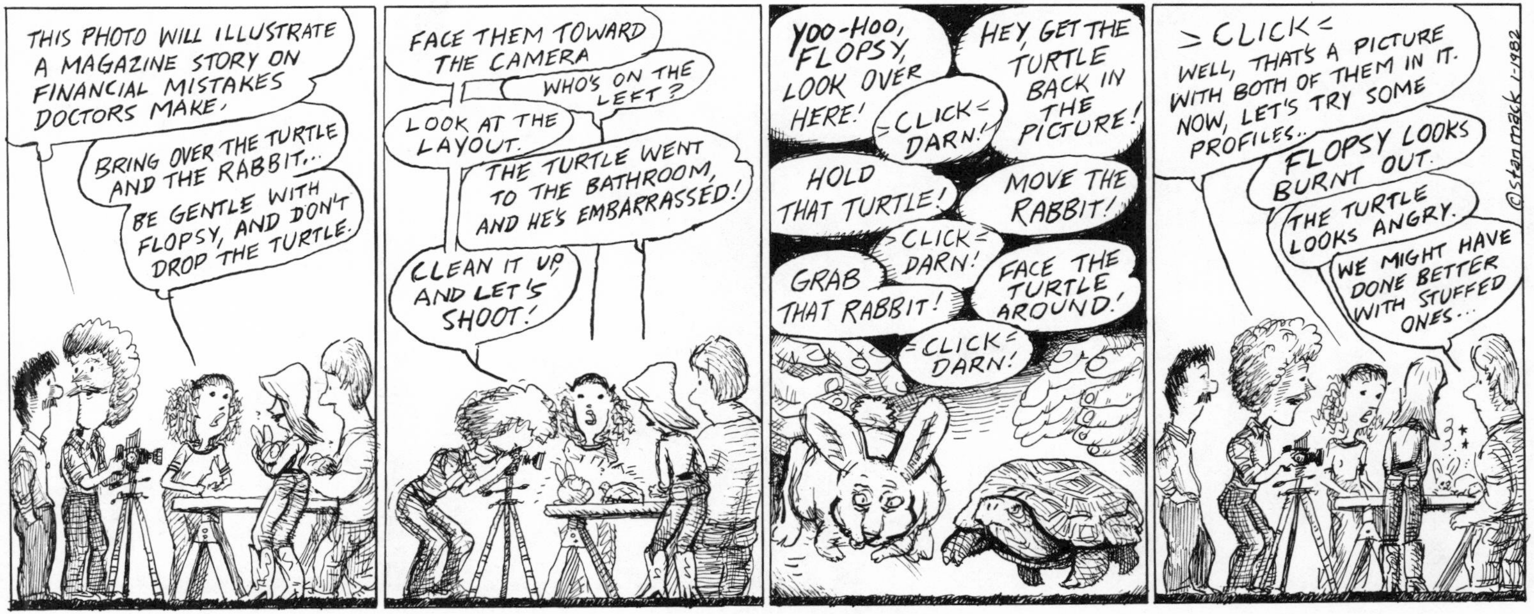
THIS PHOTO WILL ILLUSTRATE A MAGAZINE STORY ON FINANCIAL MISTAKES DOCTORS MAKE.
BRING OVER THE TURTLE AND THE RABBIT...
BE GENTLE WITH FLOPSY, AND DON'T DROP THE TURTLE.
FACE THEM TOWARD THE CAMERA
WHO'S ON THE LEFT?
LOOK AT THE LAYOUT.
THE TURTLE WENT TO THE BATHROOM, AND HE'S EMBARRASSED!
CLEAN IT UP, AND LET'S SHOOT!
YOO-HOO, FLOPSY, LOOK OVER HERE!
HEY, GET THE TURTLE BACK IN THE PICTURE!
=CLICK= DARN!
HOLD THAT TURTLE!
MOVE THE RABBIT!
=CLICK= DARN!
GRAB THAT RABBIT!
FACE THE TURTLE AROUND!
=CLICK= DARN!
=CLICK=
WELL, THAT'S A PICTURE WITH BOTH OF THEM IN IT. NOW, LET'S TRY SOME PROFILES...
FLOPSY LOOKS BURNT OUT.
THE TURTLE LOOKS ANGRY.
WE MIGHT HAVE DONE BETTER WITH STUFFED ONES...
©stanmack 1-1982

Sophisticated Lady

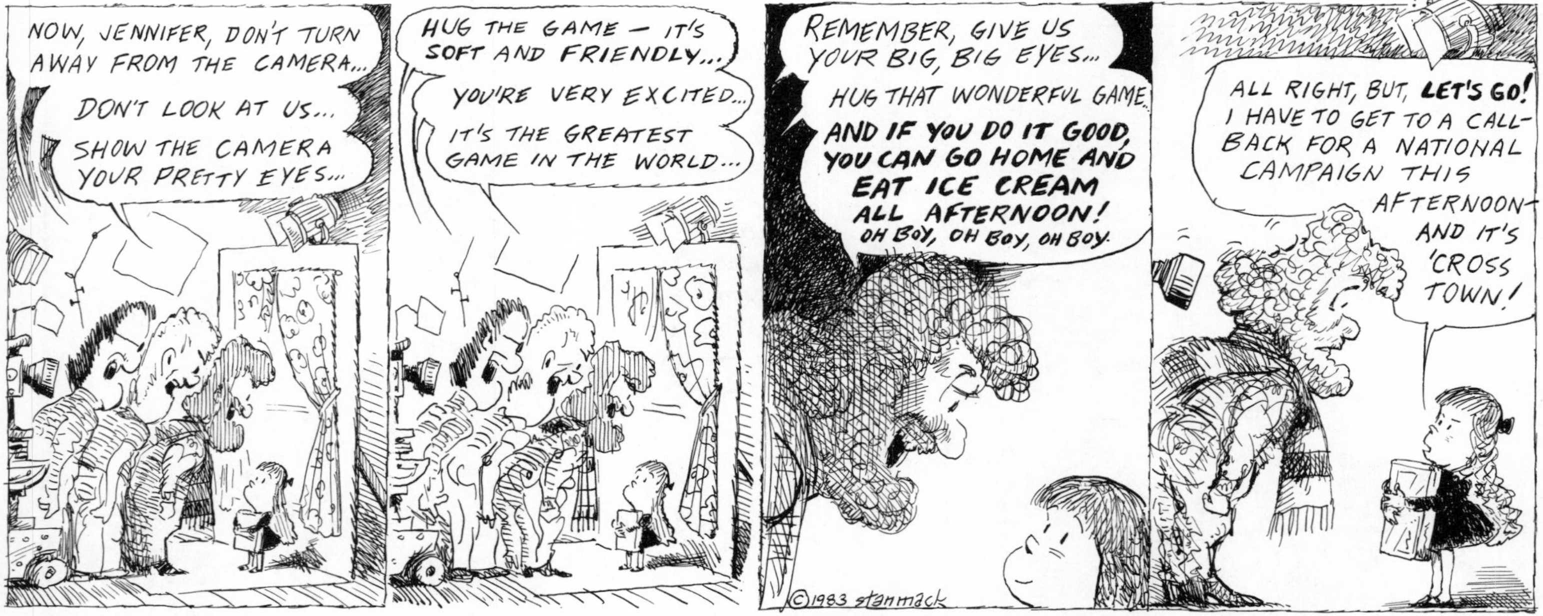

NOW, JENNIFER, DON'T TURN AWAY FROM THE CAMERA...
DON'T LOOK AT US...
SHOW THE CAMERA YOUR PRETTY EYES...
HUG THE GAME – IT'S SOFT AND FRIENDLY...
YOU'RE VERY EXCITED...
IT'S THE GREATEST GAME IN THE WORLD...
REMEMBER, GIVE US YOUR BIG, BIG EYES...
HUG THAT WONDERFUL GAME...
AND IF YOU DO IT GOOD, YOU CAN GO HOME AND EAT ICE CREAM ALL AFTERNOON!
OH BOY, OH BOY, OH BOY.
ALL RIGHT, BUT, LET'S GO! I HAVE TO GET TO A CALL-BACK FOR A NATIONAL CAMPAIGN THIS AFTERNOON–AND IT'S 'CROSS TOWN!
©1983 stanmack

Computer Collideoscope

The Spoiler

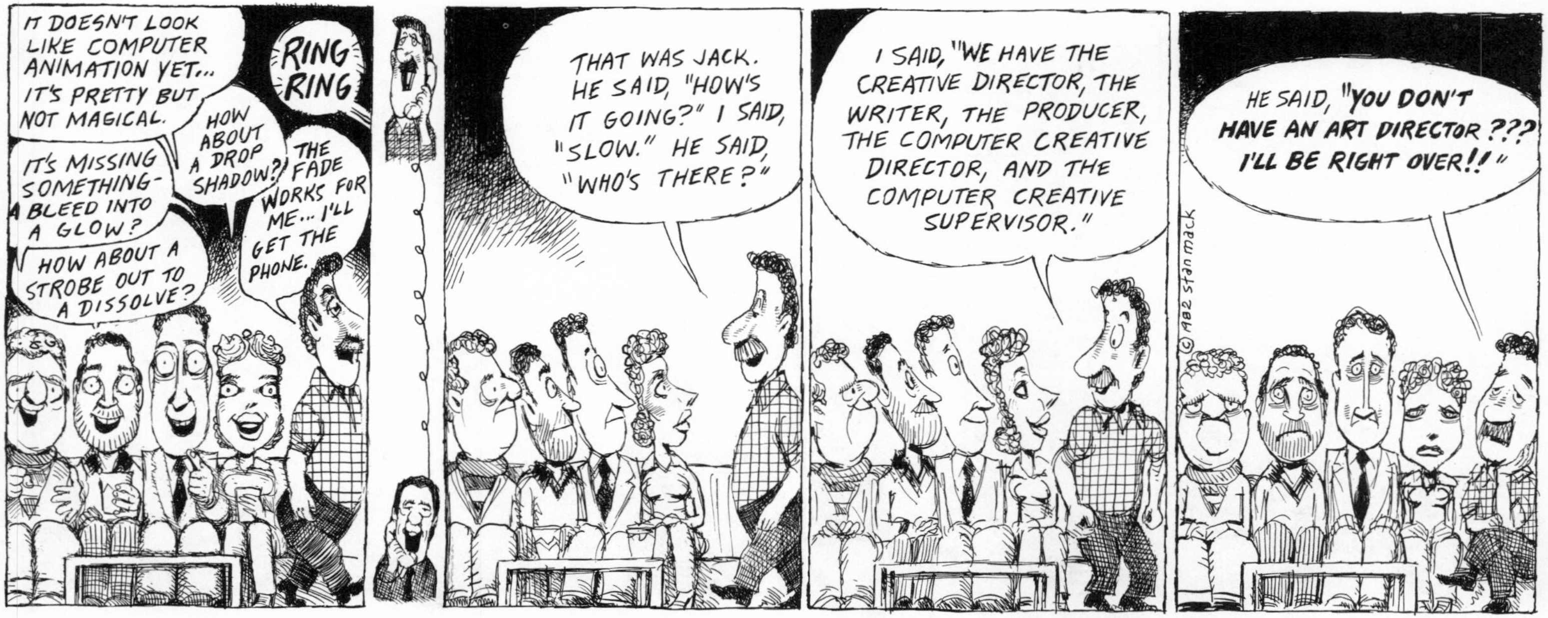
IT DOESN'T LOOK LIKE COMPUTER ANIMATION YET... IT'S PRETTY BUT NOT MAGICAL.
IT'S MISSING SOMETHING- A BLEED INTO A GLOW?
HOW ABOUT A DROP SHADOW?
HOW ABOUT A STROBE OUT TO A DISSOLVE?
RING RING
THE FADE WORKS FOR ME... I'LL GET THE PHONE.
THAT WAS JACK. HE SAID, "HOW'S IT GOING?" I SAID, "SLOW." HE SAID, "WHO'S THERE?"
I SAID, "WE HAVE THE CREATIVE DIRECTOR, THE WRITER, THE PRODUCER, THE COMPUTER CREATIVE DIRECTOR, AND THE COMPUTER CREATIVE SUPERVISOR."
HE SAID, "YOU DON'T HAVE AN ART DIRECTOR??? I'LL BE RIGHT OVER!!"
© 1982 stan mack

A Professional Cartoonist Speaks to Art Students

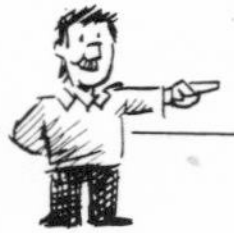

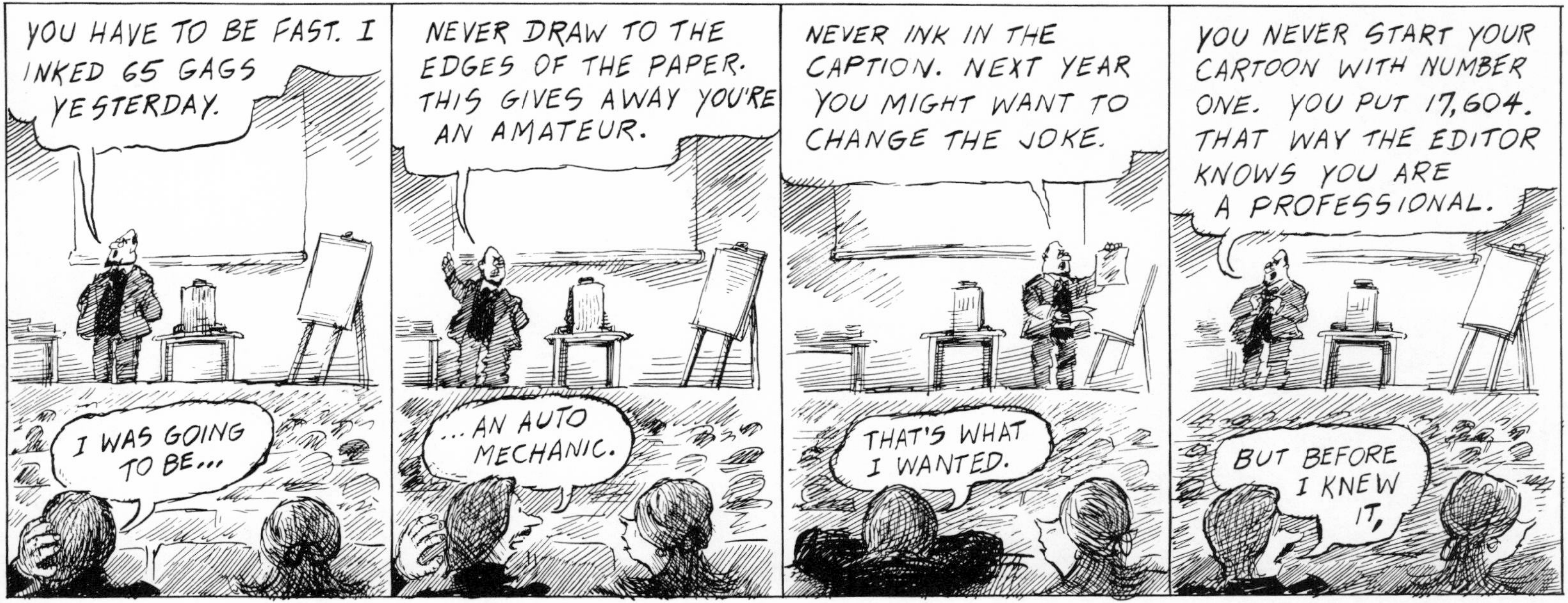
YOU HAVE TO BE FAST. I INKED 65 GAGS YESTERDAY.
I WAS GOING TO BE...
NEVER DRAW TO THE EDGES OF THE PAPER. THIS GIVES AWAY YOU'RE AN AMATEUR.
... AN AUTO MECHANIC.
NEVER INK IN THE CAPTION. NEXT YEAR YOU MIGHT WANT TO CHANGE THE JOKE.
THAT'S WHAT I WANTED.
YOU NEVER START YOUR CARTOON WITH NUMBER ONE. YOU PUT 17,604. THAT WAY THE EDITOR KNOWS YOU ARE A PROFESSIONAL.
BUT BEFORE I KNEW IT,

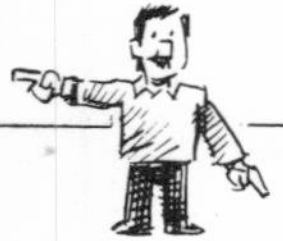

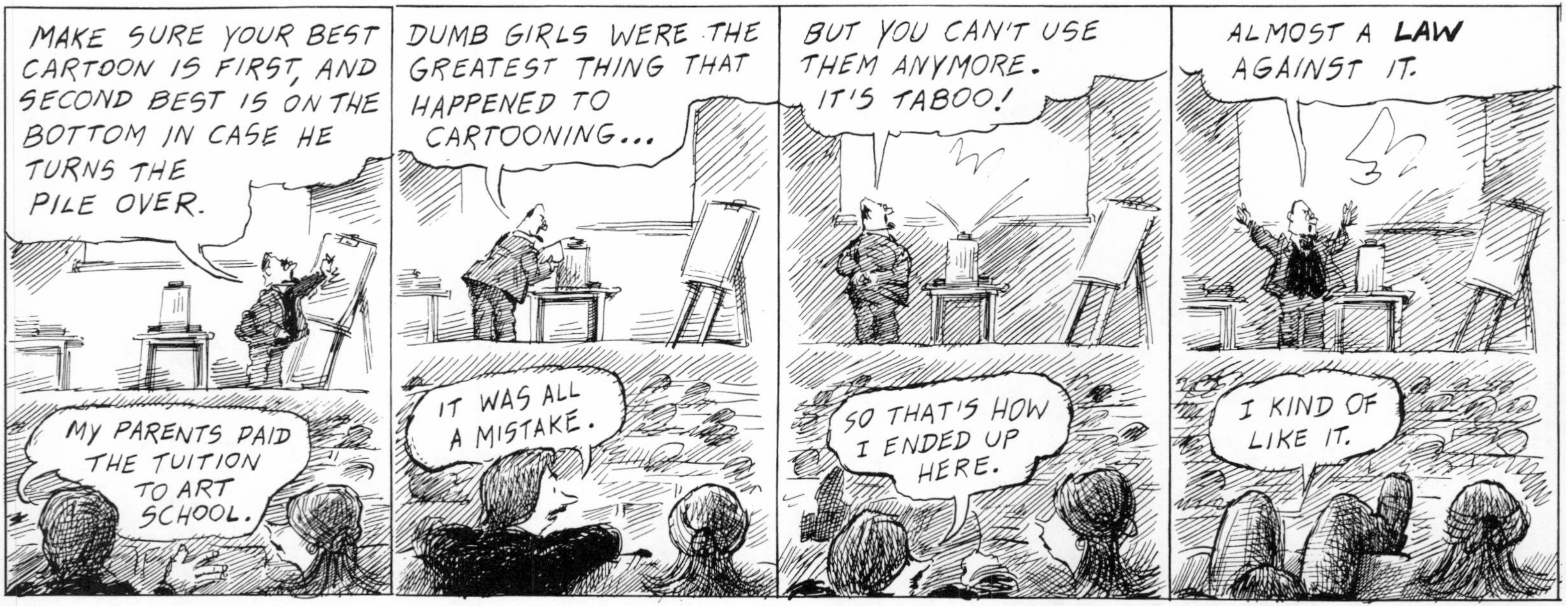
MAKE SURE YOUR BEST CARTOON IS FIRST, AND SECOND BEST IS ON THE BOTTOM IN CASE HE TURNS THE PILE OVER.
MY PARENTS PAID THE TUITION TO ART SCHOOL.
DUMB GIRLS WERE THE GREATEST THING THAT HAPPENED TO CARTOONING...
IT WAS ALL A MISTAKE.
BUT YOU CAN'T USE THEM ANYMORE. IT'S TABOO!
SO THAT'S HOW I ENDED UP HERE.
ALMOST A **LAW** AGAINST IT.
I KIND OF LIKE IT.

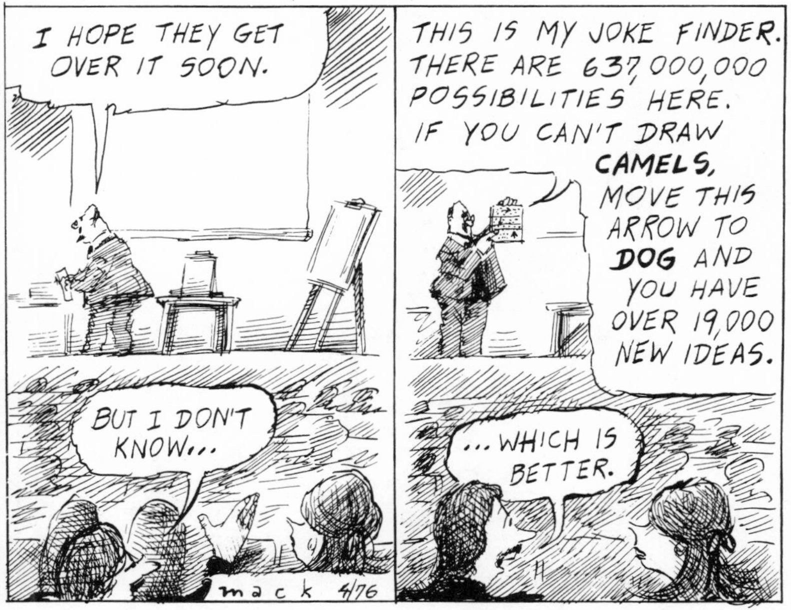
I HOPE THEY GET OVER IT SOON.
BUT I DON'T KNOW...
THIS IS MY JOKE FINDER. THERE ARE 637,000,000 POSSIBILITIES HERE. IF YOU CAN'T DRAW **CAMELS**, MOVE THIS ARROW TO **DOG** AND YOU HAVE OVER 19,000 NEW IDEAS.
...WHICH IS BETTER.
mack 4/76

Stalking the Wild Punch Line

A Non-Partisan Business

... PANAMA'S OR THE U.S.'S POINT OF VIEW. THE ILLUSTRATION, LIKE THE TEXT, SHOULD BE NONPARTISAN.

IT SHOULD NOT BE NEGATIVE TO EITHER SIDE...

... HAVE AN EDITORIAL SLANT...

...OR POINT OF VIEW...
©stan mack 11/77
... OR IMPLY THAT OUR COMPANY HAS A POLITICAL LEANING IN THIS MATTER."

Who's in charge here?

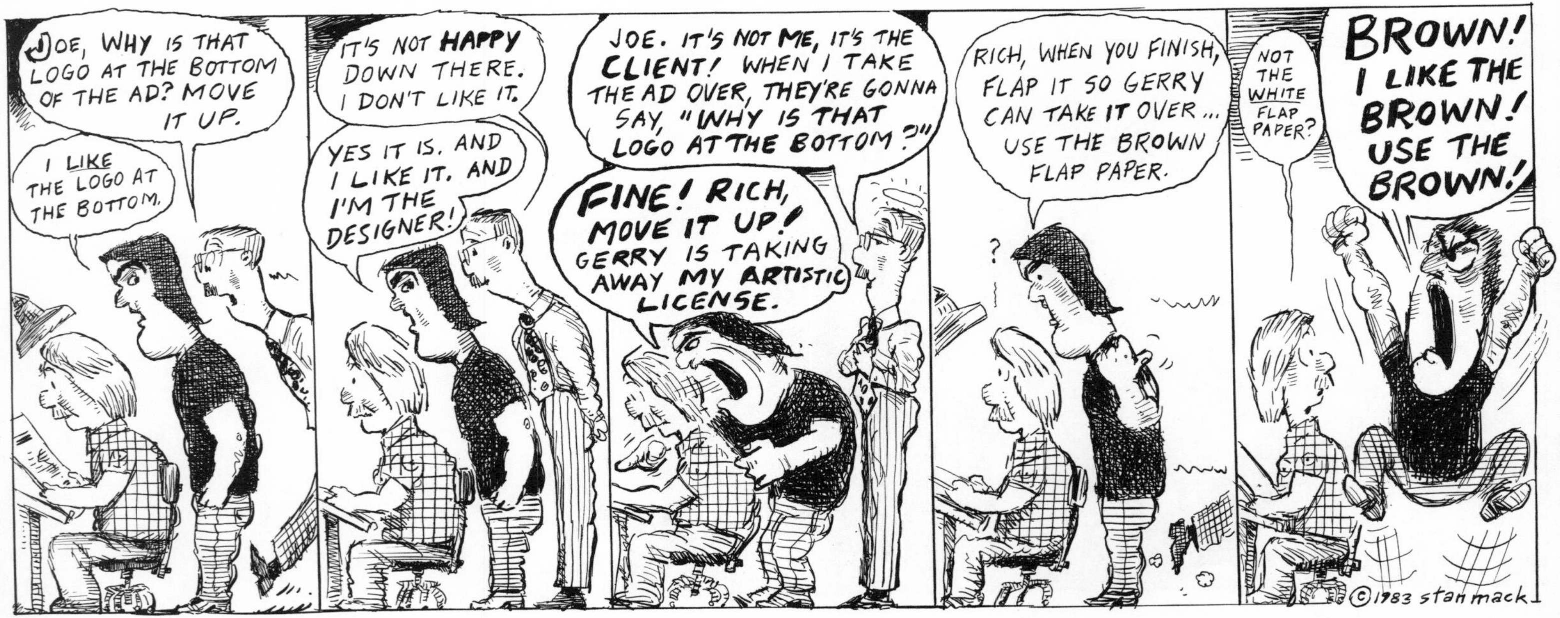
JOE, WHY IS THAT LOGO AT THE BOTTOM OF THE AD? MOVE IT UP.
I LIKE THE LOGO AT THE BOTTOM.
IT'S NOT HAPPY DOWN THERE. I DON'T LIKE IT.
YES IT IS. AND I LIKE IT. AND I'M THE DESIGNER!
JOE. IT'S NOT ME, IT'S THE CLIENT! WHEN I TAKE THE AD OVER, THEY'RE GONNA SAY, "WHY IS THAT LOGO AT THE BOTTOM?"
FINE! RICH, MOVE IT UP! GERRY IS TAKING AWAY MY ARTISTIC LICENSE.
RICH, WHEN YOU FINISH, FLAP IT SO GERRY CAN TAKE IT OVER... USE THE BROWN FLAP PAPER.
NOT THE WHITE FLAP PAPER?
BROWN! I LIKE THE BROWN! USE THE BROWN!
©1983 stan mack

The Moment of Truth

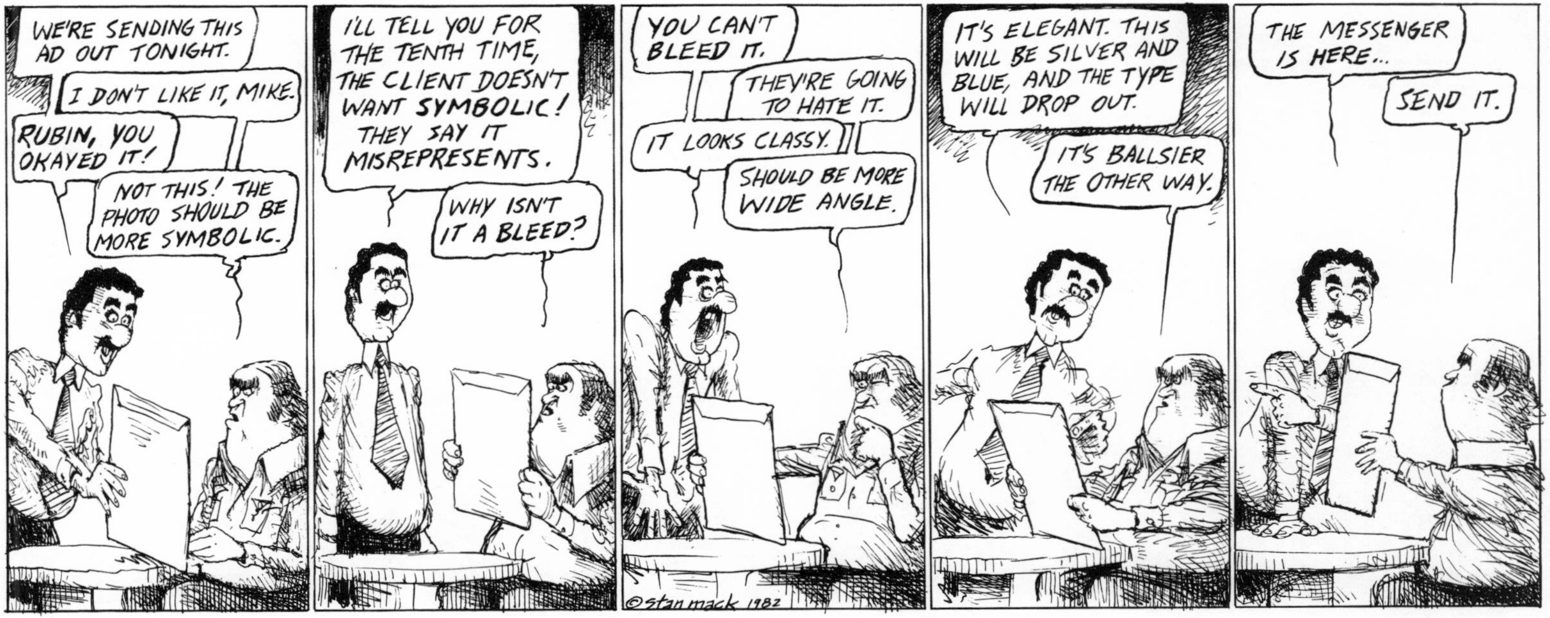
WE'RE SENDING THIS AD OUT TONIGHT.
I DON'T LIKE IT, MIKE.
RUBIN, YOU OKAYED IT!
NOT THIS! THE PHOTO SHOULD BE MORE SYMBOLIC.
I'LL TELL YOU FOR THE TENTH TIME, THE CLIENT DOESN'T WANT SYMBOLIC! THEY SAY IT MISREPRESENTS.
WHY ISN'T IT A BLEED?
YOU CAN'T BLEED IT.
THEY'RE GOING TO HATE IT.
IT LOOKS CLASSY.
SHOULD BE MORE WIDE ANGLE.
©stan mack 1982
IT'S ELEGANT. THIS WILL BE SILVER AND BLUE, AND THE TYPE WILL DROP OUT.
IT'S BALLSIER THE OTHER WAY.
THE MESSENGER IS HERE...
SEND IT.

The Patter of Little Serifs

Back to the Drawing Board

Changing Partners

MEL AND I WERE EQUAL PARTNERS WHEN WE STARTED OUR AGENCY IN A PUB, BUT I KNEW HE WAS JOCKEYING FOR CONTROL...

CLARK'S BAR

SMITH & JONES ADVERTISING

WHEN WE MOVED OUR AGENCY WE FOUND SPACE WITH TWO EXECUTIVE OFFICES OF APPROXIMATELY THE SAME FOOTAGE.

I LET HIM TAKE THE CORNER OFFICE WITH TWO OUTSIDE WALLS. I HAD ONLY ONE OUTSIDE WALL. THAT WAS MY UNDOING. PEOPLE THOUGHT HE WAS CHIEF.

© 1983 stan mack

THEN HE JUMPED INTO BED WITH OUR BOOKKEEPER AND TIED UP THE ACCOUNTS RECEIVABLE... MEL STOLE MY AGENCY.

SMITH & ADVERTISIN

"Lie Detector"

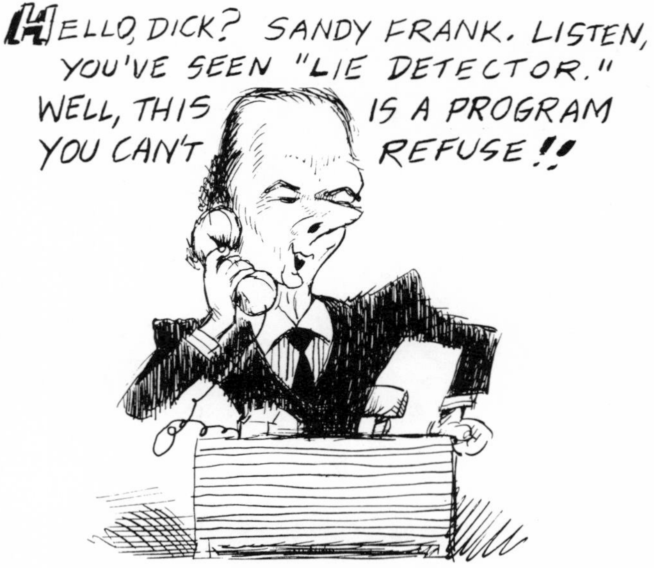
HELLO, DICK? SANDY FRANK. LISTEN, YOU'VE SEEN "LIE DETECTOR." WELL, THIS IS A PROGRAM YOU CAN'T REFUSE!!

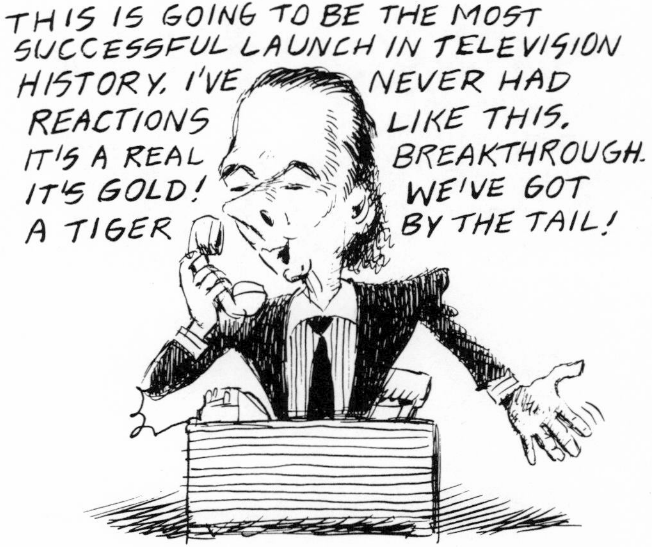
THIS IS GOING TO BE THE MOST SUCCESSFUL LAUNCH IN TELEVISION HISTORY. I'VE NEVER HAD REACTIONS LIKE THIS. IT'S A REAL BREAKTHROUGH. IT'S GOLD! WE'VE GOT A TIGER BY THE TAIL!

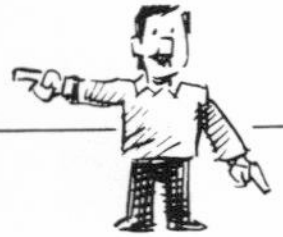

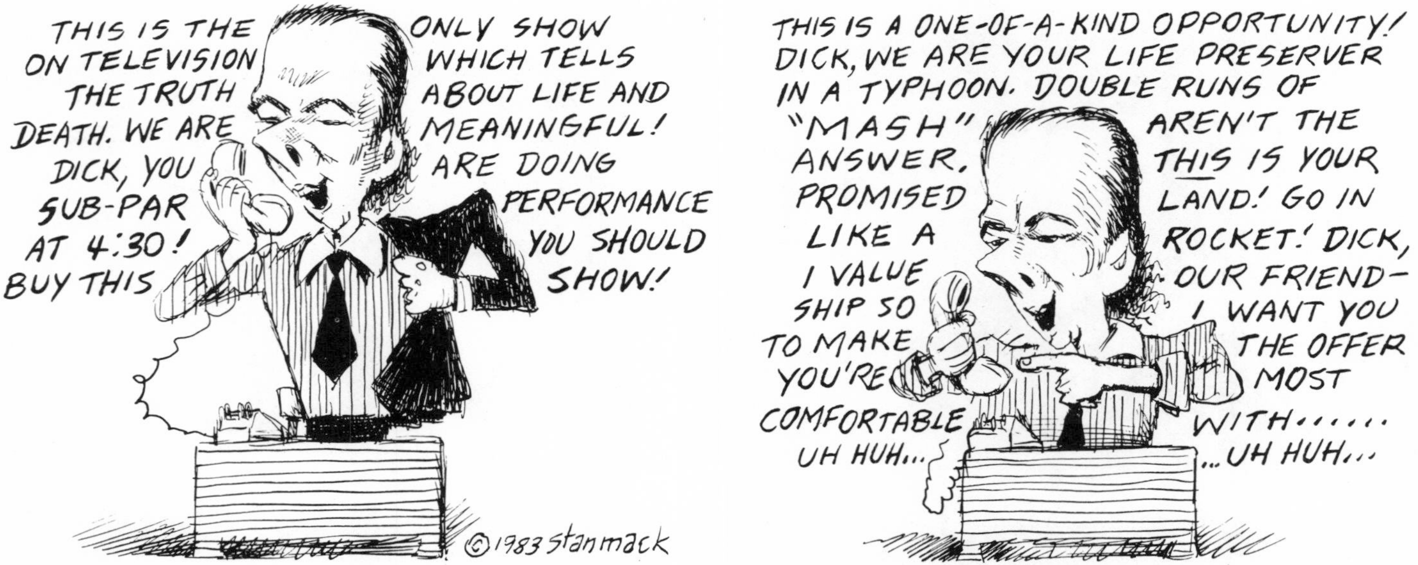
THIS IS THE ONLY SHOW
ON TELEVISION WHICH TELLS
THE TRUTH ABOUT LIFE AND
DEATH. WE ARE MEANINGFUL!
DICK, YOU ARE DOING
SUB-PAR PERFORMANCE
AT 4:30! YOU SHOULD
BUY THIS SHOW!
©1983 stanmack
THIS IS A ONE-OF-A-KIND OPPORTUNITY!
DICK, WE ARE YOUR LIFE PRESERVER
IN A TYPHOON. DOUBLE RUNS OF
"MASH" AREN'T THE
ANSWER. THIS IS YOUR
PROMISED LAND! GO IN
LIKE A ROCKET! DICK,
I VALUE OUR FRIEND-
SHIP SO I WANT YOU
TO MAKE THE OFFER
YOU'RE MOST
COMFORTABLE WITH......
UH HUH...
...UH HUH...

ALL RIGHT, DICK, IF THAT'S YOUR OFFER, I'M NOT GOING TO IMPOSE MY WILL ON YOU. BUT LET ME LEVEL WITH YOU! YOUR COMPETITION WANTS THIS SHOW BADLY! I'M GOING TO TRY MY DAMNEDEST FOR YOU, BUT YOU HAVEN'T GIVEN ME THAT ACE! I'M NOT TRYING TO PRESSURE YOU, BUT DON'T TIE MY HANDS FOR A LOUSY FEW DOLLARS! DICK, IF BEGIN CAN GET TOGETHER WITH SADAT, WE CAN GET TOGETHER! NOW, WHAT'S THE BEST DEAL YOU CAN OFFER ME?

WE'RE IN 9 OUT OF THE 10 TOP MARKETS! DICK, YOU SHOULD BE SEIZING THE OPPORTUNITY! DON'T ACT LIKE I'M BRINGING YOU THE PLAGUE! WHAT HAVE YOU GOT OTHERWISE? DRECK! DICK, I'M BEING HONEST AND CANDID! I WANT YOU TO HAVE THIS. DON'T HANG IN WITH DEAD MEAT! "LIE DETECTOR" WILL LIFT YOU ABOVE YOUR LEAD-IN! THE UPSIDE ON THIS IS ENORMOUS! THE DOWNSIDE IS NIL! GO WITH GREAT DEMOGRAPHICS! WE WILL DELIVER BIG DOUBLE DIGITS! MARRY IT TO YOUR 5 O'CLOCK SHOW AND GO DOWN THE AISLE TOGETHER. IT'S A PERFECT ADJACENCY! YOU'LL DO SO WELL, IT'LL BE A PROGRAMMER'S DREAM! LIKE... LIKE... "HAPPY DAYS" AND "LAVERNE AND SHIRLEY"! WHADDAYA THINK, DICK? YA WANT A FEW MINUTES TO THINK ABOUT IT, DICK??

Magazine Handicapping

All the News That's Fit to Buy

Perfect Pitch

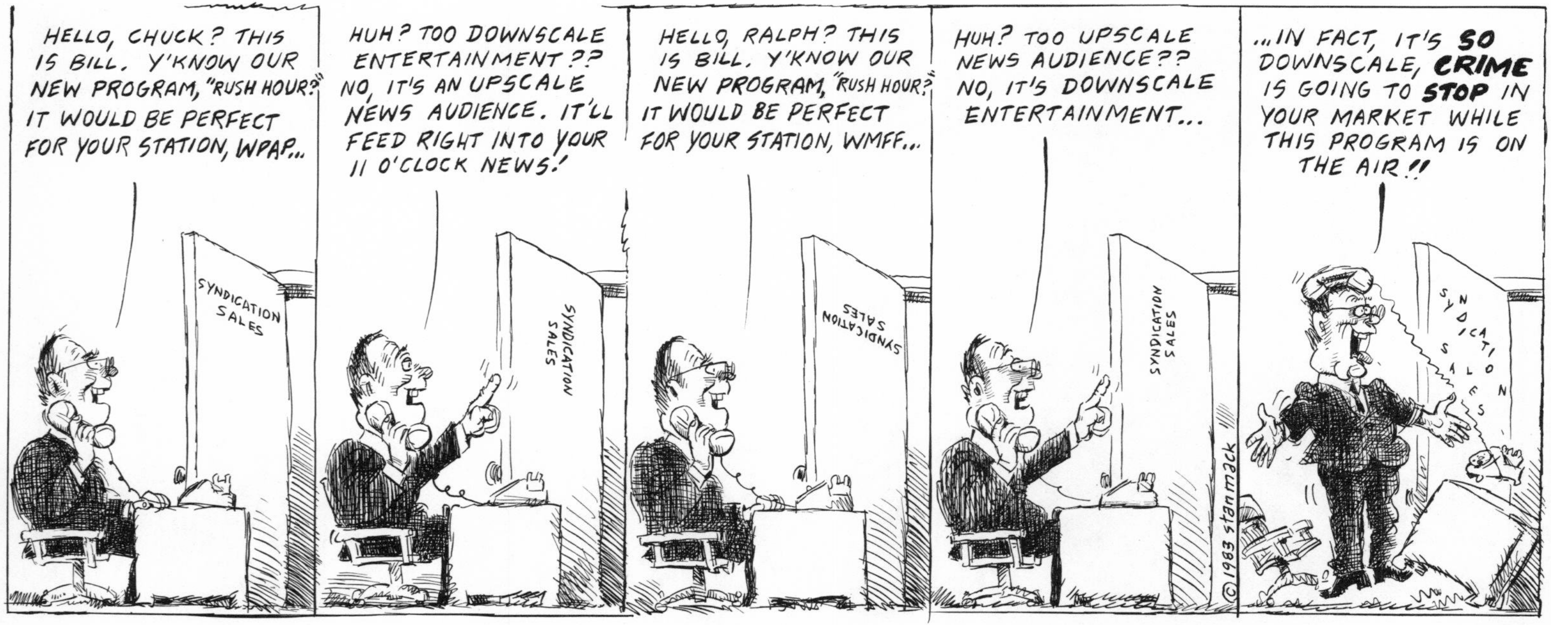
HELLO, CHUCK? THIS IS BILL. Y'KNOW OUR NEW PROGRAM, "RUSH HOUR?" IT WOULD BE PERFECT FOR YOUR STATION, WPAP...
SYNDICATION SALES
HUH? TOO DOWNSCALE ENTERTAINMENT?? NO, IT'S AN UPSCALE NEWS AUDIENCE. IT'LL FEED RIGHT INTO YOUR 11 O'CLOCK NEWS!
SYNDICATION SALES
HELLO, RALPH? THIS IS BILL. Y'KNOW OUR NEW PROGRAM, "RUSH HOUR?" IT WOULD BE PERFECT FOR YOUR STATION, WMFF...
SYNDICATION SALES
HUH? TOO UPSCALE NEWS AUDIENCE?? NO, IT'S DOWNSCALE ENTERTAINMENT...
SYNDICATION SALES
©1983 stanmack
...IN FACT, IT'S SO DOWNSCALE, CRIME IS GOING TO STOP IN YOUR MARKET WHILE THIS PROGRAM IS ON THE AIR!!

Sweet Dreams

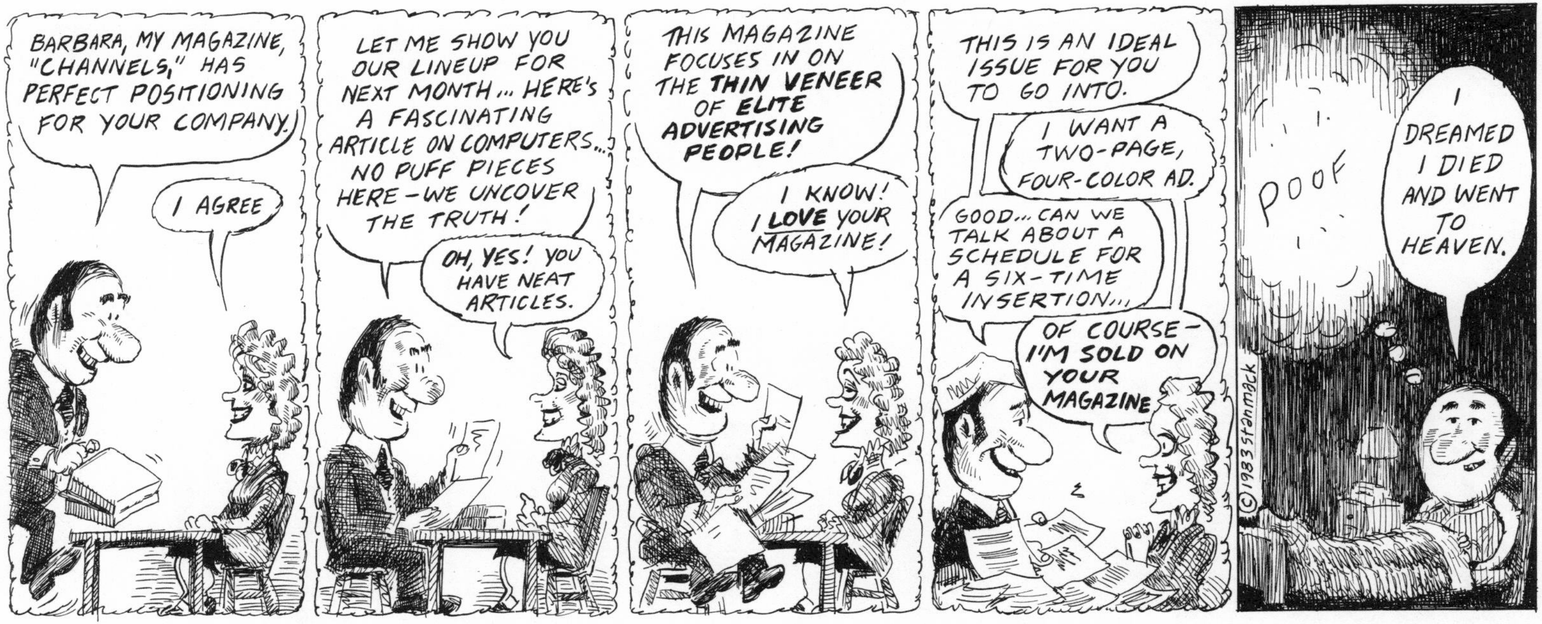

BARBARA, MY MAGAZINE, "CHANNELS," HAS PERFECT POSITIONING FOR YOUR COMPANY.
I AGREE
LET ME SHOW YOU OUR LINEUP FOR NEXT MONTH... HERE'S A FASCINATING ARTICLE ON COMPUTERS... NO PUFF PIECES HERE—WE UNCOVER THE TRUTH!
OH, YES! YOU HAVE NEAT ARTICLES.
THIS MAGAZINE FOCUSES IN ON THE THIN VENEER OF ELITE ADVERTISING PEOPLE!
I KNOW! I LOVE YOUR MAGAZINE!
THIS IS AN IDEAL ISSUE FOR YOU TO GO INTO.
I WANT A TWO-PAGE, FOUR-COLOR AD.
GOOD... CAN WE TALK ABOUT A SCHEDULE FOR A SIX-TIME INSERTION...
OF COURSE—I'M SOLD ON YOUR MAGAZINE
©1983 stanmack
POOF
I DREAMED I DIED AND WENT TO HEAVEN.

Home is Where the Desk Is

New Digs

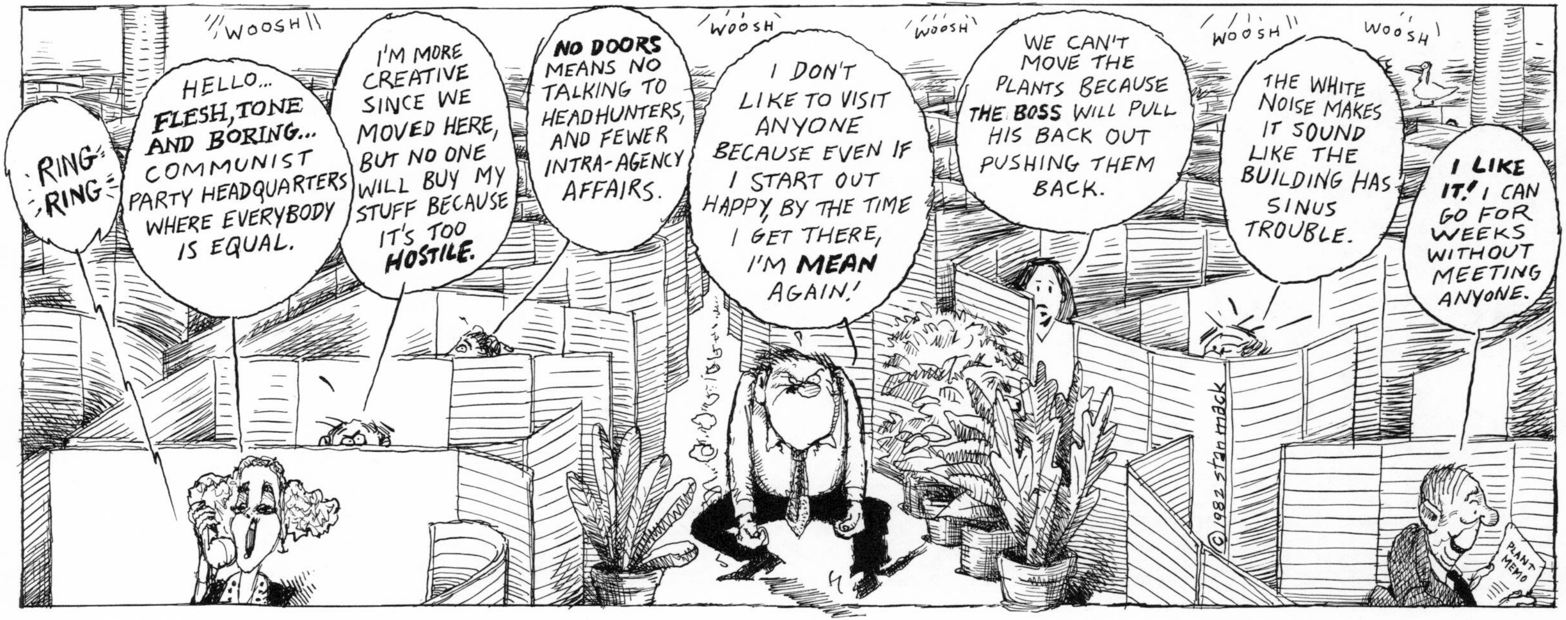
WOOSH
WOOSH
WOOSH
WOOSH
WOOSH
RING RING
HELLO... FLESH, TONE AND BORING... COMMUNIST PARTY HEADQUARTERS WHERE EVERYBODY IS EQUAL.
I'M MORE CREATIVE SINCE WE MOVED HERE, BUT NO ONE WILL BUY MY STUFF BECAUSE IT'S TOO HOSTILE.
NO DOORS MEANS NO TALKING TO HEADHUNTERS, AND FEWER INTRA-AGENCY AFFAIRS.
I DON'T LIKE TO VISIT ANYONE BECAUSE EVEN IF I START OUT HAPPY, BY THE TIME I GET THERE, I'M MEAN AGAIN!
WE CAN'T MOVE THE PLANTS BECAUSE THE BOSS WILL PULL HIS BACK OUT PUSHING THEM BACK.
THE WHITE NOISE MAKES IT SOUND LIKE THE BUILDING HAS SINUS TROUBLE.
I LIKE IT! I CAN GO FOR WEEKS WITHOUT MEETING ANYONE.
PLANT MEMO
© 1982 stan mack

Philadelphia Storyboard, Part I

Philadelphia Storyboard, Part II

Philadelphia Storyboard, Part III

Philadelphia Storyboard, Part IV

Philadelphia Storyboard, Part V

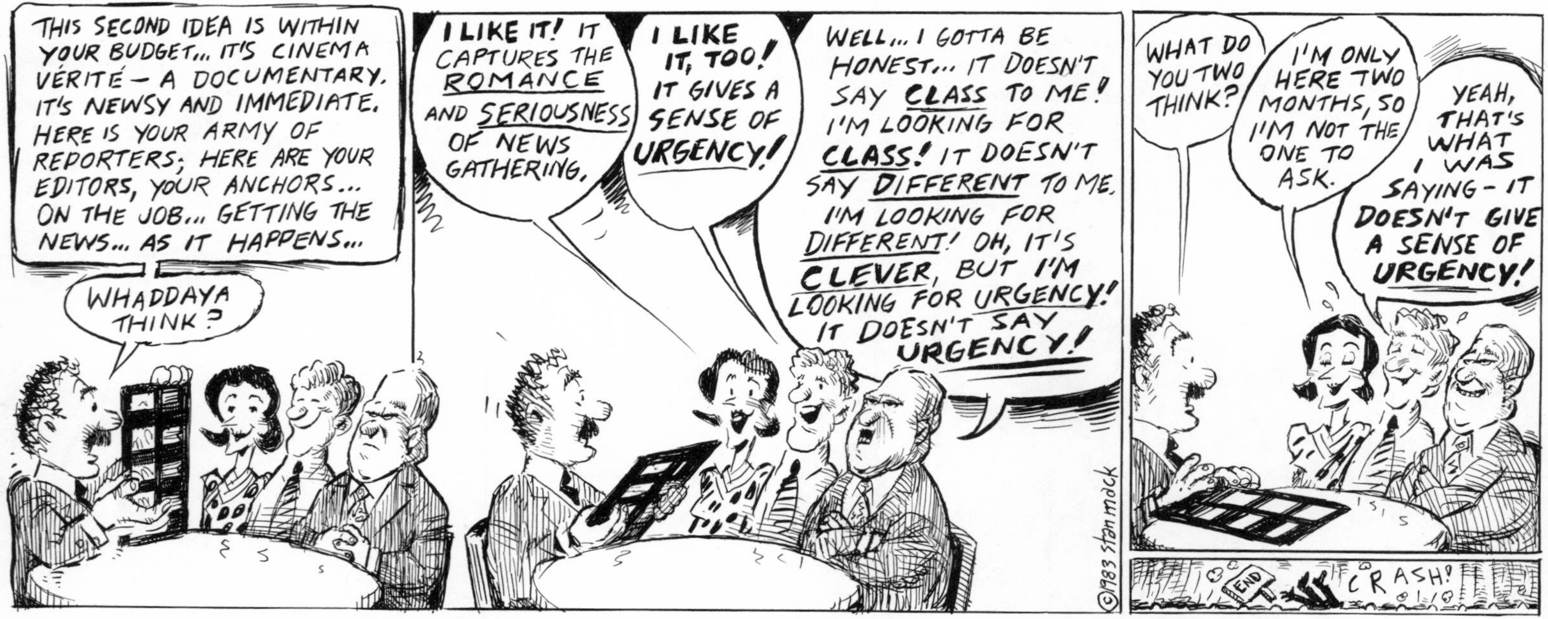
THIS SECOND IDEA IS WITHIN YOUR BUDGET... IT'S CINEMA VÉRITÉ — A DOCUMENTARY. IT'S NEWSY AND IMMEDIATE. HERE IS YOUR ARMY OF REPORTERS; HERE ARE YOUR EDITORS, YOUR ANCHORS... ON THE JOB... GETTING THE NEWS... AS IT HAPPENS...
WHADDAYA THINK?
I LIKE IT! IT CAPTURES THE ROMANCE AND SERIOUSNESS OF NEWS GATHERING.
I LIKE IT, TOO! IT GIVES A SENSE OF URGENCY!
WELL... I GOTTA BE HONEST... IT DOESN'T SAY CLASS TO ME! I'M LOOKING FOR CLASS! IT DOESN'T SAY DIFFERENT TO ME. I'M LOOKING FOR DIFFERENT! OH, IT'S CLEVER, BUT I'M LOOKING FOR URGENCY! IT DOESN'T SAY URGENCY!
WHAT DO YOU TWO THINK?
I'M ONLY HERE TWO MONTHS, SO I'M NOT THE ONE TO ASK.
YEAH, THAT'S WHAT I WAS SAYING — IT DOESN'T GIVE A SENSE OF URGENCY!
END
CRASH!
©1983 stan mack

It's a Jungle Out There, Part 1

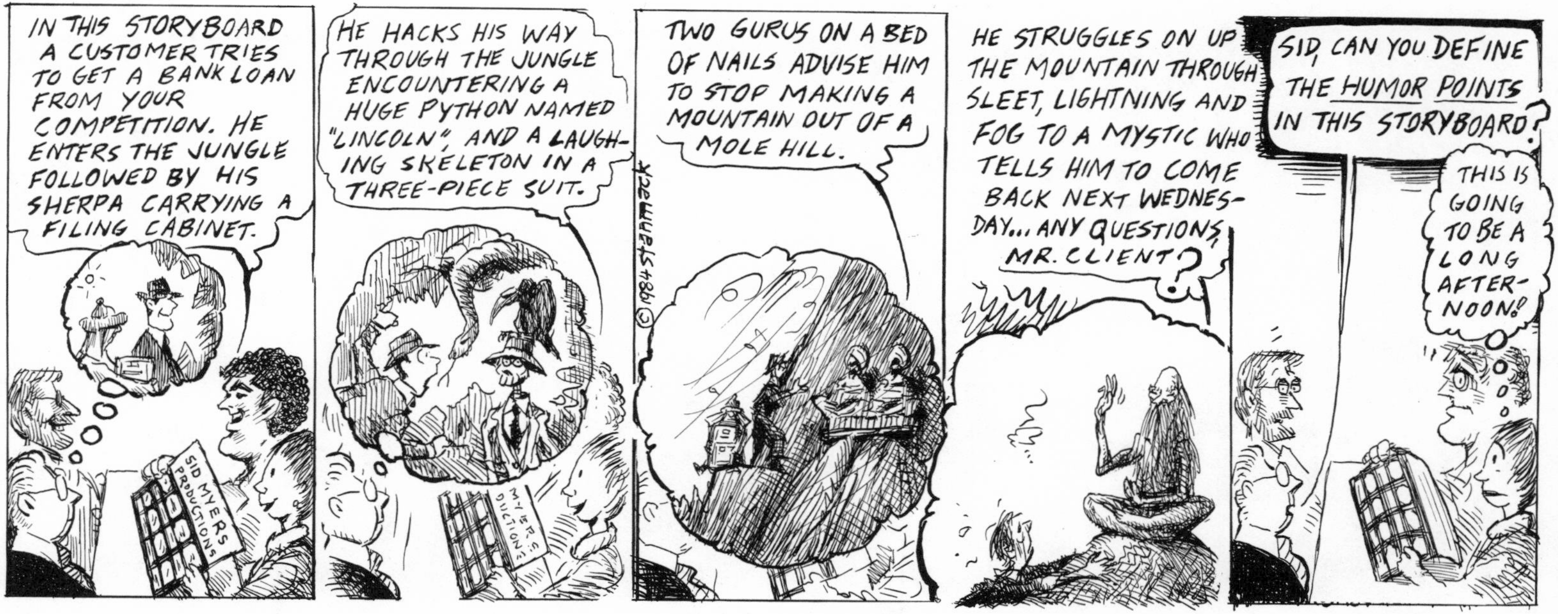
IN THIS STORYBOARD A CUSTOMER TRIES TO GET A BANK LOAN FROM YOUR COMPETITION. HE ENTERS THE JUNGLE FOLLOWED BY HIS SHERPA CARRYING A FILING CABINET.
SID MYERS PRODUCTIONS
HE HACKS HIS WAY THROUGH THE JUNGLE ENCOUNTERING A HUGE PYTHON NAMED "LINCOLN", AND A LAUGHING SKELETON IN A THREE-PIECE SUIT.
TWO GURUS ON A BED OF NAILS ADVISE HIM TO STOP MAKING A MOUNTAIN OUT OF A MOLE HILL.
HE STRUGGLES ON UP THE MOUNTAIN THROUGH SLEET, LIGHTNING AND FOG TO A MYSTIC WHO TELLS HIM TO COME BACK NEXT WEDNESDAY... ANY QUESTIONS, MR. CLIENT?
SID, CAN YOU DEFINE THE HUMOR POINTS IN THIS STORYBOARD?
THIS IS GOING TO BE A LONG AFTERNOON!

It's a Jungle Out There, Part 2

It's a Jungle Out There, Part 3

© 1984 stanmack

It's a Jungle Out There, Part 4

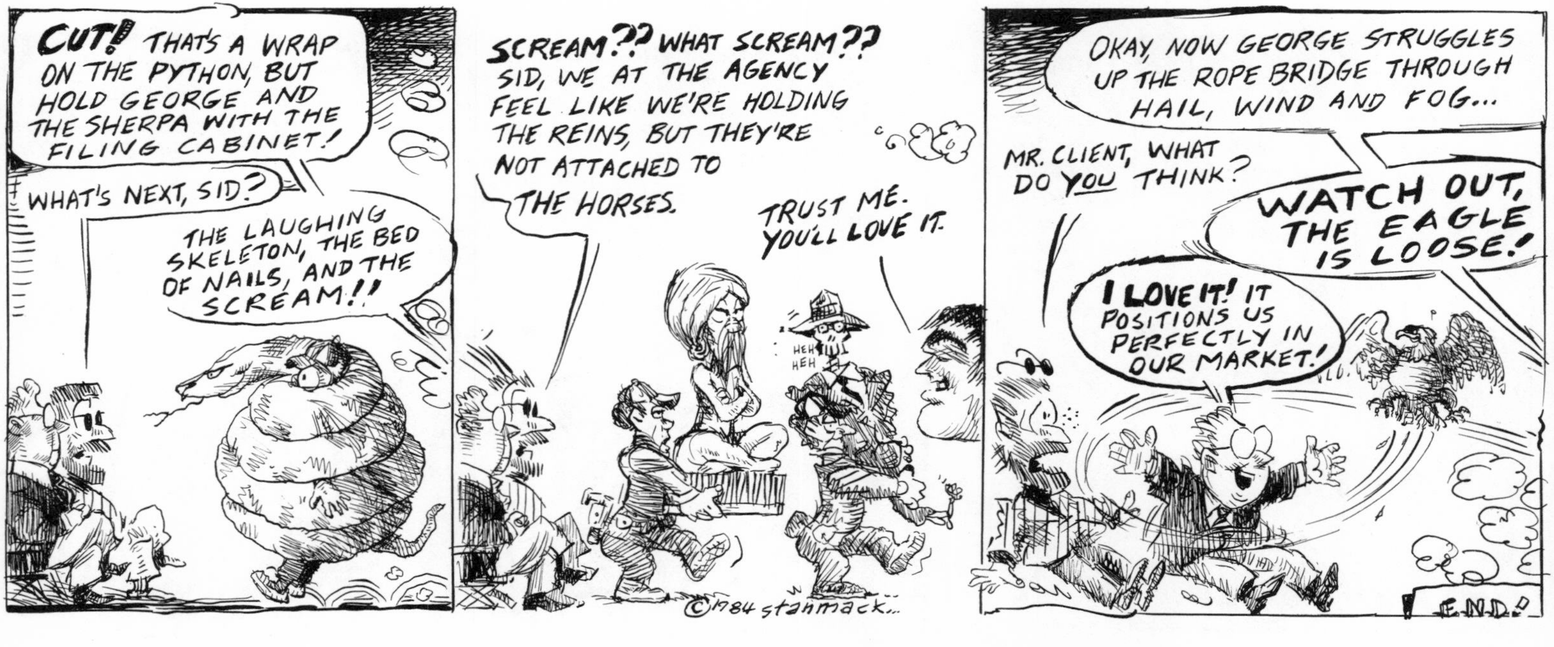
CUT! THAT'S A WRAP ON THE PYTHON, BUT HOLD GEORGE AND THE SHERPA WITH THE FILING CABINET!
WHAT'S NEXT, SID?
THE LAUGHING SKELETON, THE BED OF NAILS, AND THE SCREAM!!
SCREAM?? WHAT SCREAM?? SID, WE AT THE AGENCY FEEL LIKE WE'RE HOLDING THE REINS, BUT THEY'RE NOT ATTACHED TO THE HORSES.
HEH HEH
TRUST ME. YOU'LL LOVE IT.
OKAY, NOW GEORGE STRUGGLES UP THE ROPE BRIDGE THROUGH HAIL, WIND AND FOG...
MR. CLIENT, WHAT DO YOU THINK?
WATCH OUT, THE EAGLE IS LOOSE!
I LOVE IT! IT POSITIONS US PERFECTLY IN OUR MARKET!
©1984 stanmack...
END.

On-Hair Anchorperson

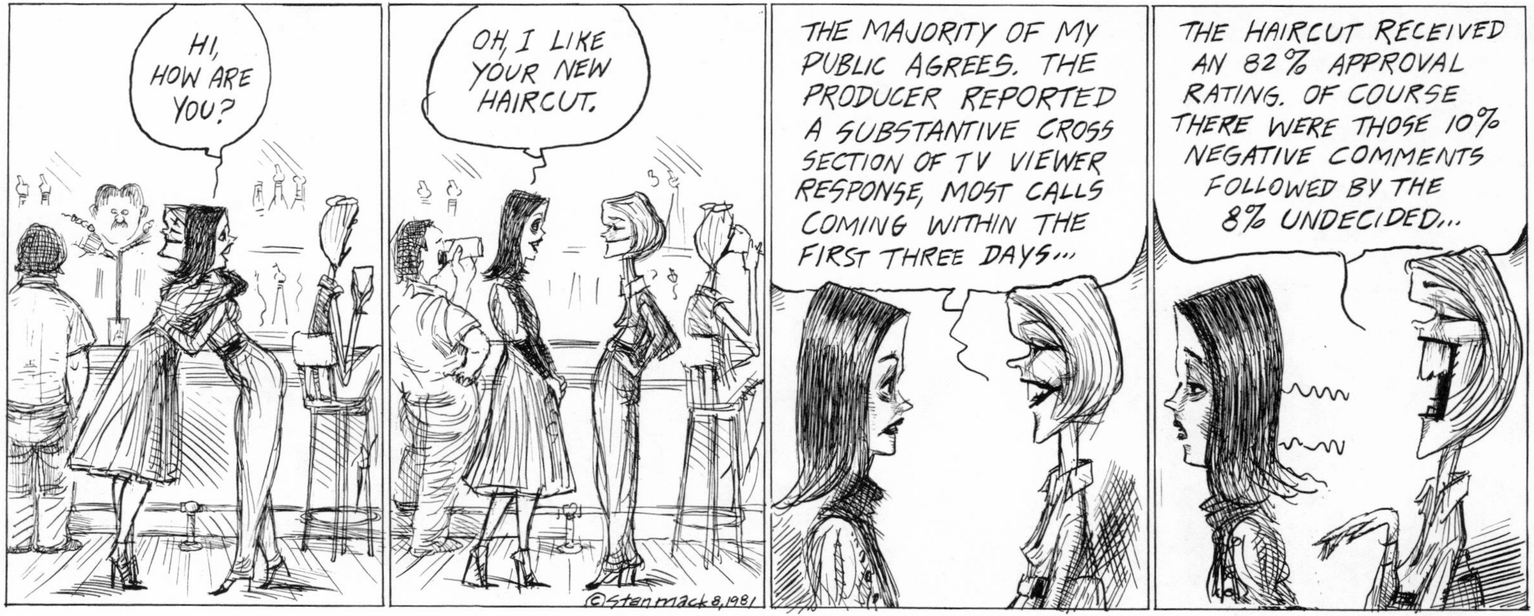
HI, HOW ARE YOU?
OH, I LIKE YOUR NEW HAIRCUT.
©Stan Mack 8,1981
THE MAJORITY OF MY PUBLIC AGREES. THE PRODUCER REPORTED A SUBSTANTIVE CROSS SECTION OF TV VIEWER RESPONSE, MOST CALLS COMING WITHIN THE FIRST THREE DAYS...
THE HAIRCUT RECEIVED AN 82% APPROVAL RATING. OF COURSE THERE WERE THOSE 10% NEGATIVE COMMENTS FOLLOWED BY THE 8% UNDECIDED...

Flack's-eye View

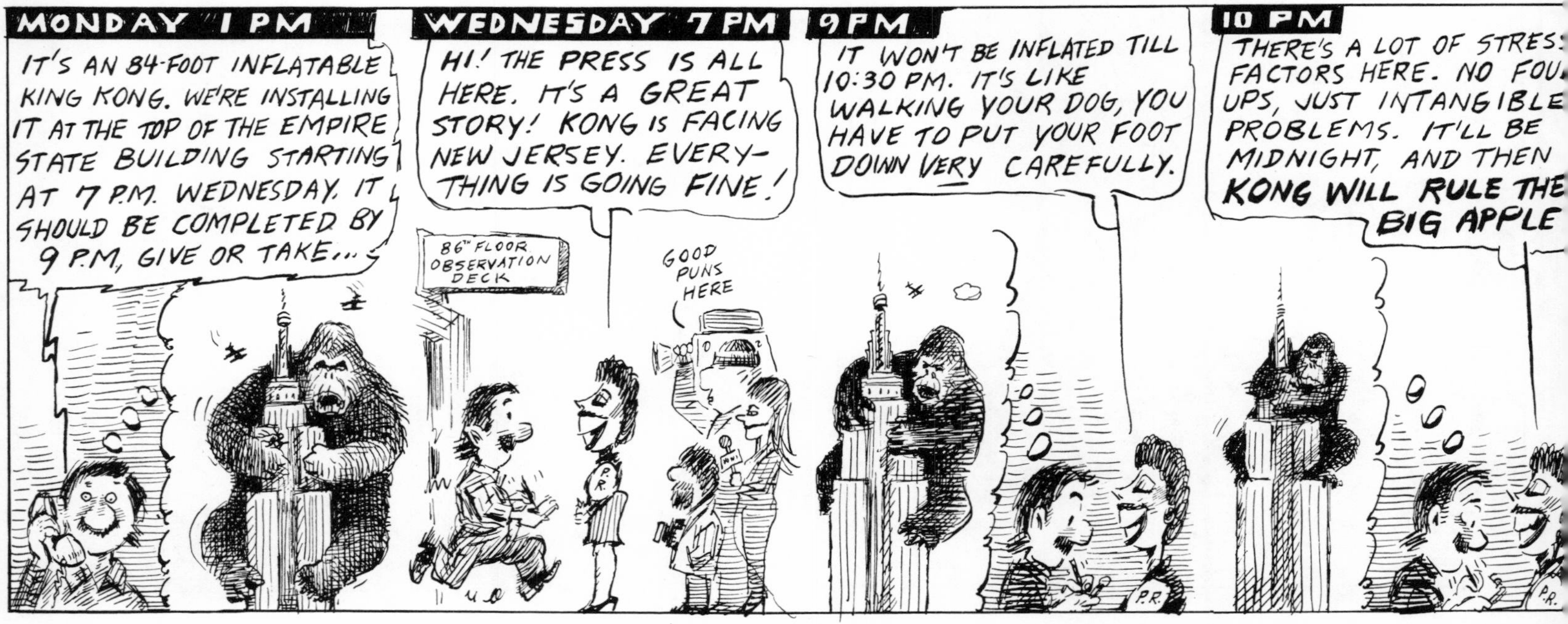
MONDAY 1 PM
IT'S AN 84-FOOT INFLATABLE KING KONG. WE'RE INSTALLING IT AT THE TOP OF THE EMPIRE STATE BUILDING STARTING AT 7 P.M. WEDNESDAY. IT SHOULD BE COMPLETED BY 9 P.M, GIVE OR TAKE...
WEDNESDAY 7 PM
HI! THE PRESS IS ALL HERE. IT'S A GREAT STORY! KONG IS FACING NEW JERSEY. EVERYTHING IS GOING FINE!
86TH FLOOR OBSERVATION DECK
GOOD PUNS HERE
P.R.
9 PM
IT WON'T BE INFLATED TILL 10:30 PM. IT'S LIKE WALKING YOUR DOG, YOU HAVE TO PUT YOUR FOOT DOWN VERY CAREFULLY.
P.R.
10 PM
THERE'S A LOT OF STRES FACTORS HERE. NO FOU UPS, JUST INTANGIBLE PROBLEMS. IT'LL BE MIDNIGHT, AND THEN KONG WILL RULE THE BIG APPLE
P.R.

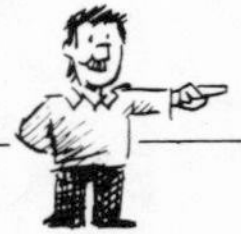

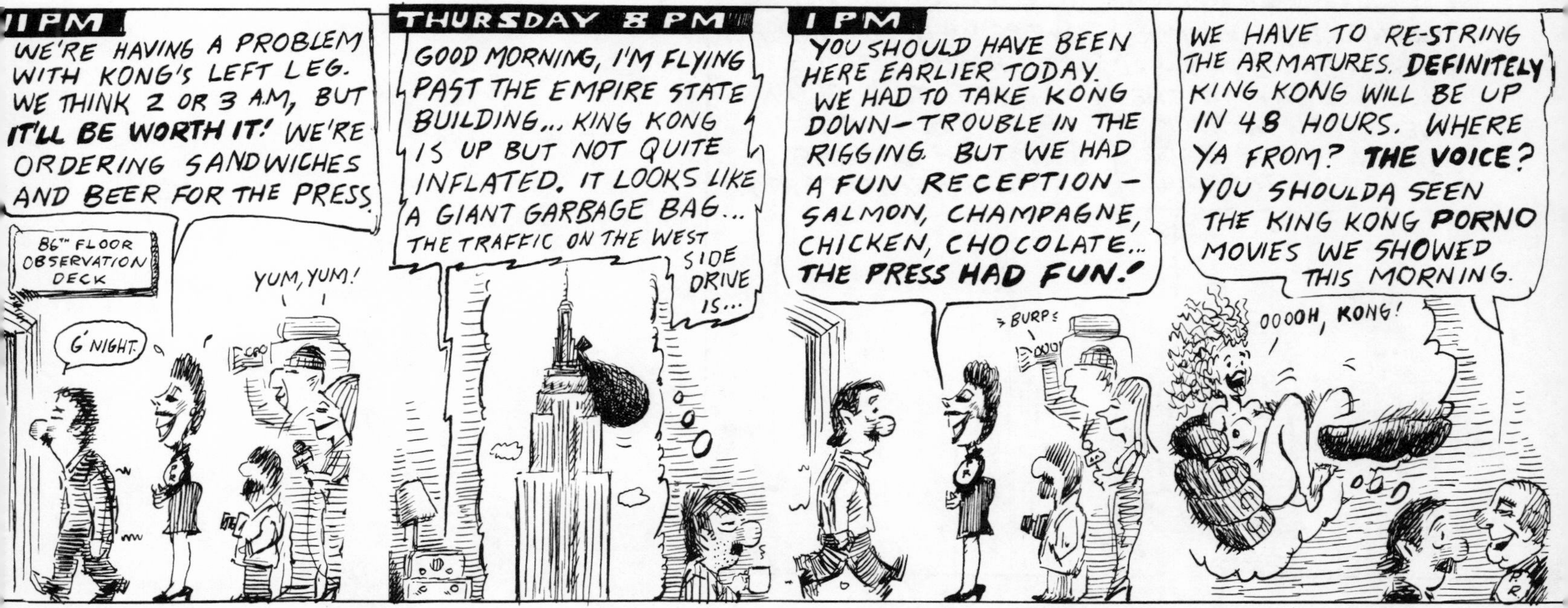

11 PM
WE'RE HAVING A PROBLEM WITH KONG'S LEFT LEG. WE THINK 2 OR 3 A.M, BUT **IT'LL BE WORTH IT!** WE'RE ORDERING SANDWICHES AND BEER FOR THE PRESS.
86TH FLOOR OBSERVATION DECK
G'NIGHT.
YUM, YUM!
THURSDAY 8 PM
GOOD MORNING, I'M FLYING PAST THE EMPIRE STATE BUILDING... KING KONG IS UP BUT NOT QUITE INFLATED. IT LOOKS LIKE A GIANT GARBAGE BAG... THE TRAFFIC ON THE WEST SIDE DRIVE IS...
1 PM
YOU SHOULD HAVE BEEN HERE EARLIER TODAY. WE HAD TO TAKE KONG DOWN—TROUBLE IN THE RIGGING. BUT WE HAD A FUN RECEPTION—SALMON, CHAMPAGNE, CHICKEN, CHOCOLATE... **THE PRESS HAD FUN!**
BURP
WE HAVE TO RE-STRING THE ARMATURES. **DEFINITELY** KING KONG WILL BE UP IN 48 HOURS. WHERE YA FROM? **THE VOICE?** YOU SHOULDA SEEN THE KING KONG **PORNO** MOVIES WE SHOWED THIS MORNING.
OOOOH, KONG!

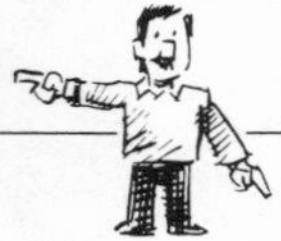

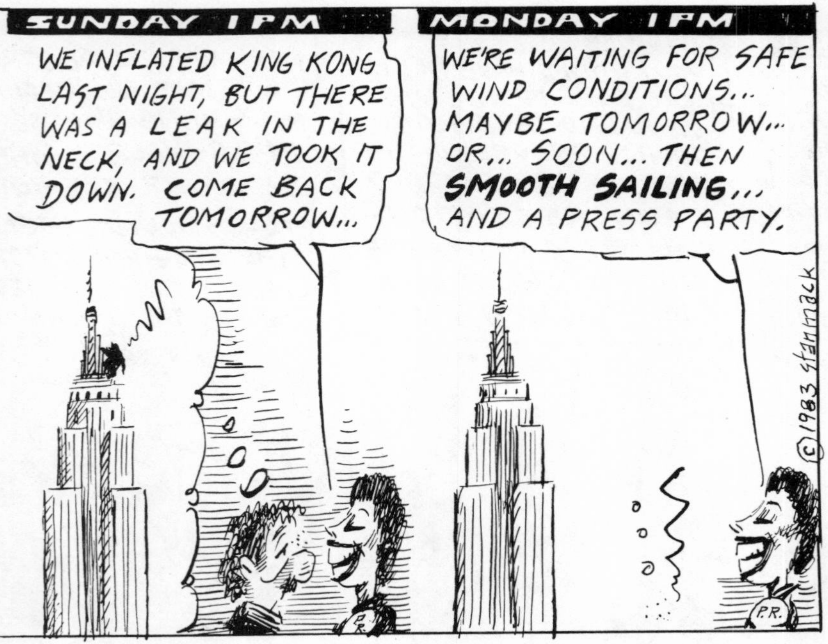
SUNDAY 1 PM
WE INFLATED KING KONG LAST NIGHT, BUT THERE WAS A LEAK IN THE NECK, AND WE TOOK IT DOWN. COME BACK TOMORROW...
MONDAY 1 PM
WE'RE WAITING FOR SAFE WIND CONDITIONS... MAYBE TOMORROW... OR... SOON... THEN **SMOOTH SAILING**... AND A PRESS PARTY.
P.R.
© 1983 stammack

Grudge? What Grudge?

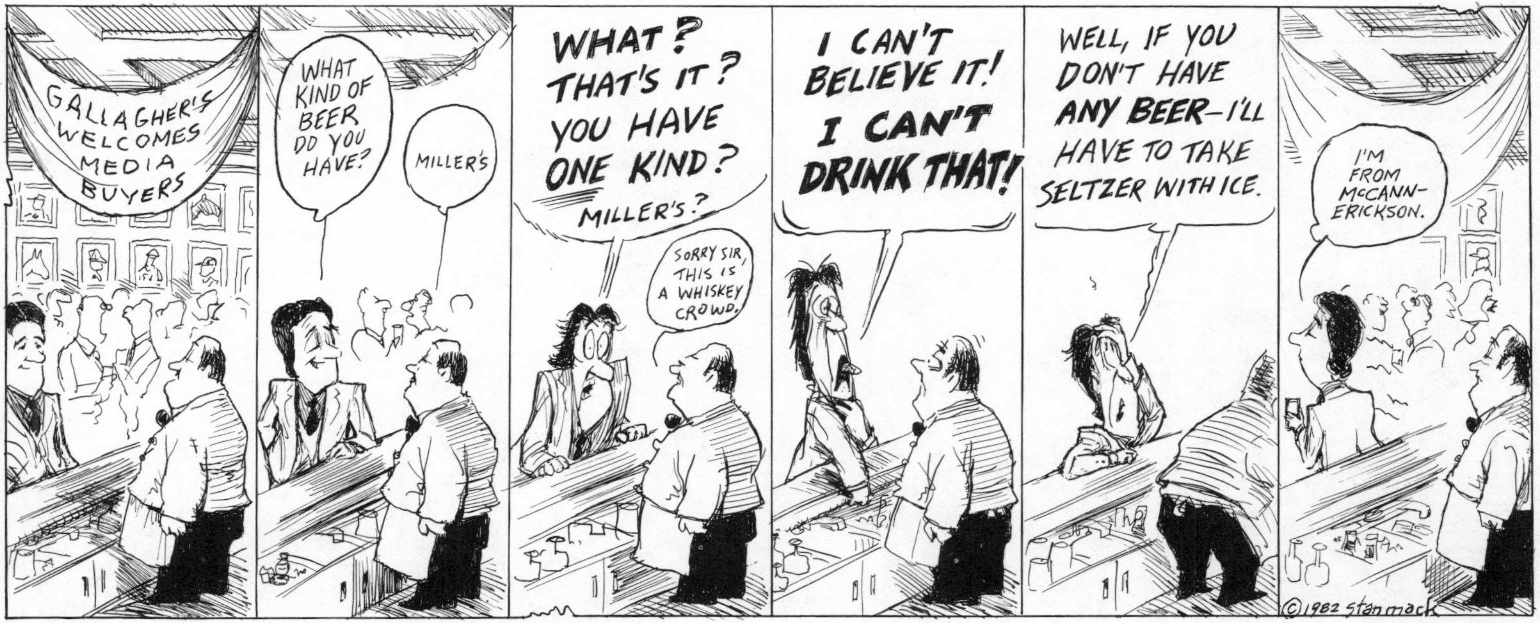
GALLAGHER'S WELCOMES MEDIA BUYERS
WHAT KIND OF BEER DO YOU HAVE?
MILLER'S
WHAT? THAT'S IT? YOU HAVE ONE KIND? MILLER'S?
SORRY SIR, THIS IS A WHISKEY CROWD.
I CAN'T BELIEVE IT! I CAN'T DRINK THAT!
WELL, IF YOU DON'T HAVE ANY BEER—I'LL HAVE TO TAKE SELTZER WITH ICE.
I'M FROM McCANN-ERICKSON.
©1982 stan mack

A Font of Wisdom

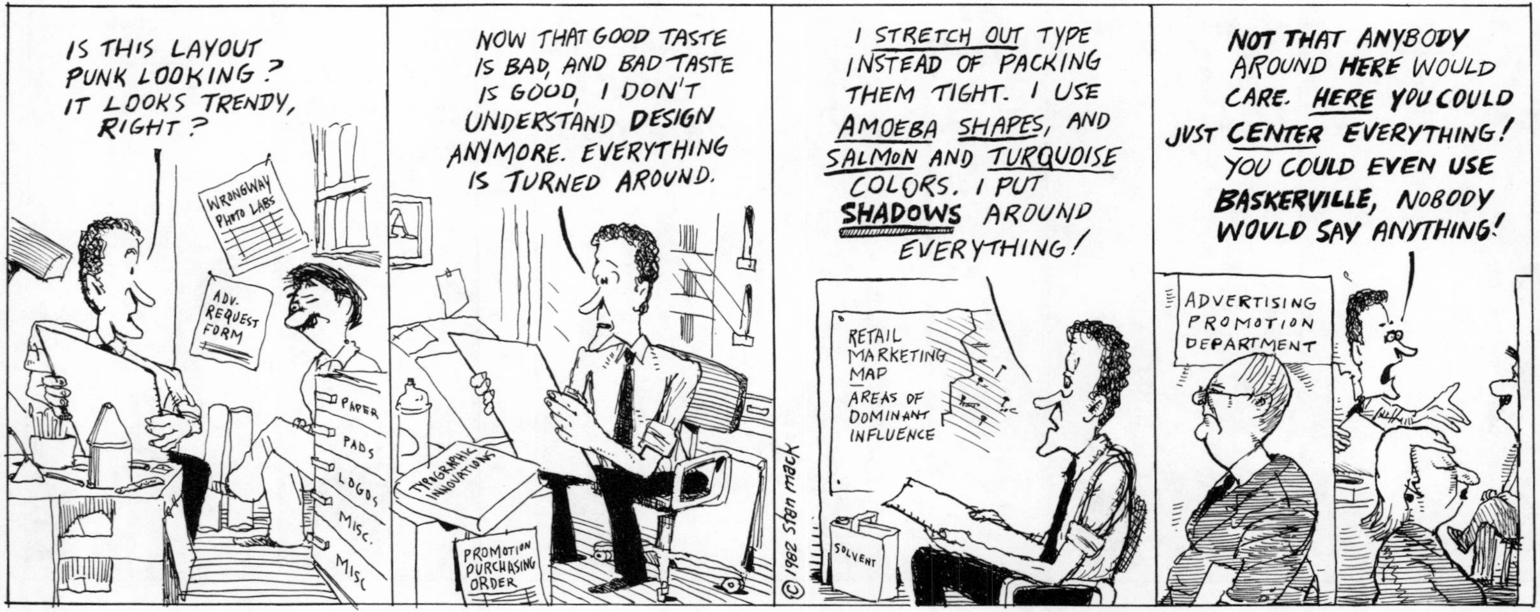
IS THIS LAYOUT PUNK LOOKING? IT LOOKS TRENDY, RIGHT?
WRONGWAY PHOTO LABS
ADV. REQUEST FORM
PAPER
PADS
LOGOS
MISC.
MISC
NOW THAT GOOD TASTE IS BAD, AND BAD TASTE IS GOOD, I DON'T UNDERSTAND DESIGN ANYMORE. EVERYTHING IS TURNED AROUND.
A
TYPOGRAPHIC INNOVATIONS
PROMOTION PURCHASING ORDER
© 1982 stan mack
I STRETCH OUT TYPE INSTEAD OF PACKING THEM TIGHT. I USE AMOEBA SHAPES, AND SALMON AND TURQUOISE COLORS. I PUT SHADOWS AROUND EVERYTHING!
RETAIL MARKETING MAP
AREAS OF DOMINANT INFLUENCE
SOLVENT
NOT THAT ANYBODY AROUND HERE WOULD CARE. HERE YOU COULD JUST CENTER EVERYTHING! YOU COULD EVEN USE BASKERVILLE, NOBODY WOULD SAY ANYTHING!
ADVERTISING PROMOTION DEPARTMENT

A Taxing Dilemma

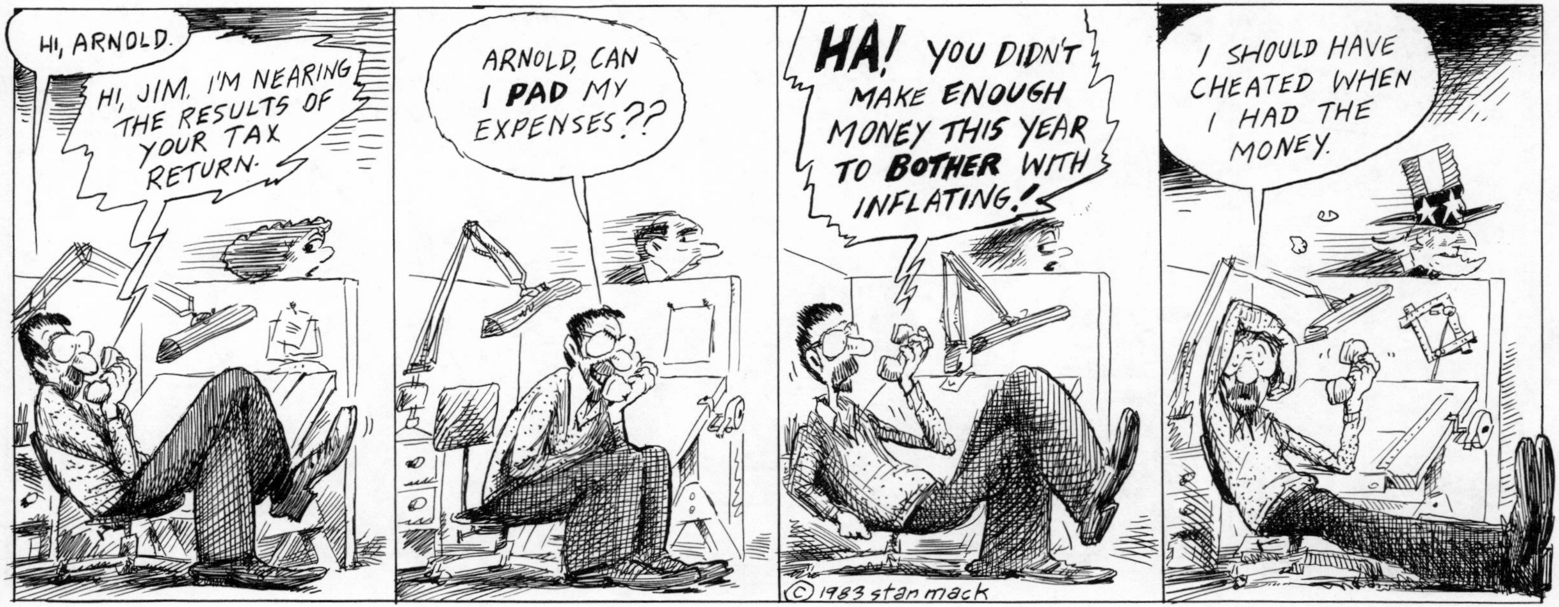
HI, ARNOLD.
HI, JIM. I'M NEARING THE RESULTS OF YOUR TAX RETURN.
ARNOLD, CAN I PAD MY EXPENSES??
HA! YOU DIDN'T MAKE ENOUGH MONEY THIS YEAR TO BOTHER WITH INFLATING!
I SHOULD HAVE CHEATED WHEN I HAD THE MONEY.
© 1983 stan mack

Homme Fatal

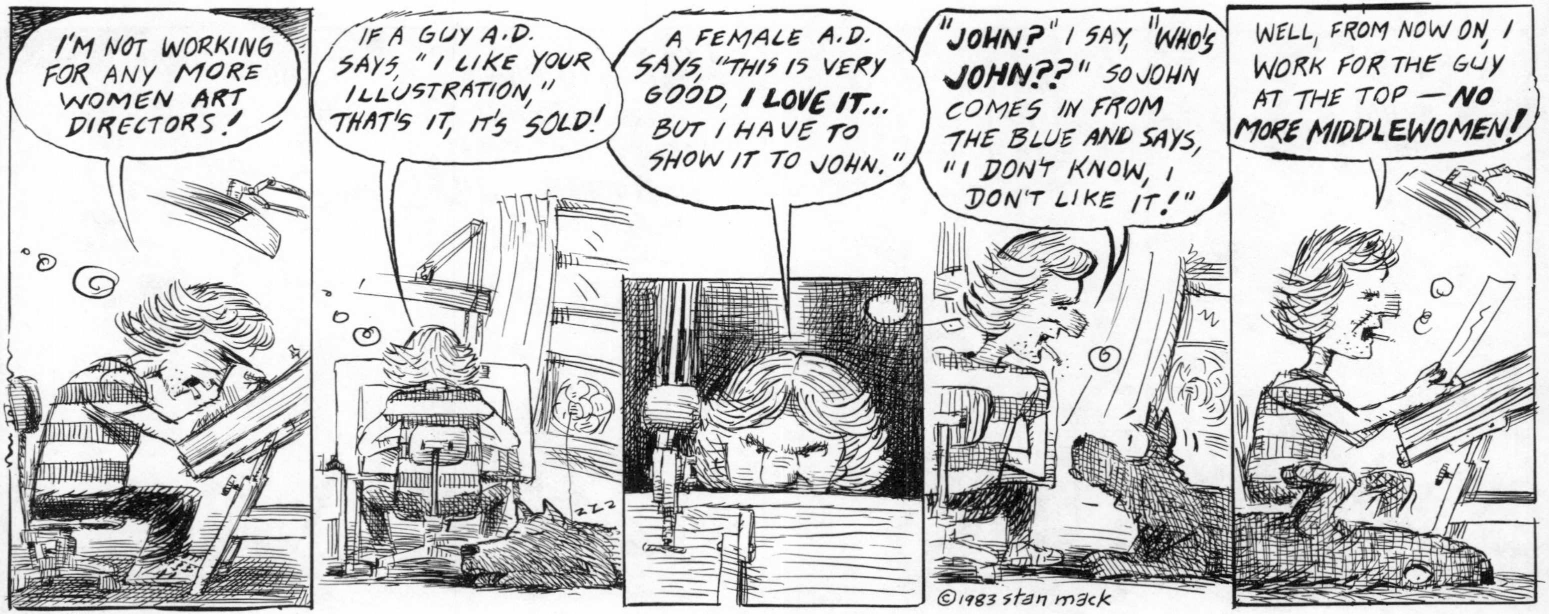
I'M NOT WORKING FOR ANY MORE WOMEN ART DIRECTORS!
IF A GUY A.D. SAYS, "I LIKE YOUR ILLUSTRATION," THAT'S IT, IT'S SOLD!
A FEMALE A.D. SAYS, "THIS IS VERY GOOD, I LOVE IT... BUT I HAVE TO SHOW IT TO JOHN."
"JOHN?" I SAY, "WHO'S JOHN??" SO JOHN COMES IN FROM THE BLUE AND SAYS, "I DON'T KNOW, I DON'T LIKE IT!"
WELL, FROM NOW ON, I WORK FOR THE GUY AT THE TOP — NO MORE MIDDLEWOMEN!
ZZZ
©1983 stan mack

Art for Art's Sake

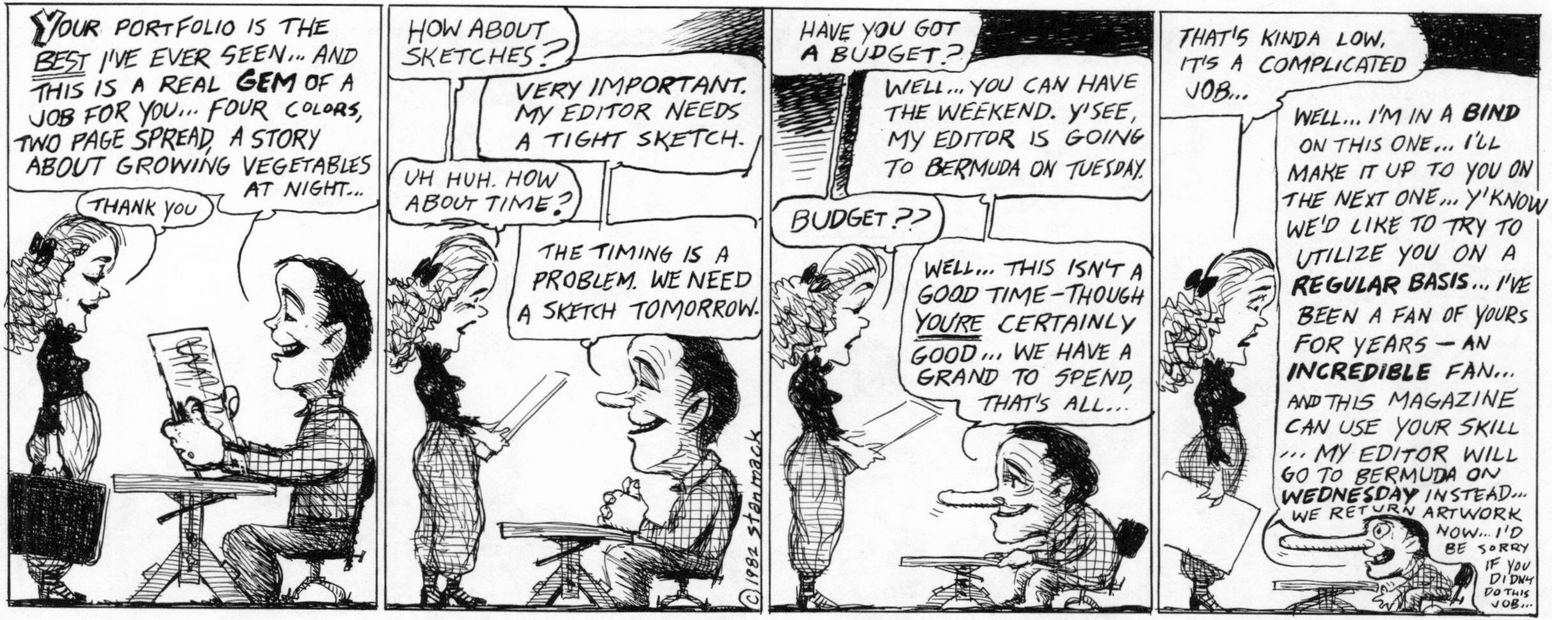

YOUR PORTFOLIO IS THE BEST I'VE EVER SEEN... AND THIS IS A REAL GEM OF A JOB FOR YOU... FOUR COLORS, TWO PAGE SPREAD, A STORY ABOUT GROWING VEGETABLES AT NIGHT...
THANK YOU
HOW ABOUT SKETCHES?
VERY IMPORTANT. MY EDITOR NEEDS A TIGHT SKETCH.
UH HUH. HOW ABOUT TIME?
THE TIMING IS A PROBLEM. WE NEED A SKETCH TOMORROW.
© 1982 stanmack
HAVE YOU GOT A BUDGET?
WELL... YOU CAN HAVE THE WEEKEND. Y'SEE, MY EDITOR IS GOING TO BERMUDA ON TUESDAY.
BUDGET??
WELL... THIS ISN'T A GOOD TIME—THOUGH YOU'RE CERTAINLY GOOD... WE HAVE A GRAND TO SPEND, THAT'S ALL...
THAT'S KINDA LOW. IT'S A COMPLICATED JOB...
WELL... I'M IN A BIND ON THIS ONE... I'LL MAKE IT UP TO YOU ON THE NEXT ONE... Y'KNOW WE'D LIKE TO TRY TO UTILIZE YOU ON A REGULAR BASIS... I'VE BEEN A FAN OF YOURS FOR YEARS — AN INCREDIBLE FAN... AND THIS MAGAZINE CAN USE YOUR SKILL ... MY EDITOR WILL GO TO BERMUDA ON WEDNESDAY INSTEAD... WE RETURN ARTWORK NOW... I'D BE SORRY IF YOU DIDN'T DO THIS JOB...

Beach, Beach, Beach

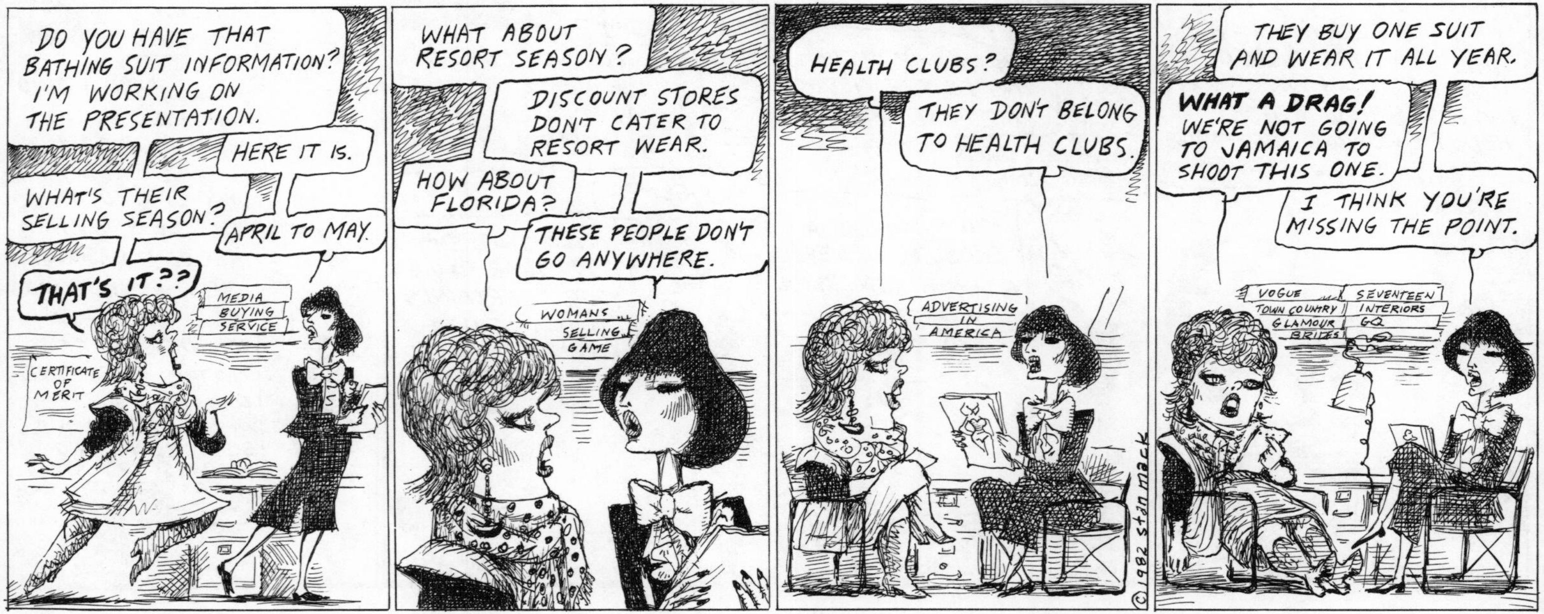

DO YOU HAVE THAT BATHING SUIT INFORMATION? I'M WORKING ON THE PRESENTATION.
HERE IT IS.
WHAT'S THEIR SELLING SEASON?
APRIL TO MAY.
THAT'S IT??
MEDIA BUYING SERVICE
CERTIFICATE OF MERIT
WHAT ABOUT RESORT SEASON?
DISCOUNT STORES DON'T CATER TO RESORT WEAR.
HOW ABOUT FLORIDA?
THESE PEOPLE DON'T GO ANYWHERE.
WOMANS SELLING GAME
HEALTH CLUBS?
THEY DON'T BELONG TO HEALTH CLUBS.
ADVERTISING IN AMERICA
©1982 stan mack
THEY BUY ONE SUIT AND WEAR IT ALL YEAR.
WHAT A DRAG! WE'RE NOT GOING TO JAMAICA TO SHOOT THIS ONE.
I THINK YOU'RE MISSING THE POINT.
VOGUE
TOWN COUNTRY
GLAMOUR
BRIDES
SEVENTEEN
INTERIORS
GQ

London Calling

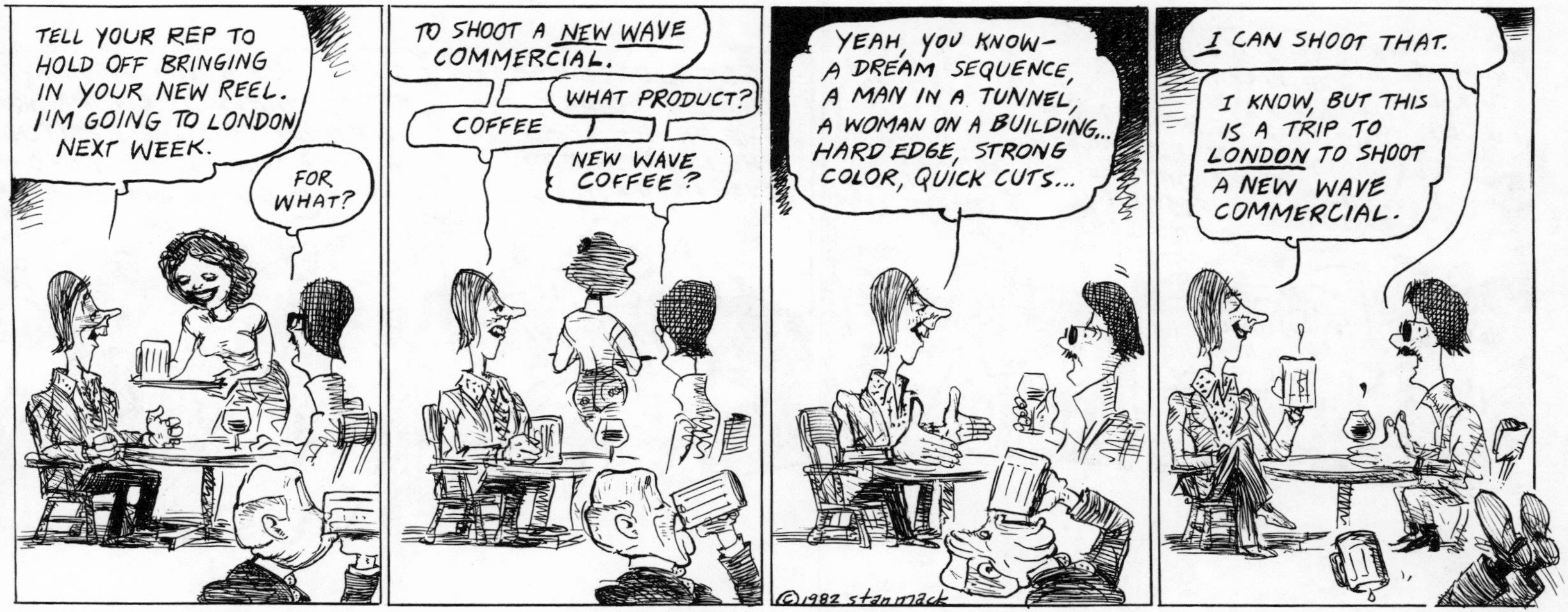

TELL YOUR REP TO HOLD OFF BRINGING IN YOUR NEW REEL. I'M GOING TO LONDON NEXT WEEK.
FOR WHAT?
TO SHOOT A NEW WAVE COMMERCIAL.
WHAT PRODUCT?
COFFEE
NEW WAVE COFFEE?
YEAH, YOU KNOW– A DREAM SEQUENCE, A MAN IN A TUNNEL, A WOMAN ON A BUILDING... HARD EDGE, STRONG COLOR, QUICK CUTS...
I CAN SHOOT THAT.
I KNOW, BUT THIS IS A TRIP TO LONDON TO SHOOT A NEW WAVE COMMERCIAL.
©1982 stan mack

A Star Isn't Born

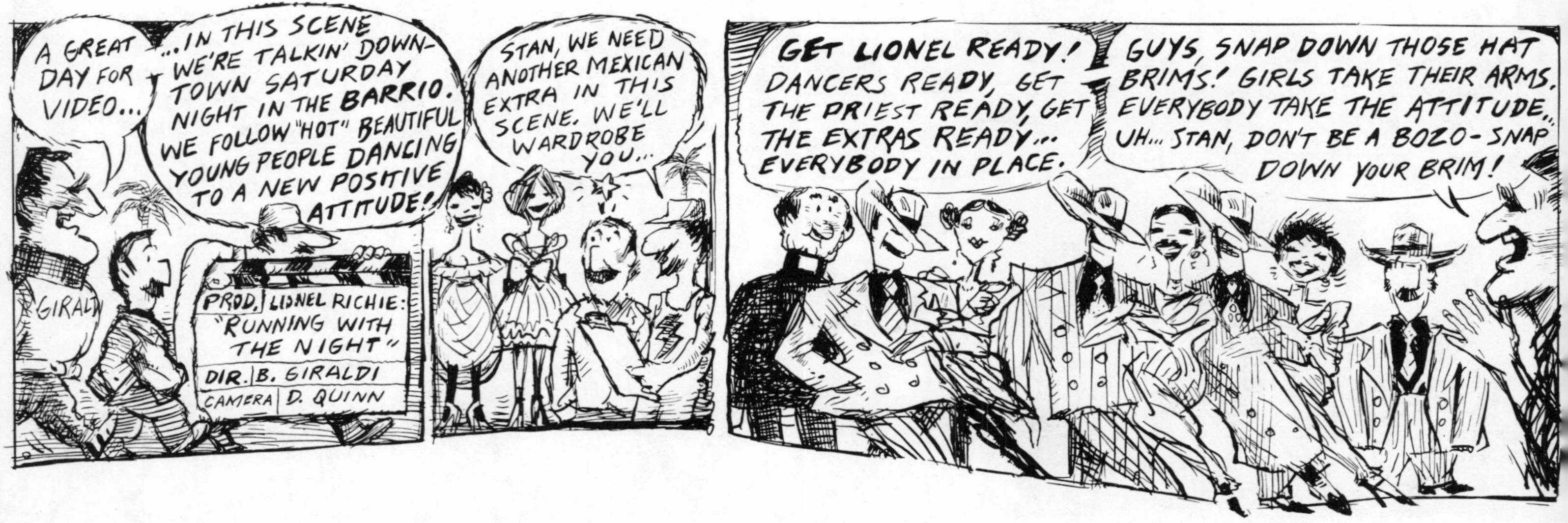

A GREAT DAY FOR VIDEO...
...IN THIS SCENE WE'RE TALKIN' DOWN-TOWN SATURDAY NIGHT IN THE BARRIO. WE FOLLOW "HOT" BEAUTIFUL YOUNG PEOPLE DANCING TO A NEW POSITIVE ATTITUDE!
GIRALDI
PROD. LIONEL RICHIE: "RUNNING WITH THE NIGHT"
DIR. B. GIRALDI
CAMERA D. QUINN
STAN, WE NEED ANOTHER MEXICAN EXTRA IN THIS SCENE. WE'LL WARDROBE YOU...
GET LIONEL READY! DANCERS READY, GET THE PRIEST READY, GET THE EXTRAS READY... EVERYBODY IN PLACE.
GUYS, SNAP DOWN THOSE HAT BRIMS! GIRLS TAKE THEIR ARMS. EVERYBODY TAKE THE ATTITUDE.. UH... STAN, DON'T BE A BOZO-SNAP DOWN YOUR BRIM!

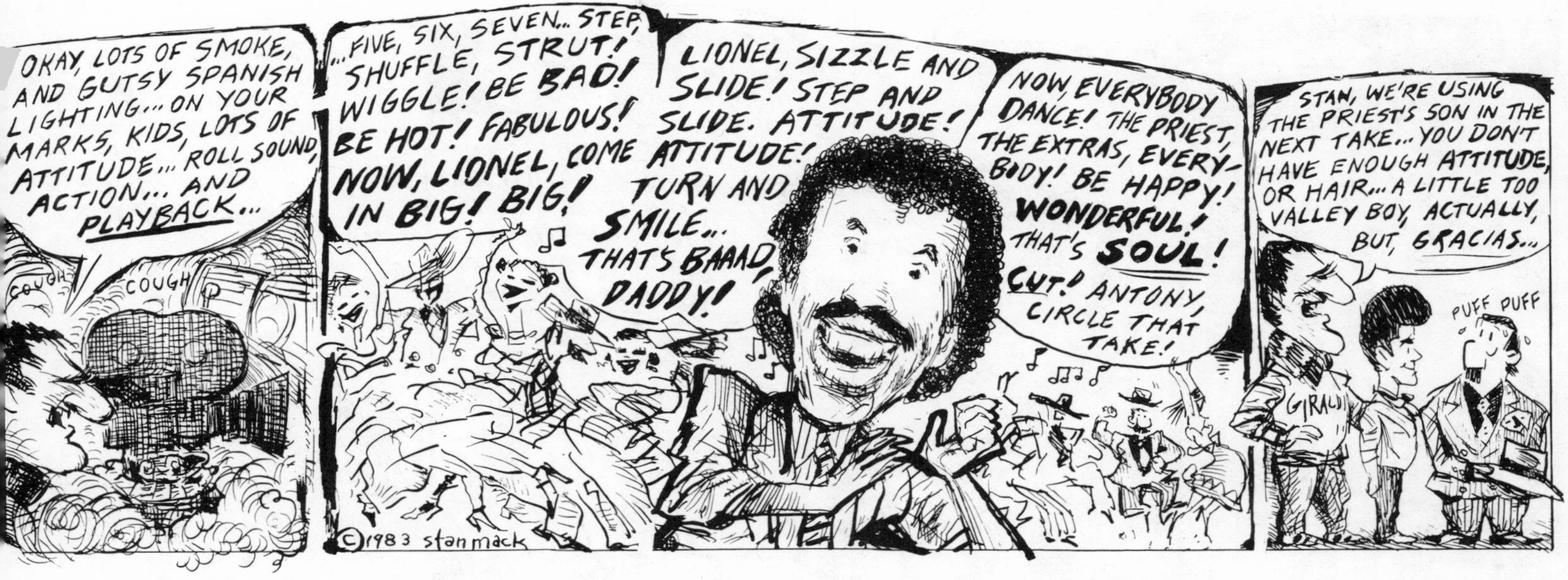
OKAY, LOTS OF SMOKE, AND GUTSY SPANISH LIGHTING... ON YOUR MARKS, KIDS, LOTS OF ATTITUDE... ROLL SOUND, ACTION... AND PLAYBACK...
COUGH
COUGH
...FIVE, SIX, SEVEN... STEP, SHUFFLE, STRUT! WIGGLE! BE BAD! BE HOT! FABULOUS! NOW, LIONEL, COME IN BIG! BIG!
LIONEL, SIZZLE AND SLIDE! STEP AND SLIDE. ATTITUDE! ATTITUDE! TURN AND SMILE... THAT'S BAAAD, DADDY!
NOW, EVERYBODY DANCE! THE PRIEST, THE EXTRAS, EVERYBODY! BE HAPPY! WONDERFUL! THAT'S SOUL!
CUT! ANTONY, CIRCLE THAT TAKE!
©1983 stan mack
STAN, WE'RE USING THE PRIEST'S SON IN THE NEXT TAKE... YOU DON'T HAVE ENOUGH ATTITUDE, OR HAIR... A LITTLE TOO VALLEY BOY, ACTUALLY, BUT, GRACIAS...
GIRALDI
PUFF PUFF

Heavy Traffic

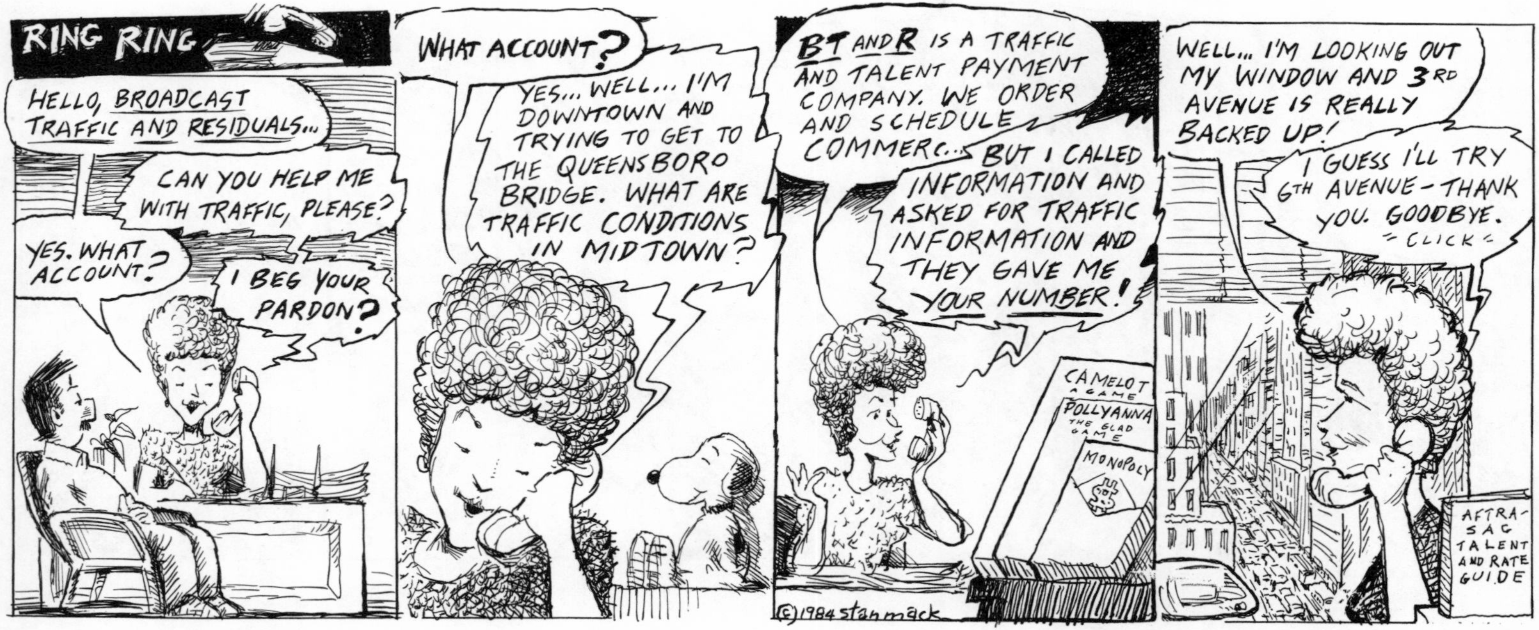
RING RING
HELLO, BROADCAST TRAFFIC AND RESIDUALS...
CAN YOU HELP ME WITH TRAFFIC, PLEASE?
YES. WHAT ACCOUNT?
I BEG YOUR PARDON?
WHAT ACCOUNT?
YES... WELL... I'M DOWNTOWN AND TRYING TO GET TO THE QUEENSBORO BRIDGE. WHAT ARE TRAFFIC CONDITIONS IN MIDTOWN?
BT AND R IS A TRAFFIC AND TALENT PAYMENT COMPANY. WE ORDER AND SCHEDULE COMMERC...
BUT I CALLED INFORMATION AND ASKED FOR TRAFFIC INFORMATION AND THEY GAVE ME YOUR NUMBER!
CAMELOT A GAME
POLLYANNA THE GLAD GAME
MONOPOLY
©1984 stan mack
WELL... I'M LOOKING OUT MY WINDOW AND 3RD AVENUE IS REALLY BACKED UP!
I GUESS I'LL TRY 6TH AVENUE - THANK YOU. GOODBYE.
CLICK
AFTRA-SAG TALENT AND RATE GUIDE

Disinflation Stalks the City

Sandwiching Ideas

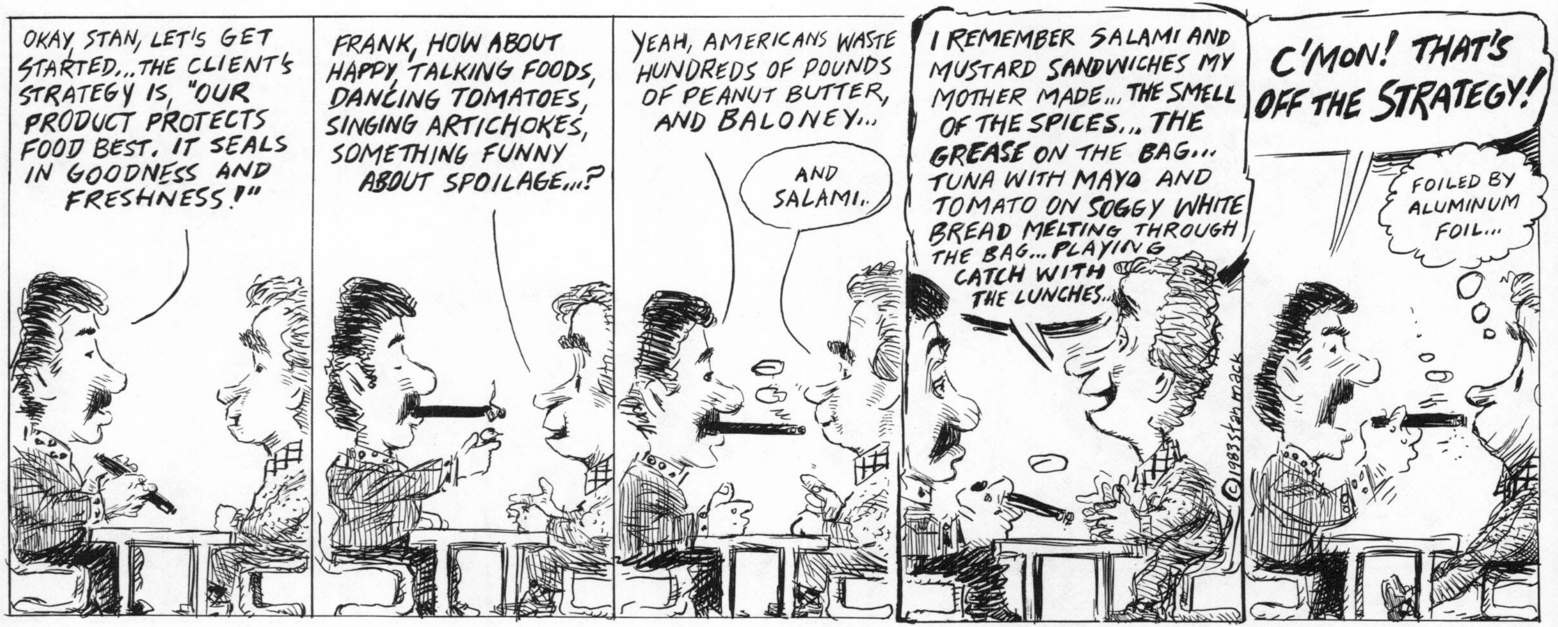

OKAY, STAN, LET'S GET STARTED... THE CLIENT'S STRATEGY IS, "OUR PRODUCT PROTECTS FOOD BEST. IT SEALS IN GOODNESS AND FRESHNESS!"
FRANK, HOW ABOUT HAPPY, TALKING FOODS, DANCING TOMATOES, SINGING ARTICHOKES, SOMETHING FUNNY ABOUT SPOILAGE...?
YEAH, AMERICANS WASTE HUNDREDS OF POUNDS OF PEANUT BUTTER, AND BALONEY...
AND SALAMI..
I REMEMBER SALAMI AND MUSTARD SANDWICHES MY MOTHER MADE... THE SMELL OF THE SPICES... THE GREASE ON THE BAG... TUNA WITH MAYO AND TOMATO ON SOGGY WHITE BREAD MELTING THROUGH THE BAG... PLAYING CATCH WITH THE LUNCHES...
©1983 stan mack
C'MON! THAT'S OFF THE STRATEGY!
FOILED BY ALUMINUM FOIL...

Packaged Goodies

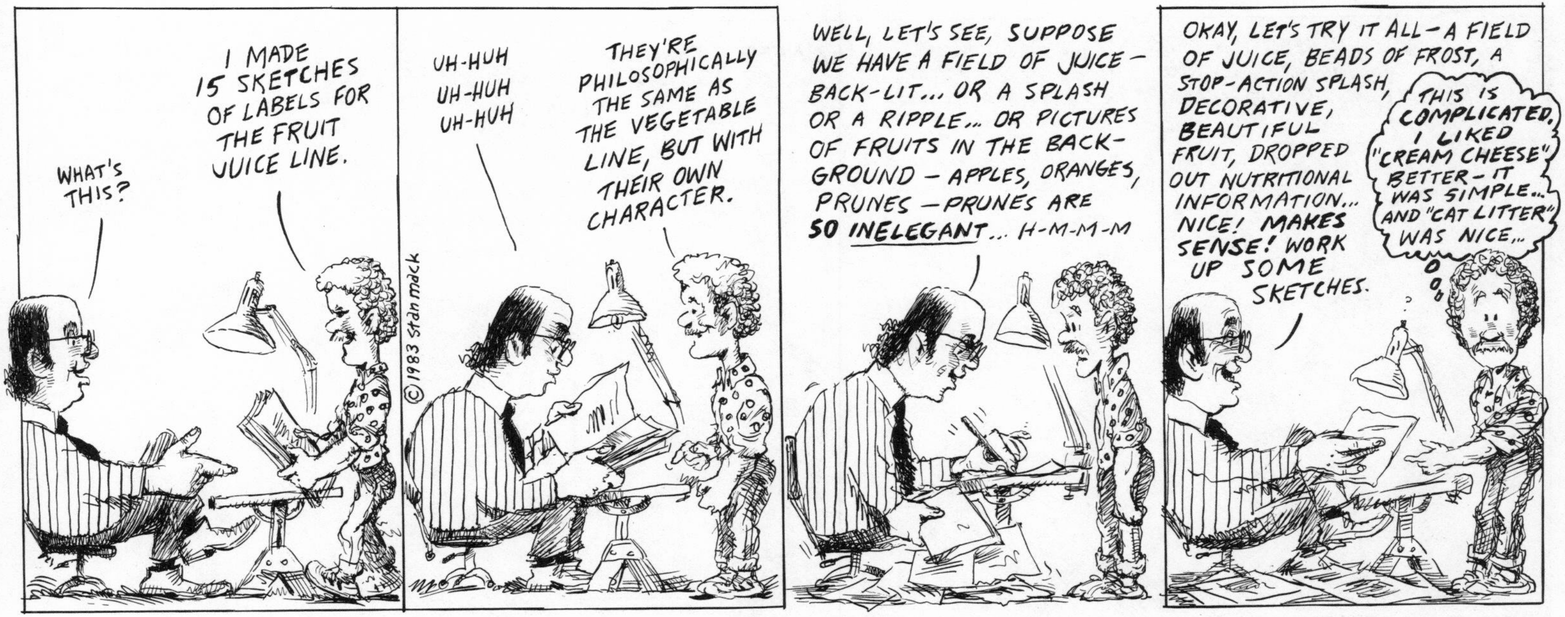
WHAT'S THIS?
I MADE 15 SKETCHES OF LABELS FOR THE FRUIT JUICE LINE.
UH-HUH UH-HUH UH-HUH
THEY'RE PHILOSOPHICALLY THE SAME AS THE VEGETABLE LINE, BUT WITH THEIR OWN CHARACTER.
©1983 stan mack
WELL, LET'S SEE, SUPPOSE WE HAVE A FIELD OF JUICE — BACK-LIT... OR A SPLASH OR A RIPPLE... OR PICTURES OF FRUITS IN THE BACK-GROUND — APPLES, ORANGES, PRUNES — PRUNES ARE SO INELEGANT... H-M-M-M
OKAY, LET'S TRY IT ALL — A FIELD OF JUICE, BEADS OF FROST, A STOP-ACTION SPLASH, DECORATIVE, BEAUTIFUL FRUIT, DROPPED OUT NUTRITIONAL INFORMATION... NICE! MAKES SENSE! WORK UP SOME SKETCHES.
THIS IS COMPLICATED. I LIKED "CREAM CHEESE" BETTER — IT WAS SIMPLE... AND "CAT LITTER" WAS NICE...

Lights, Camera . . .

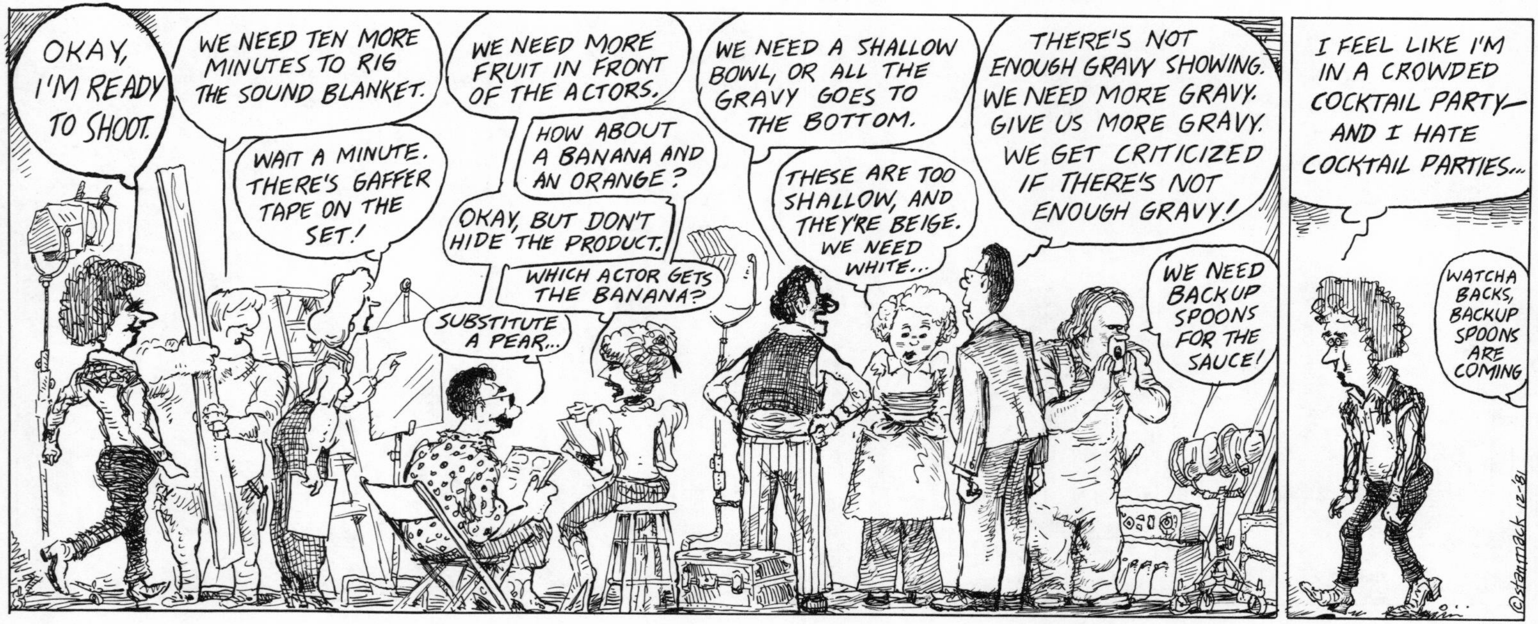
OKAY, I'M READY TO SHOOT.
WE NEED TEN MORE MINUTES TO RIG THE SOUND BLANKET.
WAIT A MINUTE. THERE'S GAFFER TAPE ON THE SET!
WE NEED MORE FRUIT IN FRONT OF THE ACTORS.
HOW ABOUT A BANANA AND AN ORANGE?
OKAY, BUT DON'T HIDE THE PRODUCT.
WHICH ACTOR GETS THE BANANA?
SUBSTITUTE A PEAR...
WE NEED A SHALLOW BOWL, OR ALL THE GRAVY GOES TO THE BOTTOM.
THESE ARE TOO SHALLOW, AND THEY'RE BEIGE. WE NEED WHITE...
THERE'S NOT ENOUGH GRAVY SHOWING. WE NEED MORE GRAVY. GIVE US MORE GRAVY. WE GET CRITICIZED IF THERE'S NOT ENOUGH GRAVY!
WE NEED BACKUP SPOONS FOR THE SAUCE!
I FEEL LIKE I'M IN A CROWDED COCKTAIL PARTY— AND I HATE COCKTAIL PARTIES...
WATCHA BACKS, BACKUP SPOONS ARE COMING
©stammack 12-'81

Rocky IV

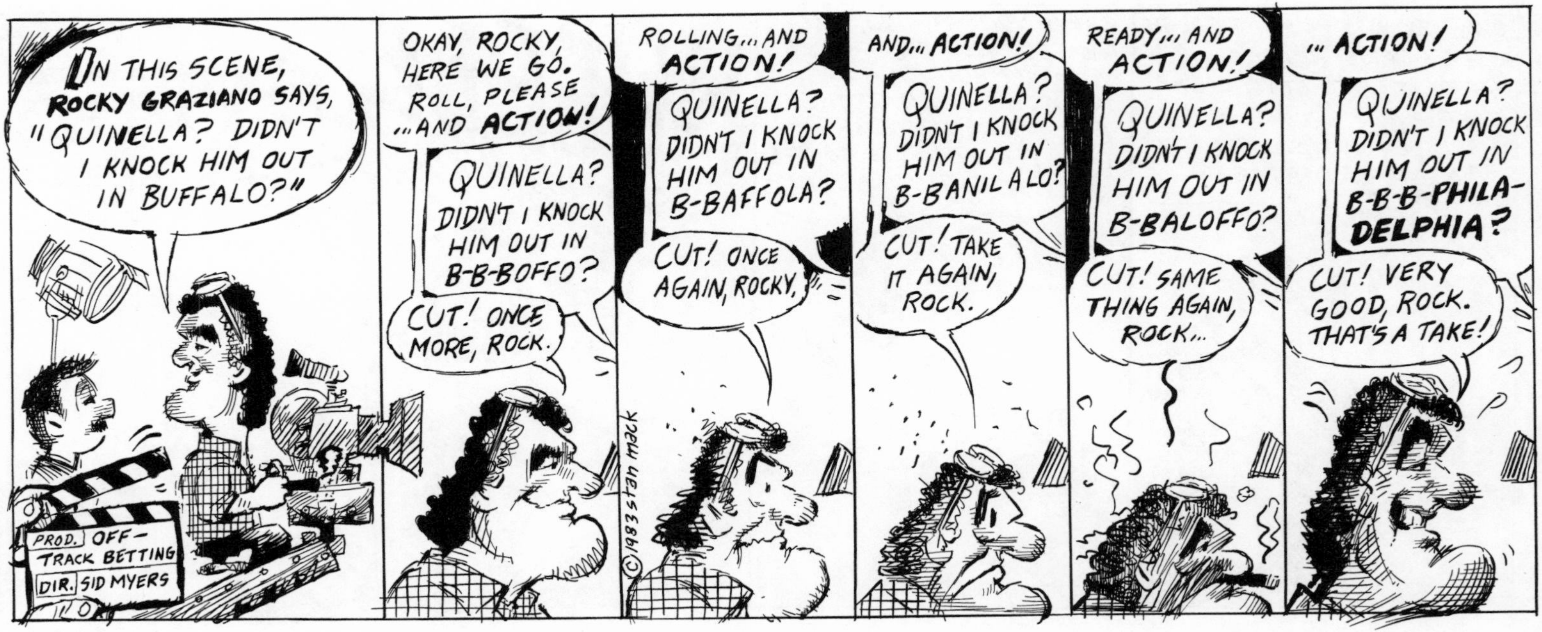
IN THIS SCENE, ROCKY GRAZIANO SAYS, "QUINELLA? DIDN'T I KNOCK HIM OUT IN BUFFALO?"
PROD. OFF-TRACK BETTING
DIR. SID MYERS
OKAY, ROCKY, HERE WE GO. ROLL, PLEASE ...AND ACTION!
QUINELLA? DIDN'T I KNOCK HIM OUT IN B-B-BOFFO?
CUT! ONCE MORE, ROCK.
ROLLING... AND ACTION!
QUINELLA? DIDN'T I KNOCK HIM OUT IN B-BAFFOLA?
CUT! ONCE AGAIN, ROCKY.
©1983 stan mack
AND... ACTION!
QUINELLA? DIDN'T I KNOCK HIM OUT IN B-BANILALO?
CUT! TAKE IT AGAIN, ROCK.
READY... AND ACTION!
QUINELLA? DIDN'T I KNOCK HIM OUT IN B-BALOFFO?
CUT! SAME THING AGAIN, ROCK...
... ACTION!
QUINELLA? DIDN'T I KNOCK HIM OUT IN B-B-B-PHILADELPHIA?
CUT! VERY GOOD, ROCK. THAT'S A TAKE!

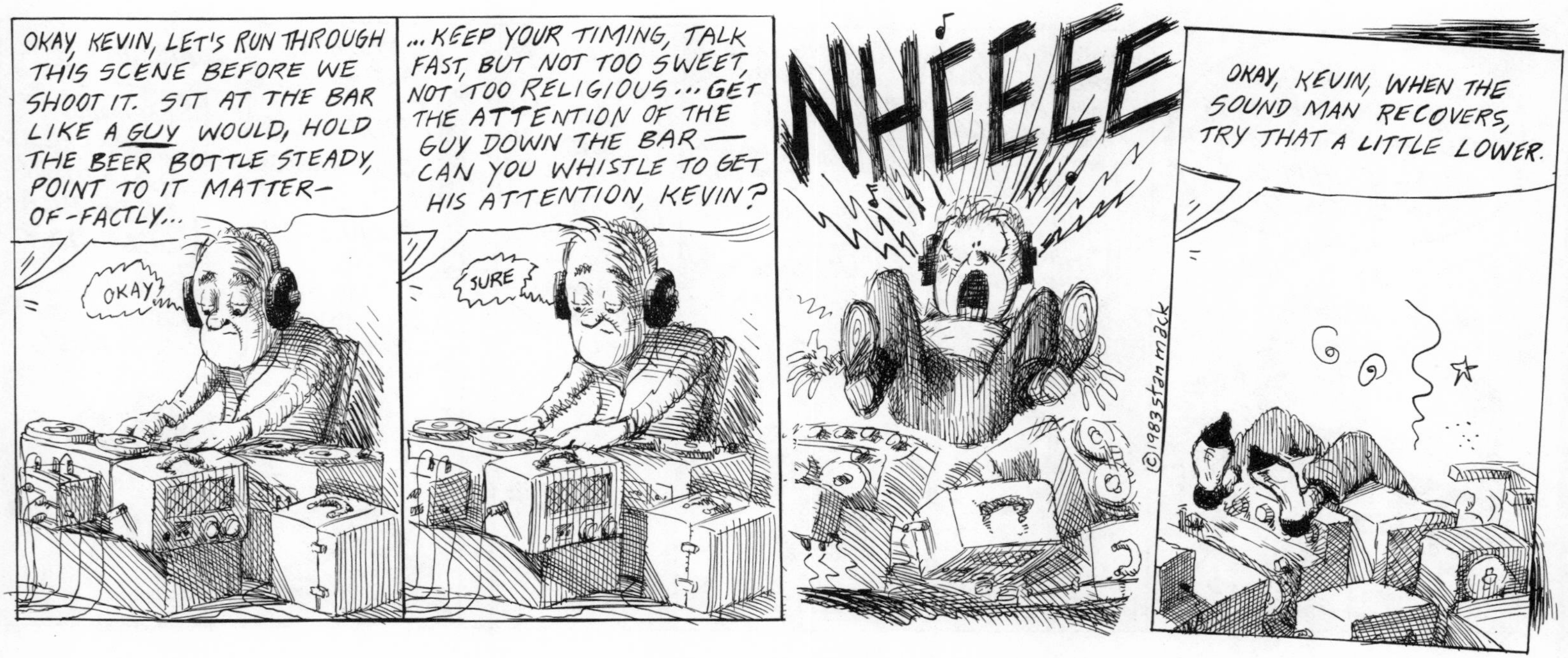
OKAY, KEVIN, LET'S RUN THROUGH THIS SCENE BEFORE WE SHOOT IT. SIT AT THE BAR LIKE A GUY WOULD, HOLD THE BEER BOTTLE STEADY, POINT TO IT MATTER-OF-FACTLY...
OKAY
...KEEP YOUR TIMING, TALK FAST, BUT NOT TOO SWEET, NOT TOO RELIGIOUS... GET THE ATTENTION OF THE GUY DOWN THE BAR— CAN YOU WHISTLE TO GET HIS ATTENTION, KEVIN?
SURE
NHÉEEE
OKAY, KEVIN, WHEN THE SOUND MAN RECOVERS, TRY THAT A LITTLE LOWER.
©1983 stan mack

The Hills Are Asleep

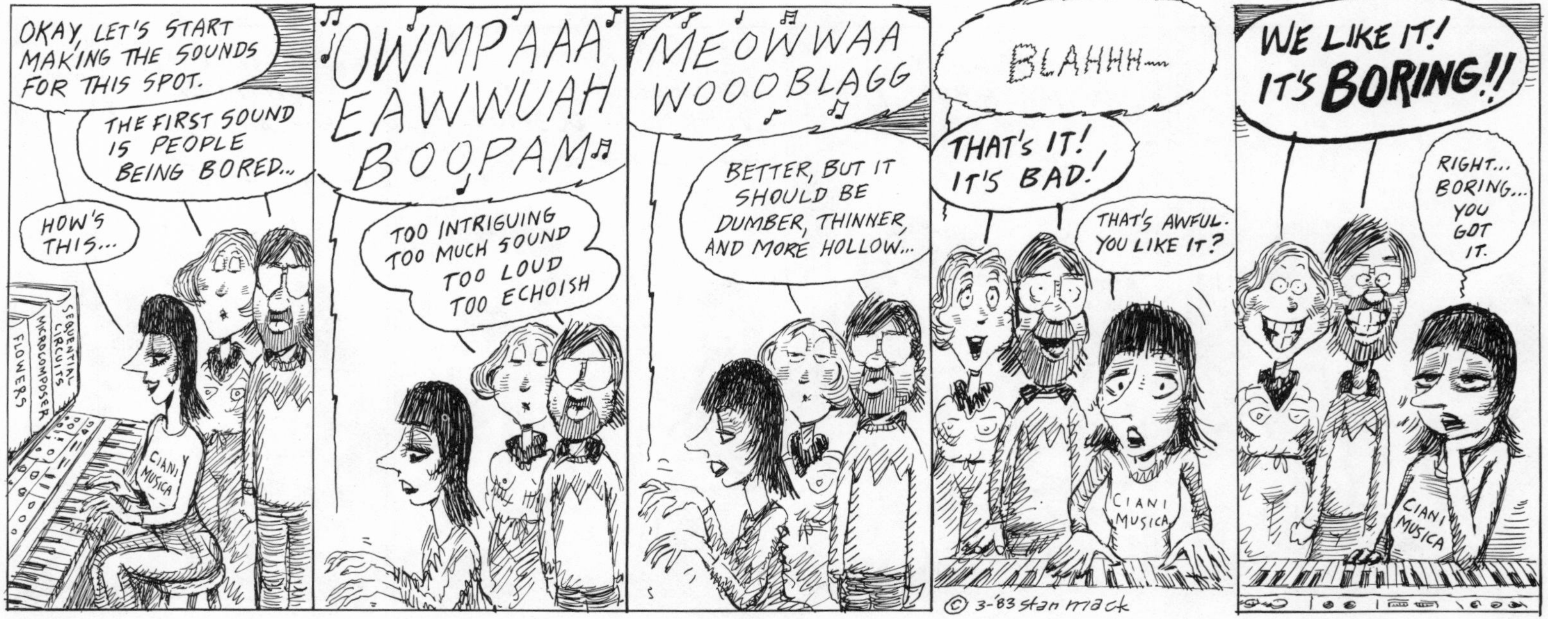

OKAY, LET'S START MAKING THE SOUNDS FOR THIS SPOT.
THE FIRST SOUND IS PEOPLE BEING BORED...
HOW'S THIS...
FLOWERS
MICROCOMPOSER
SEQUENTIAL CIRCUITS
CIANI MUSICA
OWMPAAA EAWWUAH BOOPAM
TOO INTRIGUING TOO MUCH SOUND TOO LOUD TOO ECHOISH
MEOWWAA WOOOBLAGG
BETTER, BUT IT SHOULD BE DUMBER, THINNER, AND MORE HOLLOW...
BLAHHH...
THAT'S IT! IT'S BAD!
THAT'S AWFUL. YOU LIKE IT?
CIANI MUSICA
© 3-'83 stan mack
WE LIKE IT! IT'S BORING!!
RIGHT... BORING... YOU GOT IT.
CIANI MUSICA

Preoccupational Hazard

The Eyes (Don't) Have It

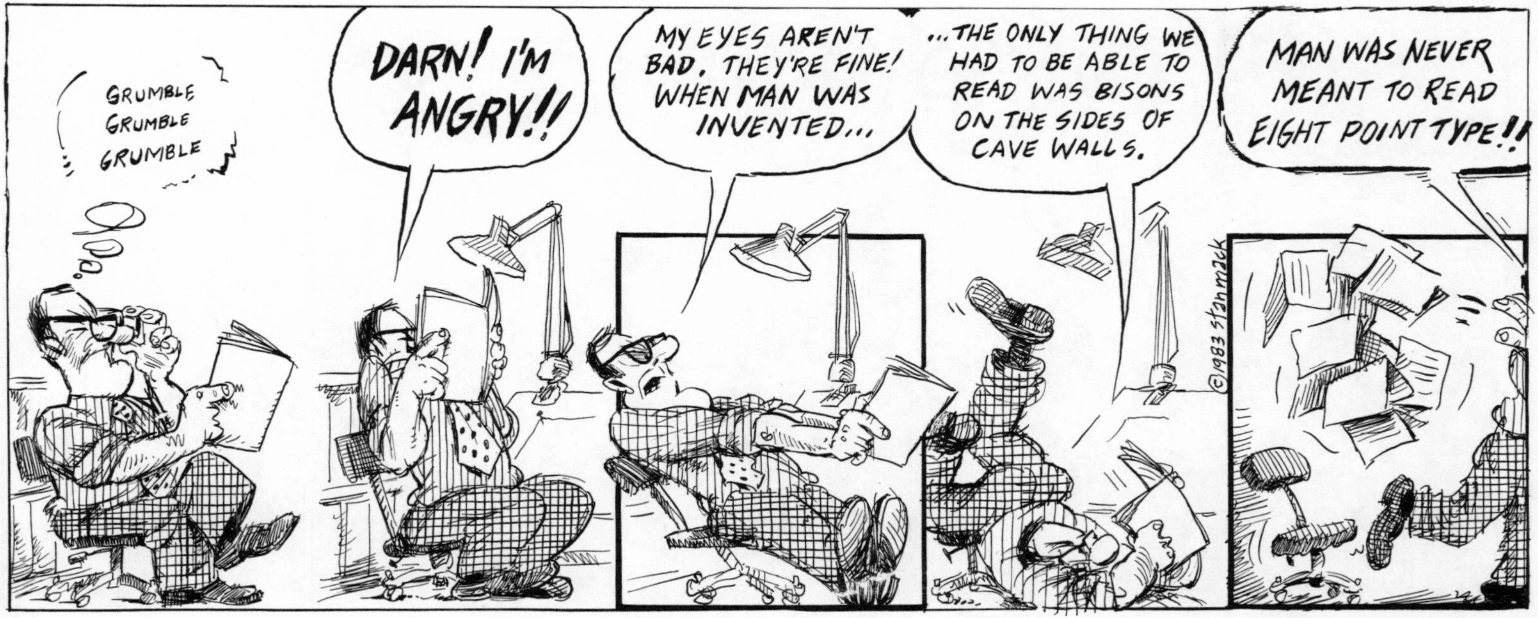
GRUMBLE GRUMBLE GRUMBLE
DARN! I'M ANGRY!!
MY EYES AREN'T BAD. THEY'RE FINE! WHEN MAN WAS INVENTED...
...THE ONLY THING WE HAD TO BE ABLE TO READ WAS BISONS ON THE SIDES OF CAVE WALLS.
MAN WAS NEVER MEANT TO READ EIGHT POINT TYPE!!
©1983 stahmack

The Five O'Clock Shadow

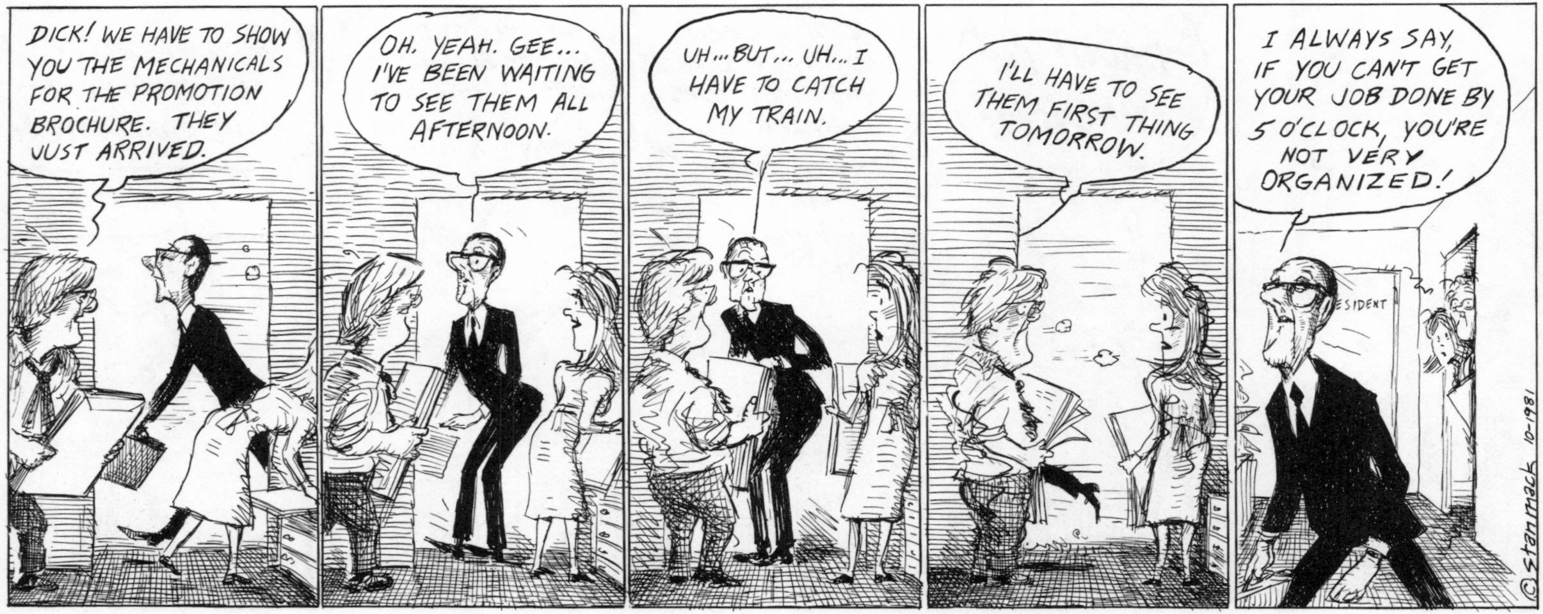
DICK! WE HAVE TO SHOW YOU THE MECHANICALS FOR THE PROMOTION BROCHURE. THEY JUST ARRIVED.
OH. YEAH. GEE... I'VE BEEN WAITING TO SEE THEM ALL AFTERNOON.
UH... BUT... UH... I HAVE TO CATCH MY TRAIN.
I'LL HAVE TO SEE THEM FIRST THING TOMORROW.
I ALWAYS SAY, IF YOU CAN'T GET YOUR JOB DONE BY 5 O'CLOCK, YOU'RE NOT VERY ORGANIZED!
ESIDENT
© stammack 10-1981

Spaced Out

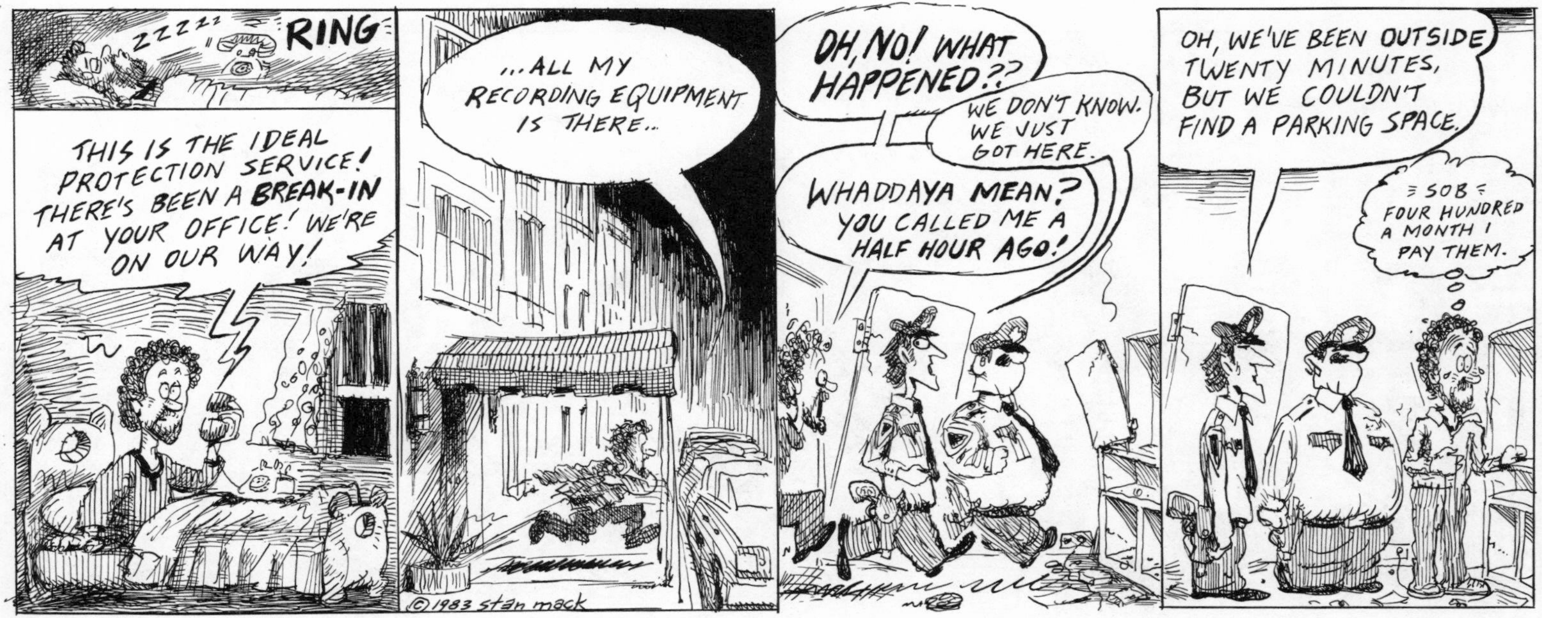
ZZZZZZ
RING
THIS IS THE IDEAL PROTECTION SERVICE! THERE'S BEEN A BREAK-IN AT YOUR OFFICE! WE'RE ON OUR WAY!
...ALL MY RECORDING EQUIPMENT IS THERE...
OH, NO! WHAT HAPPENED??
WE DON'T KNOW. WE JUST GOT HERE.
WHADDAYA MEAN? YOU CALLED ME A HALF HOUR AGO!
OH, WE'VE BEEN OUTSIDE TWENTY MINUTES, BUT WE COULDN'T FIND A PARKING SPACE.
SOB FOUR HUNDRED A MONTH I PAY THEM.
(C) 1983 stan mack

Art Misdirector

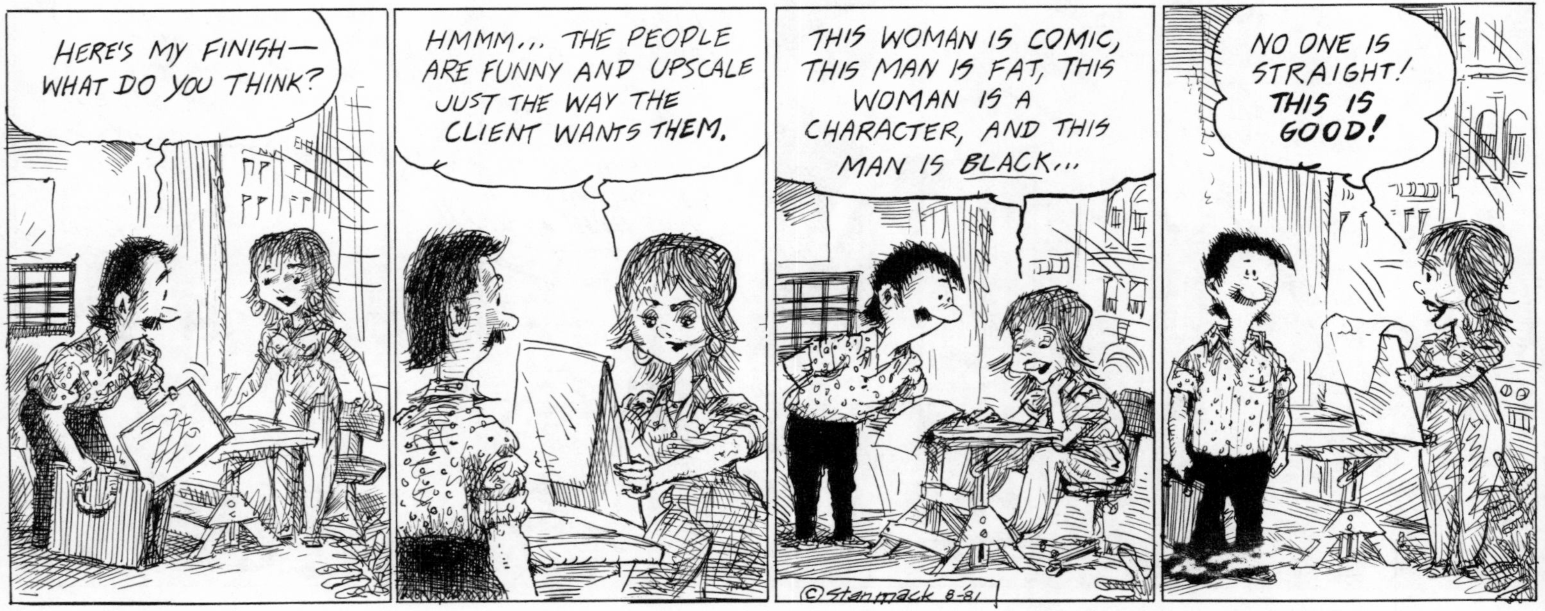
HERE'S MY FINISH— WHAT DO YOU THINK?
HMMM... THE PEOPLE ARE FUNNY AND UPSCALE JUST THE WAY THE CLIENT WANTS THEM.
THIS WOMAN IS COMIC, THIS MAN IS FAT, THIS WOMAN IS A CHARACTER, AND THIS MAN IS BLACK...
NO ONE IS STRAIGHT! THIS IS GOOD!
©Stanmack 8-81

Easy for You To Say

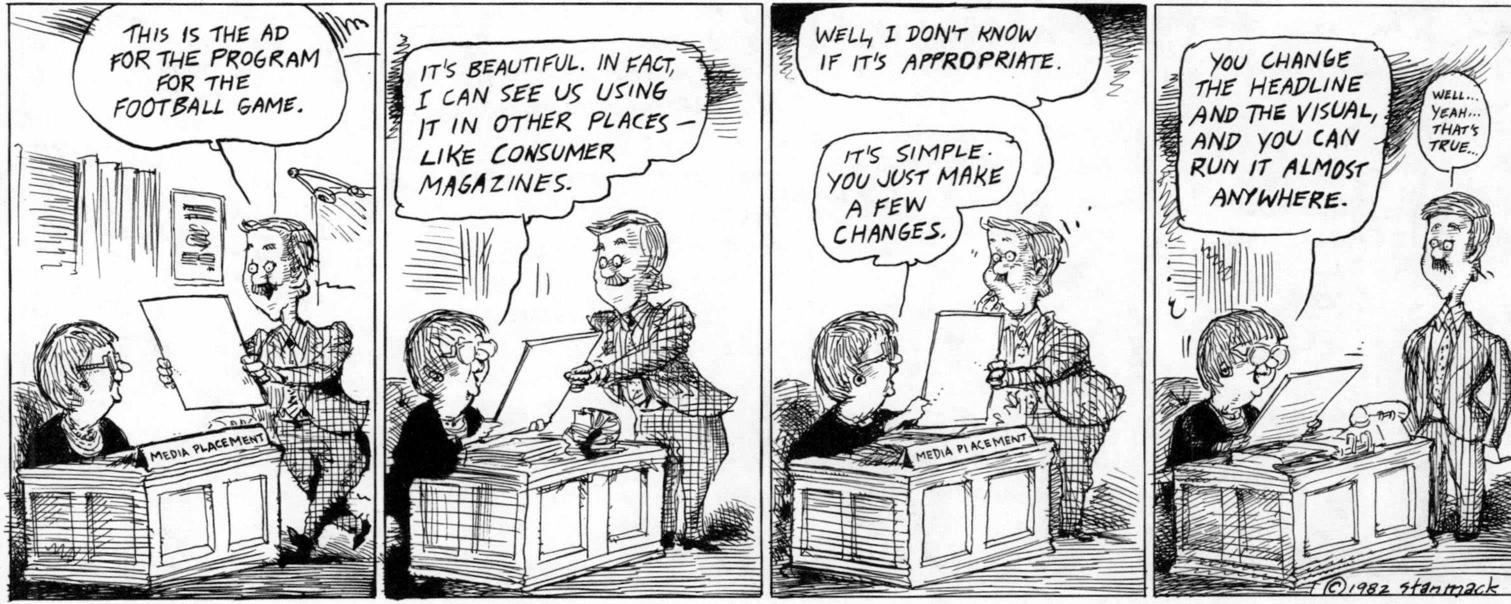
THIS IS THE AD FOR THE PROGRAM FOR THE FOOTBALL GAME.
MEDIA PLACEMENT
IT'S BEAUTIFUL. IN FACT, I CAN SEE US USING IT IN OTHER PLACES — LIKE CONSUMER MAGAZINES.
WELL, I DON'T KNOW IF IT'S APPROPRIATE.
IT'S SIMPLE. YOU JUST MAKE A FEW CHANGES.
MEDIA PLACEMENT
YOU CHANGE THE HEADLINE AND THE VISUAL, AND YOU CAN RUN IT ALMOST ANYWHERE.
WELL... YEAH... THAT'S TRUE...
© 1982 stanmack

No-Fault Separation

HI. I'VE COME TO SEE THE COLOR PROOF OF MY NEW ALBUM COVER.

AH. YOU'RE THE CHANTEUSE. HERE'S YOUR CHROMOLIN. IT LOOKS GREAT!

GARISH GRAPHIC

FIRST FLIGHT

GREAT? IT LOOKS LIKE I'VE GOT THE MEASLES! MY MOTHER'S GOING TO SAY, "CAROLE, YOU MOVE TO CALIFORNIA TO BECOME A ROCK AND ROLLER WITH A RASH??"

IT'S NOT THE FAULT OF MY SEPARATIONS. IT'S THE FAULT OF THE AIRBRUSHER, IT'S THE FAULT OF THE TRANSPARENCY, IT'S A COLOR SHIFT IN THE COMPUTER GRAPHICS, IT'S POOR MAKEUP IN THE SHOOT, IT'S YOUR AGENT'S FAULT, IT'S CHUCK'S FAULT AND HE'S NOT IN TODAY, IT'S LUNCHTIME AND I HAVE TO RUN. IT'S BEEN FUN, GIVE ME A CALL. GOODBYE.

COLOR REPRO CONFER'N ROOM

CHROMOLIN IT'S YOU I DREAD YOU'VE DONE ME IN WITH TOO MUCH RED MADE ME LOOK LIKE I'M HALF DEAD I'VE GOT THE CHROMOLIN BLUES

©1984 stan mack

Tweet Dreams

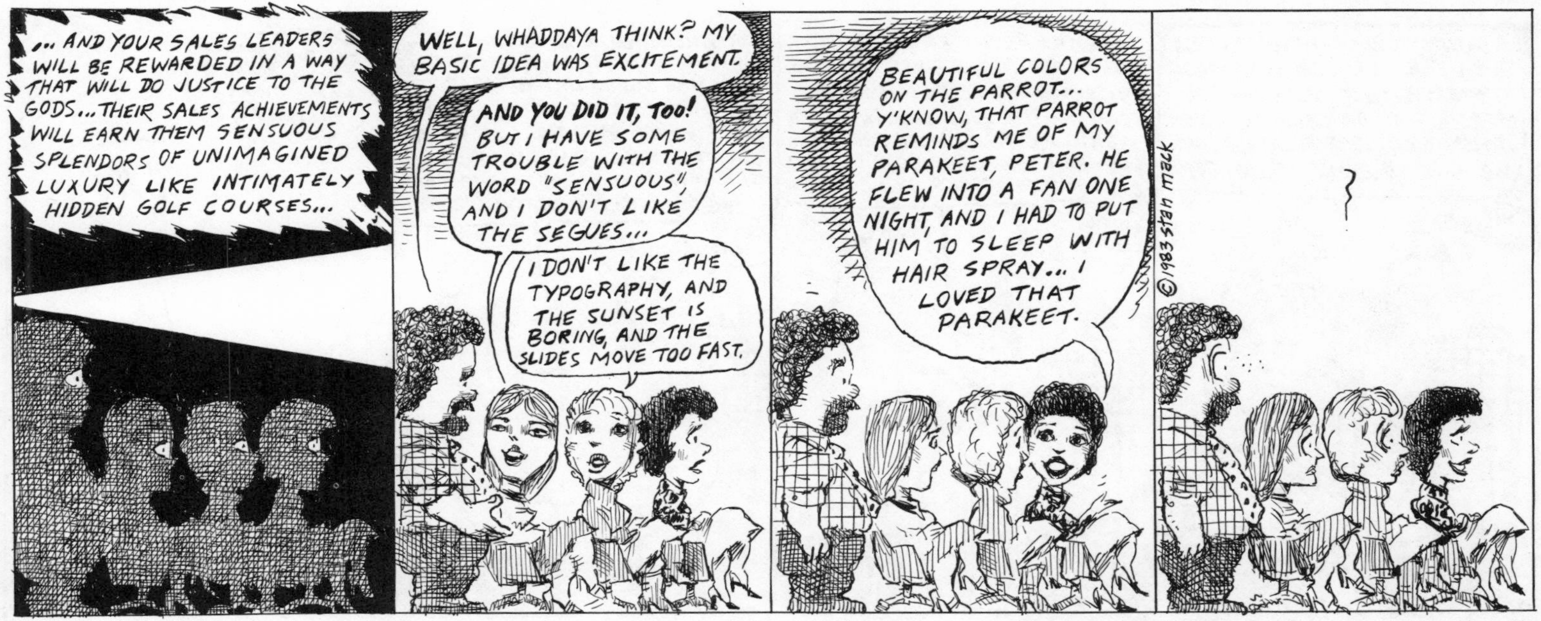
... AND YOUR SALES LEADERS WILL BE REWARDED IN A WAY THAT WILL DO JUSTICE TO THE GODS... THEIR SALES ACHIEVEMENTS WILL EARN THEM SENSUOUS SPLENDORS OF UNIMAGINED LUXURY LIKE INTIMATELY HIDDEN GOLF COURSES...
WELL, WHADDAYA THINK? MY BASIC IDEA WAS EXCITEMENT.
AND YOU DID IT, TOO! BUT I HAVE SOME TROUBLE WITH THE WORD "SENSUOUS", AND I DON'T LIKE THE SEGUES...
I DON'T LIKE THE TYPOGRAPHY, AND THE SUNSET IS BORING, AND THE SLIDES MOVE TOO FAST.
BEAUTIFUL COLORS ON THE PARROT... Y'KNOW, THAT PARROT REMINDS ME OF MY PARAKEET, PETER. HE FLEW INTO A FAN ONE NIGHT, AND I HAD TO PUT HIM TO SLEEP WITH HAIR SPRAY... I LOVED THAT PARAKEET.
©1983 stan mack
?

Reel Clear

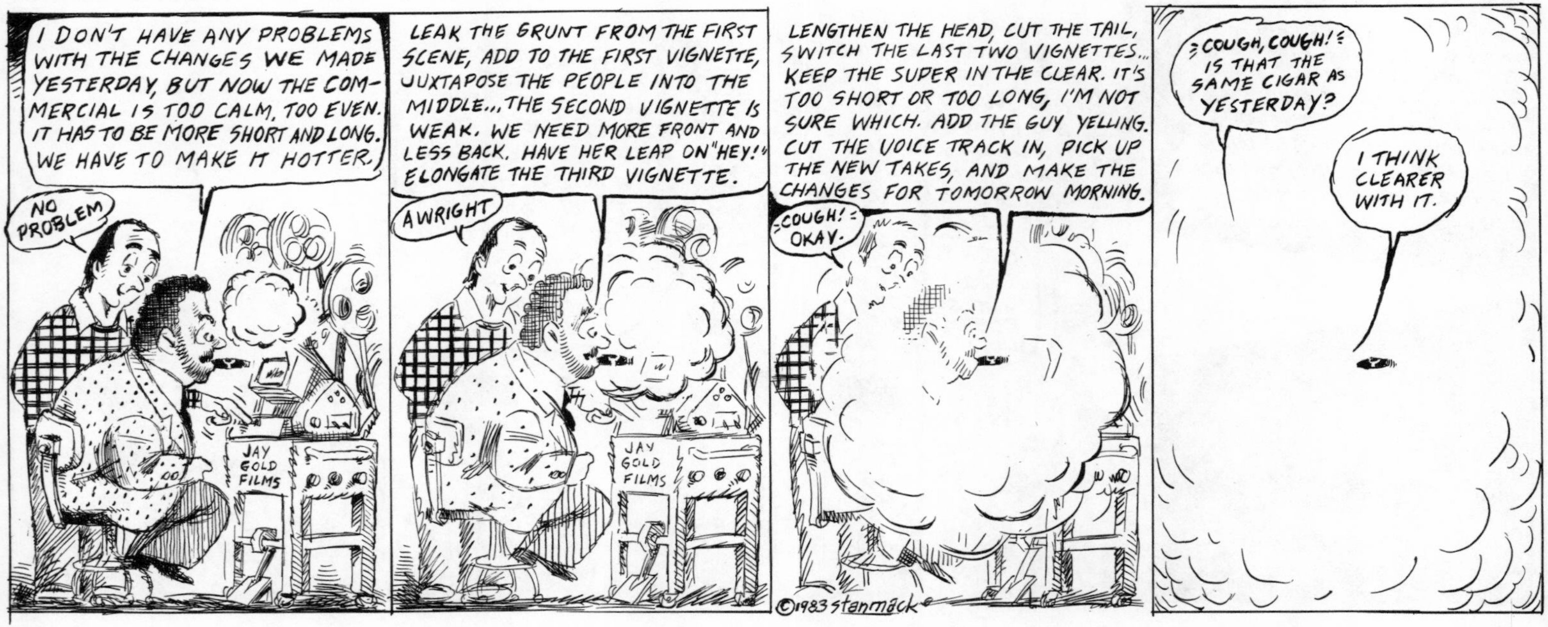
I DON'T HAVE ANY PROBLEMS WITH THE CHANGES WE MADE YESTERDAY, BUT NOW THE COMMERCIAL IS TOO CALM, TOO EVEN. IT HAS TO BE MORE SHORT AND LONG. WE HAVE TO MAKE IT HOTTER.
NO PROBLEM
JAY GOLD FILMS
LEAK THE GRUNT FROM THE FIRST SCENE, ADD TO THE FIRST VIGNETTE, JUXTAPOSE THE PEOPLE INTO THE MIDDLE... THE SECOND VIGNETTE IS WEAK. WE NEED MORE FRONT AND LESS BACK. HAVE HER LEAP ON "HEY!" ELONGATE THE THIRD VIGNETTE.
AWRIGHT
JAY GOLD FILMS
LENGTHEN THE HEAD, CUT THE TAIL, SWITCH THE LAST TWO VIGNETTES... KEEP THE SUPER IN THE CLEAR. IT'S TOO SHORT OR TOO LONG, I'M NOT SURE WHICH. ADD THE GUY YELLING. CUT THE VOICE TRACK IN, PICK UP THE NEW TAKES, AND MAKE THE CHANGES FOR TOMORROW MORNING.
COUGH! OKAY.
©1983 stanmack
COUGH, COUGH! IS THAT THE SAME CIGAR AS YESTERDAY?
I THINK CLEARER WITH IT.

Eavesdropping on a Focus Group

Who Says an Octopus Has No Arms?

Unstable Connection

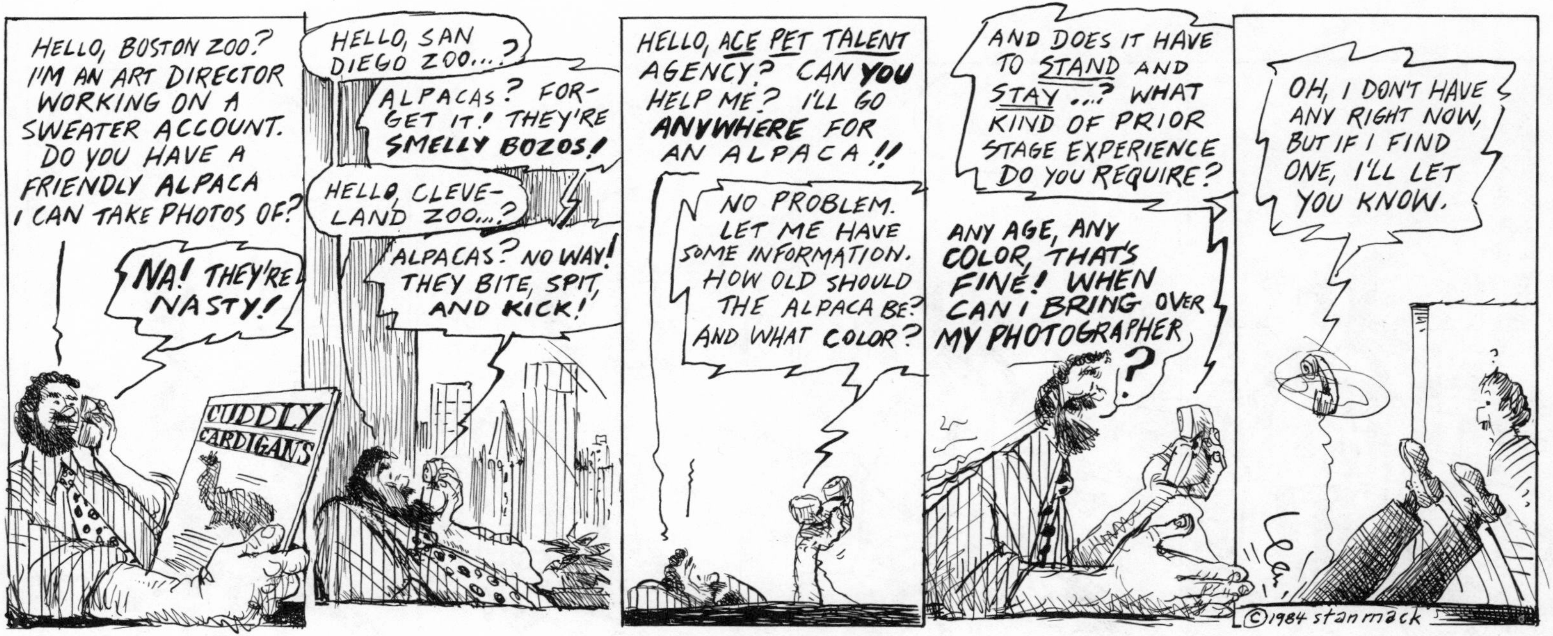
HELLO, BOSTON ZOO? I'M AN ART DIRECTOR WORKING ON A SWEATER ACCOUNT. DO YOU HAVE A FRIENDLY ALPACA I CAN TAKE PHOTOS OF?
NA! THEY'RE NASTY!
CUDDLY CARDIGANS
HELLO, SAN DIEGO ZOO...?
ALPACAS? FORGET IT! THEY'RE SMELLY BOZOS!
HELLO, CLEVELAND ZOO...?
ALPACAS? NO WAY! THEY BITE, SPIT, AND KICK!
HELLO, ACE PET TALENT AGENCY? CAN YOU HELP ME? I'LL GO ANYWHERE FOR AN ALPACA!!
NO PROBLEM. LET ME HAVE SOME INFORMATION. HOW OLD SHOULD THE ALPACA BE? AND WHAT COLOR?
AND DOES IT HAVE TO STAND AND STAY...? WHAT KIND OF PRIOR STAGE EXPERIENCE DO YOU REQUIRE?
ANY AGE, ANY COLOR, THAT'S FINE! WHEN CAN I BRING OVER MY PHOTOGRAPHER?
OH, I DON'T HAVE ANY RIGHT NOW, BUT IF I FIND ONE, I'LL LET YOU KNOW.
©1984 stanmack

A Matter of Relativity

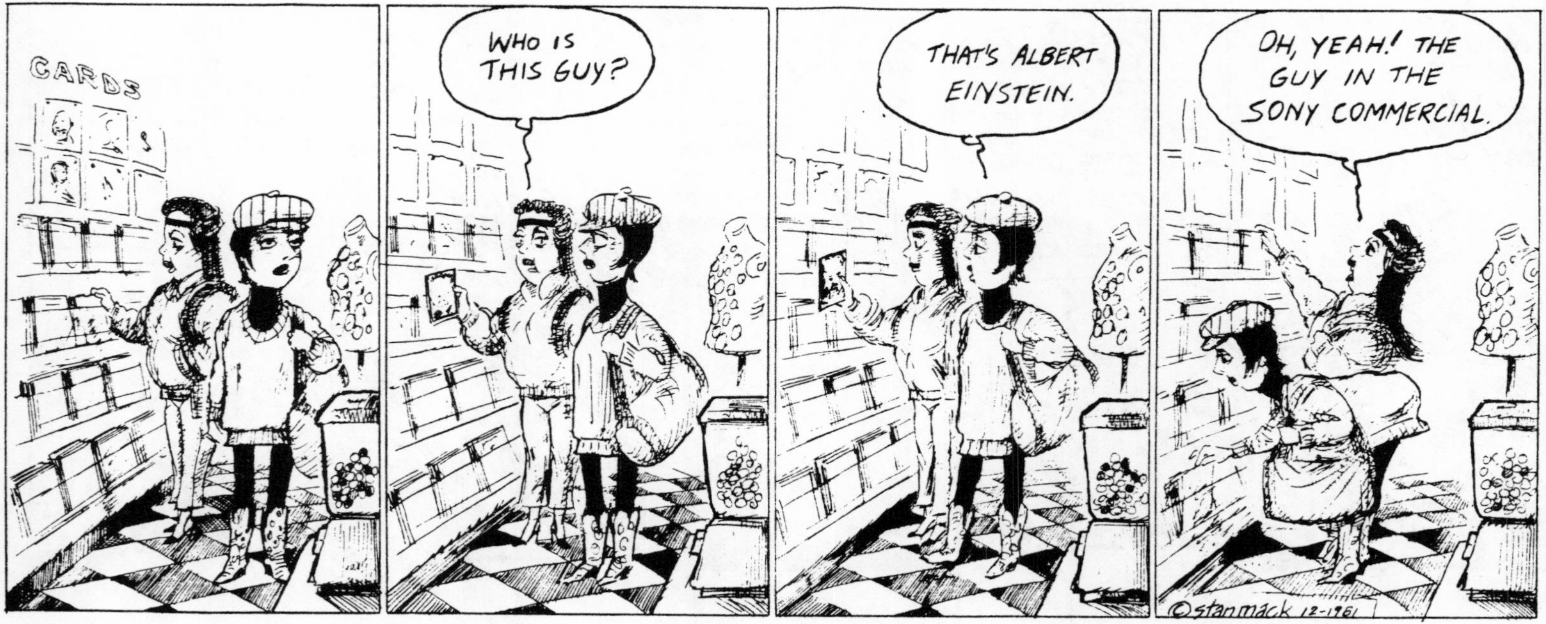
CARDS
WHO IS THIS GUY?
THAT'S ALBERT EINSTEIN.
OH, YEAH! THE GUY IN THE SONY COMMERCIAL.
©stanmack 12-1981

SO-BEA-680

Contemporary Latin American Classics

Contemporary Latin American Classics

J. CARY DAVIS, *General Editor*

EAST MEETS WEST
SOUTH
OF THE BORDER

Essays on

Spanish American life and attitudes

by D. Lincoln Canfield

Foreword by J. CARY DAVIS

Southern Illinois University Press

CARBONDALE AND EDWARDSVILLE

Feffer & Simons, Inc.

LONDON AND AMSTERDAM

Library of Congress Catalog Card Number 67–10723
Printed in the United States of America
Designed by Andor Braun

Foreword

J. CARY DAVIS

The Writer

Born December 13, 1903, in Cleveland, Ohio, D. Lincoln Canfield has passed much of his life in other parts of America—both North and South. The formative years of his youth were spent in the West: Colorado, New Mexico, California, Arizona, and Texas. In this last state he grew to manhood, graduating from Austin High School with honors (1922), and the University of Texas (A.B., 1926). From there he went to Columbia University for his Master's (1927) and the Ph.D. (1934). His early years along the Mexican border gave him his first close contacts with Spanish speakers and Hispanic-American culture, providing the impetus toward his lifelong study of these people, their linguistic traits, and ethnic character.

Dr. Canfield's professional career began at the University of Rochester as an instructor in Spanish in 1927; assistant professor 1934, and associate professor, 1942–46. From there he went to Florida State where he was professor and chairman of the Department of Modern Languages from 1946 to 1952. In 1953 he returned to Rochester where he has since been professor of Spanish and chairman of the Department of Foreign Languages (1953–62) and of the newly formed Department of Languages and Linguistics (1962–67). At intervals during this period, Professor Canfield has been a visiting professor, researcher, or lecturer at various universities and institutes here and abroad: Columbia University 1932–34; la Universidad de San Carlos, Guatemala (summer

1949); la Universidad de San Salvador (1952); the Instituto
Caro y Cuervo, Bogotá (1960); the University of Illinois
(1962–63): Alfred University (1963–64); SUNY at Buffalo
(1964–65); Southern Illinois University (1967–68); and at
NDEA Summer Language Institutes at South Dakota State
College (1961), Bradley University (1962), Bradley University in Guatemala (1963), in San Miguel de Allende, Mexico (1964, 1965, 1966), and at Utah State University at Oaxaca, Mexico (1967).

In addition, the author has traveled and studied in Spain,
France, and most of the countries of Central and South
America. His professional memberships, honors, and
achievements are many, among them the presidency of the
American Association of Teachers of Spanish and Portuguese in 1945. He has worked as a consultant with the
United States government and private industry. As a writer
his books deal largely with his specialty, linguistics, and he
is a world authority on the pronunciation of Spanish. There
are more than twenty-five printed articles to his credit, as
well as some eighteen reviews.

Much sought after as a public speaker and TV commentator, Linc—as he is affectionately known to his friends and
colleagues—has no equal as a teacher and lecturer; his class
sessions are lively, informative, and entertaining, and his
students think he is tops. He is an incomparable storyteller,
and withal, a modest man.

The Book

The first essay deals with a favorite theme of the
author's, namely, that Spanish-American culture is a curious
blend of Oriental and Western civilizations. Others consider
various phases of Latin-American culture, customs, language, and history. Some are deliberately popular in tone,
others more suited to specialized audiences. All, however,
are extremely readable, authentically based on firsthand information, and authoritative.

This book marks a new departure in the Contemporary
Latin American classics series, in that its contents are not
translations into English. Nevertheless, we feel that its in-

clusion is amply justified, and we invite the reader himself to be the judge.

Southern Illinois University
September, 1967

Contents

Introduction

D. LINCOLN CANFIELD

This little collection of essays on the coexistence of Spanish-speaking people is based on fairly frequent contacts with them and extended residence among them during some fifty years. The essays also take into consideration what the Hispanic people have said of themselves and their culture, as revealed in their literature and in their sociopolitical and linguistic writings.

Aside from contact with Hispanic acquaintances here in the United States, the author has been in the following Spanish-speaking regions, on several occasions for months at a time: Argentina, 1958; Arizona, 1916–19, 1949, 1961; Chile, 1958; Colombia, 1960; Cuba, 1947, 1957; Florida, 1946–52; Guatemala, 1949, 1951, 1952, 1963; Honduras, 1952; Mexico, 1926–66 (24 times), 1962, 1963, 1964; New Mexico, 1913–14, 1940, 1962; Panama, 1960; Peru, 1958; Puerto Rico, 1958; El Salvador, 1951, 1952; Venezuela, 1958. The author has recorded on tape many of the natives of these areas, as well as Bolivians, Nicaraguans, Ecuadorians, Paraguayans, and Uruguayans.

On four occasions he has enjoyed the research facilities of Latin-American institutions of learning and their libraries for extended periods, Mexico, 1945; Guatemala, 1949; El Salvador, 1952; Colombia, 1960; and he has visited several sections of Spain.

It has been an ever-growing conviction of the author that the basic culture of a community or nation or people lies at the grass-roots level. Culture is not just art, music, and literature, although some culture is to be found in them. Rather culture is the mode of interaction among those of the same persuasion, and the persuasion is usually their language and other systems of communication. In other words, people show their culture in their communicative behavior. Literature, music, and art are institutions, highly refined, and are many times imitations of another community and may not be typical of the people who nurture them.

The same might be said about government, education, commerce, and politics. They are institutions, whose framework may be imported from some admired nation but whose functioning is according to the native behavior pattern.

It is the writer's belief that we have too often judged other peoples by their institutions rather than by their behavior patterns, assuming that since the institutions resemble ours on paper similar actions and reactions should be expected. We have also assumed that changes may be made in the same way in which they might be made in our own society, forgetting that mode of change is also a part of the pattern of behavior. Again we have assumed that the removal of one class from power, or the dissolution of a political party, should remedy evils, forgetting that the other classes and parties within the same culture are of the same general behavior pattern.

From the study of linguistics and other communicative sciences, one learns that the individual can be changed completely speechwise if the change is made before adolescence. He may learn three or four languages without a foreign accent in any, or he may be able to talk according to the dialectal patterns of several areas of his own country. Nevertheless, it is impossible to change the speech pattern of a whole community without some overwhelming invasion or conquering force. The same observations might be made of the entire pattern of culture. Children become "foreigners" easily and quickly, but nations are slow to change.

Latin America has been judged by its institutions: its governments, its education, its commercial dealings, its diplomats. Actually, more often than not, these do not represent Latin America, nor does the so-called ruling class, and the proletariat would represent it even less. Latin America is a *modus operandi*; many systems of communication, nurtured and perpetuated for centuries in Spain and Portugal and America. The Hispanic systems of communication, like those of the Eastern Mediterranean and North Africa, seem to the Anglo-Saxon to be characterized by a certain egocentrism and an attractive personalism. Latin America has very charming people, a high birthrate, and a measure of civic irresponsibility.

University of Rochester
February 10, 1967

East Meets West, South of the Border

The personal flourish
in Hispanic culture

Introduction

The fastest growing population of the world today is that of Latin America. An increase from the present two hundred million to six hundred million by the year 2000 is a current estimate. Moreover, the people of Latin America since the sixteenth century have characteristically been grouped together in urban clusters, separated by scantily settled territory. These urban nuclei today exert a strong attraction, and rather than expand into a new pioneer zone, the Hispanic American tends to move toward the center. Given the unprecedented concentration of people in the cities, overpopulation in relation to production becomes a virtual certainty. In these conditions poverty becomes a dynamic factor and a part of the pattern of the culture. So does the rejection of one class by another along with very poor intersocietal communication.

The annual rate of increase seems to be highest in the predominantly tropical regions of Latin America, which, incidentally, are the areas of considerable sociopolitical unrest—the average for all Hispanic America is 2.4 per cent, as against 1.7 per cent for the United States, and it reaches 4 per cent in Costa Rica.

What are the chief elements of continuity in the civilization of these people whose nations constitute our greatest trade area and who will presently outnumber their North American neighbors two to one? What will be the effects of this population explosion on relations with the Great Powers? What of proud nationalism in the face of aggressive capitalism and communism? Or is it to be romance, rumba, and revolution?

It is the writer's contention that the fundamental elements of the nature of Latin America and the answers to the above questions should be sought at the grass-roots level: in the behavior pattern of the common people, rather than in the institutional framework of these nations, much of which is adopted or imposed. Not only is the behavior pattern of the people the essence of the so-called national character, but it is the vital force in the interpretation, acceptance or rejection of such institutions as education, religion, commerce, government, the law itself. Since we are an institutional people, we often ascribe to institutions traits that are actually of the people who maintain the institutions. The behavior pattern of Latin America is eminently Hispanic and is, therefore, non-Western in many of its elements.

One of the most tangible and tenacious aspects of the basic culture pattern of a people is language. By its very nature it is society-centered and environmentally perpetuated, and since thinking, especially argumentative or reflective thinking, is talking to one's self, our society affects our way of thinking, and the people who speak one language tend to develop certain common ways, postures, and attitudes. As the anthropologist Edward Hall (*The Silent Language*, 1959) points out, culture is actually communication, and communication is culture. But mankind, in his collective existence, communicates not only through language but through association, in his pattern of subsistence, in bisexuality, in temporality and territoriality, in learning, at play, and in his exploitation or use of materials. It is in these "message systems" that we should look for the real nature of men and peoples. These systems of interaction and interstimulation are unstudied, informal, and one is generally not aware of them. They are usually learned in childhood and as much from the community as from the home. Such things as art, literature, and music are formalizations, as are the institutions of law, religion, etc. Again, we are too prone to judge peoples by their institutions rather than their pattern of behavior.

Américo Castro ("The Spanish People," *Texas Quarterly*,

1961) insists that to judge peoples is to familiarize one's self with their *vital structure*. Some societies have developed over the centuries definite attitudes in favor of cooperation, collective effort, organization. Others have put more emphasis on person-to-person relations, on the enjoyment of leisure, and have thought of work as a handicap. By examining carefully this behavior structure, this culture pattern, we can understand better, perhaps, how the building of a Spanish Empire was possible for a people who have a disinclination for science, for technology, and for a workable democratic social organization, and how their descendants in America, in spite of all sorts of admixtures of race and color, have fairly common attitudes and ways of life and seem to be faced with the same problems in the collective entity.

The Hispanic behavior pattern

What is the nature of the Hispanic behavior pattern? What are the elements of its continuity? Castro refers us to his *Structure of Spanish History* (1954) and the original *La realidad histórica de España* (1948 and 1959), in which he stated that a confused sense of values had prevented historians from realizing that Spaniards are not a completely Occidental people. He feels that they actually came into being in a process starting in the eighth century and continuing through the Muslim Occupation, as a conglomeration of three castes of believers: Christians, Moors, and Jews. Their language is Latin in origin, and their connections are with the West, but their mode of existence, their culture pattern, came about as a result of the intermingling of Christians, Moors, and Jews from the eighth century to the end of the fifteenth.

From this long experience they have the Oriental feeling that nationality and religious faith are inseparable. Spain and Latin America today bear a closer resemblance to the Muslim countries than to any of the Western nations, including France and Italy. This integration of nation and faith extends to the person, who concedes value and authentic reality to whatever can be encompassed and dominated by his will. He is interested in the expression and representation of his own life, not in theories and thought about the world outside the reach of his senses. Thus he seems to convert the abstractly desirable into his own reality. Castro has called this personal absolutism, but other Hispanic writers have referred to it as individualism or personal pride. The great essayists Ortega y Gasset (*Invertebrate Spain*, 1921) and Unamuno (*The Tragic Sense of Life*, 1921) have been concerned with this quality, while Madariaga (*Englishmen, Frenchmen, Spaniards*, 1929) has spoken of his countrymen as people of passion (suffering) who act and react in a climate of *honor personal*. Indeed, *honor personal* is the chief theme of Spain's great Golden Age dramas.

The net results of Spain's Mediterranean past and her struggle with, and absorption by, Semitic peoples is that the Spanish-speaking person of today is by habit a personalist of passion rather than an institutionalist of action, a spectator and victim rather than an author and actor. And in his concern to check his own subjectivism he indulges in manifestations of the pompous and grandiose, in revolutions and counterrevolutions. His has been a history of palpitations rather than calculations!

Peter Boyd-Bowman recently completed a geobiographical study of the original Spanish settlers of America after examining the Spanish records of some 40,000 *pasajeros a Indias* of the sixteenth and early seventeenth centuries. He concluded that the great majority of these 40,000 was from the part of Spain that was longest under Semitic influence: Andalusia and Extremadura. And because so many of the people who migrated to the New World in the first century and a half were from southern Spain and Portugal, the traits inherited environmentally from the Moors and other Semitic peoples become important in a study of Latin America.

A product of contacts with many peoples, especially peoples of the Near East and Africa, the Andalusian is perhaps the most personalistic of all Spaniards, the most suffering, the most irreverent, and yet the most fanatical. He can dedicate himself alternately to frivolity and to solemnity with hardly a change of face. He takes life as it comes. It is for him a dance for today, not a march toward tomorrow! He has a wonderful capacity for pleasure from passion, whether it be the *flamenco* or a bullfight. At the same time volatile and indolent, sensual but unashamed, they have made Sevilla a sort of mecca for those who want escape from the trials and frustrations of ordered society.

Although the Andaluz is very talkative, his speech is filled with hyperboles, and his euphemisms are the most picturesque in a country and society that is much given to euphemistic expression and double meanings. And yet this suppleness of expression may become a liability in social-interaction.

This southern Spaniard conquered territory and founded great cities in America (Mexico, Lima, Buenos Aires, Havana, Santiago), but he took little thought for the welfare of those who dwelt in them. If there had been no foreign assistance, Castro reminds us, such splendors would still be lighted by candles and oil lamps. Spanish America—and Portuguese America, too—was made by preaching, not teaching. Its population today is almost all Christian, but less than half of these people are literate!

Spanish influence in America was strong and direct for three centuries, through *conquistador*, colonizer, priest, and merchant. Although indigenous and African elements have entered the stream of basic culture, and although there has been a wholesale mixing of races, the Iberian pattern, as nurtured during the Middle Ages, is still the common denominator.

The behavior pattern of Latin America is that of Spain and Portugal in a new setting. It is a functional system of human activity with components that are actually forms of communication, the most obvious of which is language, but which include many other manifestations of societal interaction, association, learning, recreation, and exploitation. George Foster's *Conquest and Culture* (1961) portrays the strong similarities that exist today between Spain, especially Andalusia, and the nations of Latin America.

The Spanish Christian's desire to maintain his *honor*, which to us is "face," is still sensed in the rejection of learning and technology, and the tendency to regulate to inferior status those who work with their hands. It must be emphasized that this attitude, along with his proverbial idleness, is an indirect consequence of the Christian desire to avoid being confused with Jews and Moors. From the end of the fifteenth century on, it was considered dishonorable to be descended from Jews or Moors. Everyone shied away from intellectual activities, inasmuch as almost all of these had been cultivated by the Jewish caste and by their descendants, the New Christians.

It is not strange, then, that the Spaniard early established a pattern for the exploitation of lands and mines which involved the Indians as an involuntary working force under devices and arrangements known as the *repartimiento,* the *encomienda,* and the *mita,* the latter especially designed to supply a steady flow of laborers to the mines. Assignments were made to particular Spaniards, and although the Church instigated the setting up of protective regulations to safeguard the interests of the natives, the service amounted to legalized slavery. Under such conditions concubinage grew and did not cease with the conquest or with the termination of the colonial period. The prevalence of miscegenation of many sorts produced new races, and with much less race prejudice than in northern societies whole mestizo populations were created, Paraguay being a good example.

In all of this, again, it is the person-to-person relation that distinguishes the Spaniard and his American offspring, and even if there have been Indian elements in the culture of some of the Latin-American nations, the modern world processes and the very personalist nature of Spanish culture will gradually complete the conversion to *Hispanidad* of the rest of the millions of native Americans who may have kept their original ways for years after the conquest.

The basic continuity of Hispania is, therefore, the personalist behavior pattern, a pattern which is not of one's own making—it is given to him by society—and yet it drives him to formulate the policy, as it were, of this same society. Castro tells of a Madrid streetcar motorman, who, seeing a pretty girl walking along the sidewalk, slowed down to her pace in order to pay her the compliments *de rigueur.* The streetcar was thus transformed into something like a horse, docile to the will and designs of its rider. This sort of conversion Castro calls a "centaurical" joining, and although it has produced admirable results in art and literature and brought about the conversion of millions of Indians and Negroes to the beliefs and language of Spain and Portugal, one sees the immediate possibilities of laws and other public services being joined "centaurically" to the personal will of those who administer them! This has happened only too often.

Personal absolutism may modify all aspects of communication and interaction. The personal flourish may have a profound effect on business transactions, professional procedures, and national enterprise. The concept of public education may have difficulty in remaining public, and political life may be completely converted to the direct action associated with *honor personal.*

The Spaniard may seem to be alternately Don Quijote and Sancho Panza. Many of the exploits and adventures of the *conquistadores* are comparable to the *locuras* of Don Quijote, and yet Hispanic people have shown very realistic points of view in international relations on many occasions, and their rich store of proverbs might be indicative of a pragmatic philosophy. Far from being security happy, the Hispanic person is assured only of the importance of fate and his is a tragic sense of life.

As Madariaga insists, the Spaniard is a man of passion who may do things according to the light of intuition, and, although his chief sin is envy, he is usually generous. Men are the center of his universe, not mankind, and he shows unusual interest in helping particular individuals but not a community chest. He is on guard against those outside the intimate group and is moved only by an urge to surge!

Personal flourishes as a way of life

One of the most interesting phases of Hispanic personalism is the *rúbrica* or personal flourish that one writes beneath his signature—and with which he may cash a check without the signature. All legal documents say at the bottom, "Signed and flourished on . . . (date)." And one might refer to the dramatic flair that characterizes most Hispanic action and interaction as a *rúbrica*: attitudes, postures, gestures, oratory; even the journalism of Hispanic America abounds in a euphemistic and hyperbolic expression which would shock the cold and factual Anglo-Saxon with his understatement and abbreviations. Let us examine first the system of gestures and facial expressions and filigree attitudes that make Hispanic existence a dance for today, not a march toward tomorrow.

The gesture which means "come here," for instance, is quite the opposite of that used by English-speaking people. It is made with the arm extended but with the palm of the hand downward. A movement is made earthward rather than skyward, similar to "go away" in English, and, as is usually the case in these matters, the female does this with more delicacy—just a finger, perhaps. Now that we have examined the hither sign, let's see how one gesticulates the idea of good-bye. The hand is raised in front of the face but with the palm toward the face or to one side. Then one agitates the fingers.

To say "no" without saying it, the index finger is waved back and forth in front of the face. At the bullfight, the same gesture, somewhat amplified, is used by members of the audience to inform the authorities that the bull seems to be too much of a Ferdinand. For this, the whole arm, handkerchief in hand, is used!

The interrogative attitude manifests itself with a rather complicated gesture. First one opens the eyes to the point of bulging, the head is raised with a brusque movement, and the hands, palms up, are extended at the sides with a quick movement. To emphasize or reiterate the question, the brusque movement is repeated. One may ask a question from two blocks away!

Perhaps the most intricate of all gestures of the Hispanic people is the one that means simply "so-so," not too good, not too bad. For this attitude one uses the head, the eyes, the eyelids, the mouth, the shoulders, and one hand! First the head is tilted to one side, the corners of the mouth are turned down, the eyebrows are raised, but the eyelids are lowered about halfway. Then the shoulders are shrugged, and the right hand is extended and turned from side to side, showing first the knuckles and then the palm.

To represent the quality of avarice or to single out a stingy person, one doubles the right arm and then taps the elbow with the other fist or hand, while the act of paying the bill is represented by the thumb, nail up, on the curved index finger. The hand is moved downward.

To represent eating or the indication of appetite, one bunches the fingers of one hand and moves these toward the mouth with a wrist motion. To drink, especially alcoholic beverages, is portrayed by pointing the thumb on one hand at one's face, fingers folded down to the palm. In Mexico, the little finger seems to stand up under these circumstances! (These are graphic representations of the Spanish leather wine bottle, *bota*, carried slung over one shoulder, and the double-spouted drinking jug called a *porrón*—EDITOR.)

So it is that gesture and facial expression form part and parcel of the Hispanic way of life, the filigree attitude; but they are not the only *rúbricas*. One courts a girl with a *rúbrica*, he eats with one, he drives a car—and honks the horn—with a couple of them, and he may even get on a bus with a beautiful flourish.

The male passenger boarding a moving bus gives one of the most artistic of all flourishes, at times approaching in daring and execution the dance of death of the bullring. As the bus approaches, he maintains a stance similar to that of a good matador awaiting the charge of the bull, and when the front fender of the vehicle nears his body, he bends slightly backward in the middle without changing his foot position. As the hulk lurches past him he extends both arms, grasps the bars of the window just forward of the central door (which is open) with his right hand and uses the other for any available contacts on the inside. He may have a package in his left hand and a cigarette in his mouth, but with the utmost grace he plants his left foot in any space to be found on the step, swings the other foot out in a beautiful arc over the receding pavement, and accommodates himself among the other hangers-on. There have been several "strokes" devised by the young bucks of some Hispanic communities for the process of alighting, among them the sidestroke and the backstroke, the latter being referred to affectionately as the *angelito*, since one lands with his wings spread.

Hispanic custom with regard to passing on the sidewalk is another manifestation of the person-to-person psychology in situations of interaction. It has long been the habit in order to show respect to a person approaching from the opposite direction to give this individual the inside. This is in contrast to the American institution of right versus left. I recall the occasion of the little old maid Morelian schoolteacher, whom I was accompanying down the street of that Michoacán city, when we met two gentlemen acquaintances of hers. They not only doffed their hats but took the outside of the walk, finally stepping off into the street as we passed, "Para servirle." She said to me, "Did you see those two gentlemen who give me the sidewalk? One is the superintendent of schools, the other is one of our veteran teachers."

Related to this and also a part of the flourish of Hispanic existence is the professional *rúbrica* that now and then is so evident. We once had occasion to visit a doctor. Our daughter, then eight, had fallen out of a tree, hurting her nose. It might have been broken. This particular physician had a waiting room equipped with a speaker from his adjacent office, and he called his patients in by numbers assigned to them by the receptionist: *número dos, número tres,* and so on. We were *número ocho,* and we finally went in. He got up from his desk, took off his overcoat (which he hadn't bothered to do before), hung it on the coatrack, put on a clean, white coat, went over to the sink, reached for the liquid green soap and began to scrub his hands very thoroughly—up to the elbow, shook them off, dried them, then put on a pair of rubber gloves, picked up the green soap bottle, washed again, talking all the time about the accident. Next, he put on a gauze mask, then went to his cabinet, got out all his instruments and laid them on a glass-top table. With a bottle of alcohol he sprinkled the instruments and lighted a match! One might call this the crepe suzette of

medicine! To our eight-year-old daughter this was certainly
fire and brimstone. He finally got her up on the examining
table, and using just one of the instruments, he opened a
nostril, looked inside, and said, "Well, this doesn't seem to
be very serious. I would say that it isn't broken, since it is
not off the track nor does it crunch."

One of the most picturesque manifestations of the His-
panic *rúbrica* is the use of names of rather fertile imagina-
tion for stores and saloons: The Surprise, The Temple of
Love, The Violet, American Ping-Pong, The Little Cheap,
The Ideal, The Port of Liverpool, The City of Chicago, The
Two Worlds, I Feel like an Aviator, I'm Going Again, and
I'm Laughing Now.

The close relation of religion to life and custom is seen
in the women's names that are appellations of the Virgin:
Mary of the Anguish, Mary of the Angels, Shelter, Reme-
dies, Help, Pillar, Conception. And so many men are Jesús
as well as Joseph Mary, and then there is a friend whose
name translated is John of God Flowers, and the baggage-
man, a husky fellow, who was Margarito Flores.

Education

Let's take a look at education south of the border.
A typical curriculum of a secondary school shows that all
students may be studying Spanish, English, history, algebra,
solid geometry, physics, psychology, literature, and geography, at one time. Before a child graduates from a secondary
school of this type he will have had four sciences, several
years of mathematics, three foreign languages. Everybody
takes everything, but is everybody in school?

When one examines the laws of the Latin-American countries in this regard, he learns that compulsory attendance
is the rule. When one examines the facts, he finds that not
even half of those who should be in school are there. As one
Latin American has stated it, "The law is obeyed, but not
carried out."

In only a few countries of the twenty republics do 50 per
cent of those who should be in school actually attend! (In
Mexico and Cuba, where great strides have been made in

recent years, the percentage is still close to 50.) Why do these conditions exist? The fundamental reason is lack of interest on the part of the individual in the enforcement of law for the good of the group. To say that shortage of personnel and equipment is the fundamental reason for these conditions is naïve. In Colombia, the average education of the public-school teacher is that of the fifth grade, and there are several hundred thousand children without schooling. The sad part of this picture is that the population explosion is complicating the matter.

A typical total education program is that of Uruguay: six years of elementary school, six years of secondary, divided into a four-year general course and a two-year pre-professional course for those who will enter the university. The student receives a *bachillerato* at the end of secondary school which entitles him to enter a university. But it should be noted that this means, in terms of the United States, a graduate school. *There is no four-year college.* A degree of doctor of medicine is obtained after six or seven years beyond high school; the same is required for the degree in civil engineering. A doctor of chemistry degree takes five years beyond high school. The degree Dr. Fidel Castro has would correspond to the A.B., or, at the most, an M.A., in terms of American education, and probably represents some sixteen years of schooling.

To the people of Latin America, the matter of education is the task of the nation, not the community. The government usually has a *secretaría* or *ministerio* headed by a cabinet member, and although private education may be tolerated, it is "incorporated" and must abide by certain government regulations. Where the Catholic Church still exerts considerable influence in education, notably in Colombia, lay education turns out to be Catholic-guided.

One of the greatest dangers of nationally directed education is that it implies a *doctrine d'état*, especially since teachers and professors are very often government employees or officials. Then, too, if the university seems to represent government authority, the students are apt to oppose its policies.

Most Latin-American universities are national and are

financed by the national budget. Faculties tend to be part-time, and the problems of improving standards are often exacerbated by this fact and because of the traditionally powerful role of students in the management of the university. Characteristically, student representatives sit on their ruling councils, often in such numbers as to make effective formulation of curricula and disciplined administration exceedingly difficult, if not impossible. A recent case in point is the complete surrender of the Universidad Libre of Bogotá, Colombia, to Marxism through student manipulations. The student-inspired crisis (a word which often appears in university affairs in Latin America) at the Universidad de la Habana has put that institution in the column of communism, and has become an instrument of the *revolución.*

At the university level, some very interesting things take place, quite outside the basic academic program. The students use the strike, for example, to bring to the attention of the public their desire for reform of curriculum, or change of administration. Having witnessed several strikes in Mexico, Cuba, El Salvador, Venezuela, and Colombia, I shall describe one that took place in San Salvador a few years ago.

It happened that a student came to class one morning in an intoxicated condition and proceeded to call the professor several names—without euphemistic glossing. The professor went right out and got the police, thus making a national issue of the affair. The boy was arrested and the students called a university-wide strike in protest. As usual, most of those who followed the strike order did not know what the issue was but welcomed the opportunity to leave their books. At the police station officialdom felt the pressure of the students, so they quietly edged their prisoner out the side door, took him by car to the border of Honduras, from which country he had been excluded sometime before.

During the week that the strike continued, it was revealing to watch activity at the university. The students would mill about the buildings, calling meetings, making speeches to each other, dropping chalk on the bald-headed men who might pass, and whistling at the girls. They finally decided to bury in effigy the professor who had caused the student to be arrested in the first place. Having built a little coffin, they paraded the "body" through the central part of the city, took it to the cemetery, had several orations, and buried it. There was no protest from the public, press, or parents, and, as a sidelight, it should be noted that the professors reported to the campus each day during the strike, to sign the roll, since they were paid "by the class." Otherwise, they had a tendency to cut their own classes!

During six months of 1960, I witnessed seven strikes in the universities of Colombia. In at least two of these, the students succeeded in unseating the rector himself. A committee of the National Congress promised "to study the problem"!

Hispanic disinclination for science and technology, which Américo Castro attributes to caste differences, is quite evident in Latin America. A recent report of the American Council of Learned Societies shows that the state of research in the universities is deplorable, although there are a few bright spots, and a great many Hispanic doctors and technicians have been eminently successful in a more rigorous intellectual climate. In spite of this sad situation, the title doctor is used very loosely, all congressmen being so designated in Colombia, along with practically anyone who has attended a university, who wears glasses, or carries a briefcase!

The elements of the pattern of behavior seem trivial on first examination, but they turn out to be basic manifestations of collective qualities that really make institutions what they are.

Economy

For the first time in years of Pan-American relations and conferences, social progress has been elevated to a position alongside economic development as one of the objectives of inter-American efforts and one of the important reasons for American loans. This new emphasis seems to recognize that the greatest economic resource of any country is its people, and while social progress may depend basically on economic progress, it cannot be assured in good time unless the strengthening of institutions brings about equitable sharing of the fruits of national economic, social, and political processes of the nation.

The Act of Bogotá, signed by most of the American Republics on September 13, 1960, states that "the preservation and strengthening of free and democratic institutions in the American Republics requires the acceleration of social and economic progress . . ." The Punta del Este Conference of August 1961 has formulated the Alliance for Progress, signed by all delegates except "Che" Guevara, representing Fidel Castro. This agreement calls for billions to be spent in the next ten years to raise the standard of living and better the lot of the underdog in Latin America.

While the Alliance for Progress provides for increased participation on the part of Latin-American people and monies, Latin-American economies continue to crumble, inflation and city-crowding complicate the population explosion, and the Hispanic way of life continues to militate against material progress. We must realize that although production must be increased, and although taxation and other public responsibilities have to be taken seriously in a free society, none of these things will ever flourish until there is respect and concern on the part of the individual for the welfare of the whole! The problem is a moral one.

Just as in education, the Hispanic individualism militates against the conduct of large-scale economic enterprise. And its egocentric social system produces extremes of wealth and poverty, discourages the growth of stabilized business, and perpetuates rigid class stratification. In turn, political compromises are difficult.

Under such circumstances, an organization seems too impersonal, the machine a real indignity which leaves no room for personal prowess. Although there are other factors, such as climate and lack of energy sources, the poverty of Latin America is not a result of insufficient national income, or vice versa, but rather these conditions and many others are simply aspects of a behavior pattern of personal absolutism.

Oscar Lewis describes on page xxvi of *The Children of Sánchez* (1961) what he calls the culture of poverty.

The economic traits which are most characteristic of the culture of poverty include the constant struggle for survival, unemployment and underemployment, low wages, a miscellany of unskilled occupations, child labor, the absence of savings, a chronic shortage of cash, the absence of food reserves in the home, the pattern of frequent buying of small quantities of food many times a day as the need arises, the pawning of personal goods, borrowing from local money lenders at usurious rates of interest, the use of second-hand furniture and clothing.

Mexico, with a revolution under its belt, with billions of American dollars over the past twenty years, in tourism and in industrial investment, still presents the sad picture of bad distribution of wealth, a population probably 40 per cent illiterate and a life expectancy of less than forty years. The 100,000 at the top of Mexico's economic structure receive billions more than the 10,000,000 at the bottom of the pyramid, who average about three hundred dollars annually.

While our Marxist apologists shout against the ravages of American imperialism and exploitation of Latin America, we note that much of the economic development, both industrial and of natural resources, has been brought about over the years by foreign capitalists and investors; wherever they have been most active, standards and general progress have been greatest.

In some countries of Latin America, income taxes are light, or nonexistent, and, in most, inadequately collected. Guatemala instituted its first income tax in 1963. Taxes on wealth in the form of land are low, but taxes on corporate profits are commonly very high. Many foreign firms have recently been taxed out of business, while local taxes are so ineffective that lotteries prove to be the most dependable source of income. As an item of curiosity, a large Latin-American daily published a general account of taxes collected in the country, noting that of 55,000 firms, only 11,000 paid taxes. American oil firms in Venezuela pay high taxes, heavy royalties, and hire thousands at good wages—in an industry that probably would not have been developed without the foreigner.

Economic development requires objective planning and

painstaking execution, highly trained technical and managerial personnel, and the cooperation of society. As Américo Castro has indicated, the disinclination of today stems from caste differences of the Middle Ages. While many Hispanic Americans shudder at the thought of the impersonal community chest of the North Americans, the person-to-person almsgiving means that there are beggars and hangers-on in most Spanish-speaking countries, and in some of the capitals of Latin America hundreds of urchins roam the streets, begging by day and stealing by night, and often sleeping wrapped in newspapers in the doorways of closed shops. Due to the altitude, the temperature drops to near freezing in some of these cities.

As Oscar Lewis points out, most of the poor of Mexico City, for instance, have a very low level of literacy and education, do not belong to labor unions, are not members of a political party, do not participate in medical care, maternity and old-age benefits of the national welfare agency, and make very little use of the city's banks, hospitals, department stores, museums, art galleries, and airports. Lewis believes that over the years such groups of people develop critical attitudes toward values and institutions, a mistrust of government and of those in high position, and a cynicism which extends even to the Church. One could insist, however, that the critical attitudes toward government and those in high position are traditional in Hispanic society and that even those in high position have the same cynicism. One could insist, too, that the very social disorganization of which Lewis writes is a part of this pattern.

The society of the Spanish-speaking people places great emphasis on family connections, family cohesion, and family loyalty. This means the presence of nepotism and the general lack of the merit system in civil service. But in spite of this situation the phenomenon of the absent father is a crucial one in a society that is known for the authoritarian status of the father. As Oscar Lewis notes in his *The Children of Sánchez*, the considerable influence of women in the family turns out to be a corollary of their supposedly low status, because the mistress is so common, as are free unions, and many children know not their fathers. A man spends lots of time proving he is a real male, and *machismo* becomes his philosophy of life, while matrifocality develops at home.

As has been noted in regard to university professors, many professional people of Latin America hold down two or more jobs, one of which may be a political post. Authors are no exception. In fact, many politicians double as authors and literary critics. Hence it is that since independence, the literature of Spanish America has become more and more sociopolitical in its orientation.

Domingo Faustino Sarmiento, statesman, writer, and finally president of Argentina, wrote *Facundo*, later translated by Mrs. Horace Mann, before the middle of the nineteenth century, to decry the tendencies of *caudillismo*, or petty dictatorships in his country. Novels depicting urban conditions of Santiago, Mexico, and Caracas were written by Alberto Blest Gana, Federico Gamboa, Rufino Blanco Fombona, and many others; and since 1920 a large part of the literature of Spanish America, even much of the poetry, deals with political, economic, and social problems.

With the new methods of communication, especially the movies and the radio, many illiterate people have been reached; there is a new interplay of influences, and there has emerged a "literature of the common man," some of it Marxist-inspired, most of it concerned with the destruction of society's elite and the exaltation of the common people and their social justice. These things are reflected in the blasts at the military, the landowners, illiteracy, religious fanaticism, and Yankee imperialism. Aristocratically oriented literature, therefore, has been replaced by writings that deal with people of today and in circumstances and problems of today's Latin America. Trends are toward secularism, realism, nationalism, and the use of the vernacular.

Religion

Although the Catholic Church of Spain held a privileged position in colonial society, and although it was powerful economically, it was not blind to the problems and injustices of the era. While the Church was used by the crown as an instrument of colonization, its position today in many of the countries of Latin America is that of defender of the masses and advocate of the revolution. This may be especially true in the very places where it held considerable secular power in another day.

The Roman Catholic religion, which is nominal to more than 90 per cent of Latin Americans, is another institution that has the mark of the original intermingling of Christians, Jews, and Moors during the reconquest of Spain. Strangely, Hispanic Catholicism bears the scars of a Semitic past. The Oriental concept of nationality and religious faith as inseparable is the chief heritage and is very much in evidence among Spanish-speaking people, who, if they can't come together under a single mystique, can't come together at all: hermetic traditionalism, or the burning of churches and the killing of priests.

The religious situation of Latin America represents the vigorous interpenetration of the objective and personal. The integration of the Indians, and later the Negroes, is the egocentric Oriental tendency to encompass and dominate through the will of the *person*. Because of this latter characteristic one finds great contrasts, at least on the surface, among the nations of Latin America.

As contrasts, Mexico's anticlerical laws prohibit Catholic schools, and the ones that exist are winked at and are called private; and, although the teachers are often clerics and are called *padre* by the students, they aren't allowed to wear their robes on the street. Colombia, Peru, and Ecuador present very conservative trends. In Colombia, a child must have a birth certificate signed by a priest in order to enter a public school. The concordat between Church and State is a serious matter and all sorts of tensions arise from it. Protestants, Jews, and other non-Catholics are permitted to establish private schools, but Catholic students who enter such schools must identify themselves as of some other religion.

In contrast to this, one recalls the great *manifestación* of 1926 in Mexico City, when some 300,000 Mexicans, mostly Catholics, marched in support of President Plutarco Elías Calles, who had closed the Church in a conflict over the

enforcement of religious laws that descended from the re-
forms of Benito Juárez. Feeling ran high in those days, and
the interesting paradox is that several Mexican presidents,
born as Catholics but now Masons, were conducting the
affairs of a country that was and is 90 per cent Catholic.
And just a few years later, a pamphlet in a Catholic church
of this same country said, among other things: "Don't talk
to any Protestant, because they are all liars. It is treachery
to the Fatherland to listen to a Protestant."

It is estimated that only some 20 per cent of the Catholics
of Latin America are practicing Catholics, and these mostly
women, but of course much hinges on the interpretation of
practicing. It is certainly true that it is quite rare to see men
in church in Latin America in any numbers.

Here again, as in education, in commerce, and in politics,
the vital force is personal, subjective, not concerted and
objective. One understands why the Church in Cuba has
not proved to be a deterrent to communism. One may understand, too, why North Americans, including Catholics,
are sometimes shocked by the bleeding figures, the depic-
tions of the suffering of martyrs, the fireworks, the sky-
rockets and burning *castillos*, along with parades in which
special Virgins are venerated—beautiful cathedrals, much
gold leaf, many articles of extreme value, in the midst of
abject poverty.

The Hidden Convent of Santa Mónica, in Puebla, Mexico,
is an interesting example of the development of these institutions within the conflict around the Church and its
privileges. Its existence was discovered in 1935 by a federal
detective, quite by accident, at which time he learned that
it had been operating secretly for some sixty years. Rumors
of a secret convent in the neighborhood were common, and
the detective was sent to investigate. He gained entrance to
a private home, and accidentally discovered a button hidden
behind a flower pot. He pressed the button, and a section
of shelves moved aside, revealing the hallway of a convent.
This was the beginning of a startling revelation: the cells
of the nuns, the heart of the founder preserved in alcohol,
the refectory, kitchen, the mother superior's bathroom, and
all the rest. Apparently, some sixty nuns had lived there for

many years, practicing their vows in secret and in defiance
of the law. They had been fed and maintained by the residents of the homes within which the convent was built,
contrary to the law, in a country whose people are nearly
all Catholics!

Contrast to this the villages of Colombia, where the priest
is the boss—often because nobody else assumes responsibility—and where it is necessary to get his permission for
activities and projects that are completely secular. The
Peace Corps youths who go to Colombia are forewarned of
this situation.

Politics

In the political realm, Hispania tends toward direct
action and dictatorship. Fidel Castro is simply one of some
seventy dictators on the Latin American scene since Simón
Bolívar. Most of these men originally entered their responsibilities as elected leaders or as popular heroes. José Ortega y Gasset, speaking of these conditions, attributes them
to what he calls personal pride, the essence of which is a
feeling of not belonging to the whole. Therefore, the individual does not share the confidence of the others.

Américo Castro reminds us that in Portugal a dictator
has been in power for more than thirty years, and in Spain
for more than twenty. To cry out against such a situation is
naïve. It is more useful to relate it to the way in which the
Hispanic people have developed their collective existence.
As this essayist states, political disasters are not physical
phenomena like a bolt of lightning or a drought; they are
magnifications of what goes on within the individual, the
family, the village, the city and the region. And the Spanish-
speaking person of today goes back politically to the centuries of coexistence with Moor and Jew, to constant preparations for war, but also to the need of sharing a common
life with other castes. Hence the personal absolutism, the
individualism, the disintegrating centrifugal force.

The strange rationalization of the new Cuba is depicted
in the following passage from *El Mundo* (Havana), January
1965.

A Communist is, necessarily, a man of a high sense of humanity; a man capable of making Justice triumph and of fighting and giving his life for a happier humanity, with equal rights and opportunities for all, whatever their geographical origin or the color of their skin.

For the free world, for the representative democracies, *Communist* can be anyone who in any way opposes imperial aggression; who fights against wars or simply who opposes the devices of those who may command in a given moment. It's a question of a convenient label which authorizes the hounds of the regime to employ against the one so classified the most brutal means of repression.

If in any subordinate country of Latin America there arose a man to condemn the war of agression which the United States is carrying on in South Korea [sic]; if this man were to oppose publicly the projects of the U.S.A. to get backing from the countries of the Hemisphere and were to say that the money would be better spent on a school or a hospital of the many that are needed, the label of "Communist" would not be long in coming.

Today throughout Latin America, one hears the cry ¡*revolución*! The leading political parties of many nations have the word as a part, at least, of their official designation, and students, writers, intellectuals continue to speak of the need for *revolución*. And yet one finds upon examining the history of these countries that there have already been many. Some Mexicans speak now of a *revolución* against their almost sacred social revolution. What do they mean? Apparently the general thought is to turn society over and give the little fellow a better chance—always at the expense of some vague combination of exploiters and oppressors, the Church, the foreign imperialists, the military, the oligarchy, the rich, etc. As a Spanish friend has said, they always want to turn the tortilla over, only to find, once they have, that it is burned on both sides and is still just a tortilla.

The Castro revolution is the result of all this, combined with a dangerous alignment with the Communist bloc. This type of change leads to civil war, it drives out talent and capital, and it tightens the oppressive measures that are always latent in the Hispanic collective behavior. One of the best testimonies of the rapid disintegration of Cuban society is to be had in the official organ of Castro's *revolución*, a paper of this same title. (The writer has a rather large collection, sent by a Cuban correspondent.) These newspapers depict a strange combination of the old Hispanic euphemistic flourish, highly subjective, combined with a crude and disrespectful Marxism that twists and deforms the truth to meet its own vindictive ends.

The Guatemala revolution of July 18 and 19, 1949, witnessed by the writer, brought home in political terms and social implications the Hispanic character of the participants. On this sunny day, July 18, your *seguro servidor* was walking to the Facultad de Humanidades in Guatemala City where he was visiting professor of philology during the summer session. On the way, he intended to mail a letter at the post office, but upon reaching this edifice, he was momentarily shocked from his usual absent-minded professorial state by the fact that the doors of the building were closed and the employees were out on the balconies in what seemed to be a rather festive spirit. Small groups in the street were alternately whispering to each other and shouting or waving to the men and women on the balconies. A question to one of those on the sidewalk elicited this reply, "The mail carriers must be on strike"; but the roar of two motors overhead, and a swiftly passing shadow made one wonder if the mail carriers had an air force! An army fighter plane had just buzzed the post office.

Walking down the street, this gringo was told by another group that there were *bullas* (hullabaloo), and as he progressed the statement became more emphatic: *bullas pues*! At the Facultad de Humanidades, when the question was put to the officials, the dean and the rector went into a huddle. They conferred for a moment, put their heads out of the window, looked up and down the street, and finally said, "¡*Bullas, pues!*"

Some of my students and I decided to go directly to the United States Embassy—Uncle Sam always knows the answer. Reaching the building, we were ushered into the reception room and seated. One employee whispered to another, "Shall we tell them?" The other said, "I guess we'd better." Finally, the first spokesman advanced and said portentously, "Well, if you must know what's going on here in Guatemala, they are having what they call *bullas*."

We scattered to the private homes where we were staying, and as soon as I got to mine, I was handed a note that had come from the embassy of El Salvador, sent by a young lady resident of the house who worked there. It said simply, "Don't go out on the street; the Thing has come."

It happened that one of the young ladies in our group was ill and needed a prescription filled. Seeing the opportunity of finding out what was going on, I took the prescription to the principal drugstore, situated in the central part of the city. While I was waiting for the prescription to be filled, one of the employees came out and pulled down the iron shutters, which he padlocked to the sidewalk. I looked out the front door, and there on the sidewalk was a man with a machine gun, who at that moment started shooting at the National Palace down the street. I walked home at about twenty miles an hour!

Once in the house, some of our group went up to the *azotea* (flat roof of Semitic type). We could see very little, but we heard two or three machine guns, and it was evident that some dissident group was shooting at both the National Palace and the National Police headquarters, which housed the well-trained Guardia Civil. As we stood on the roof, looking down over this situation of civil strife, two artillery shells whistled overhead, and a house, not far away, went up in the air. With darkness came more machine guns, a host of Mauser rifles, mortar shells, and Sherman tanks. Our house was only two blocks from the Civil Guard headquarters. The din continued all night long, and I found out "by the dawn's early light" that four of the largest members of our party had huddled together all night in one double bed —with two more under it! The siege lasted all the next day and the following night and ended with the capitulation of the rebel group. Apparently they had been attempting to avenge the death of an assassinated colonel by simply ousting the president of the Republic of Guatemala.

The informality of organization of the rebel force and the individualism of action were apparent as we watched the ragtag army from the front door, many of them urchins of the street, firing their booming Mauser rifles at the four-story Guardia Civil building, two blocks away. Most of these fellows were in civilian clothes. Few knew why they were fighting.

As if it were a game, one of these men decided that he would change corners to get closer to the target. In order to negotiate the distance with comparative immunity he carried a dirty bath towel, which he waved periodically at the enemy, as if to say, "No fair shooting, boys, until I get to the next corner." Evidently the Guardia Civil was playing under a different set of rules, for he was hit in the leg by a hollow-point bullet as he came opposite our doorway—only about three feet from our "standing committee." Before fainting into my arms, and with the blood pouring from his leg, he exchanged pleasantries with the boys on the corner that he never reached: "They touched me, boys." "They did?" As a result of yelling *ambulancia* at the top of my lungs, this victim was finally taken to a hospital, one of hundreds who were either killed or wounded that day.

It is a pitiful illusion to think that such affairs as this are revolts of "the people" against "the oppressors," or that there are basic principles involved. Nor should one be too moved by the grandiose things stated by the official newspapers, such as the account of the above episode which appeared several days after the cessation of hostilities:

> From perfectly informed sources we received today this version of the action of the police corps during the events which moved the citizenry deeply, on the 18 and 19 of the current month, in defense of constitutionality . . .
>
> At the stroke of midnight the scene changed, to convert itself into tragedy, because the attackers assaulted the edifice of the police, employing heavy artillery and letting function pieces of 37 and 75, with the fury of real demons.

One might add to the ever-present political instability the growth in this century of a spirit of nationalism and a concomitant reliance on the state as the instrument for doing good for society. Socialism to many is the answer just as

Fascistlike movements characterized the 1930's. Either is a welfare state and perhaps the example of the extreme development of this sort is the Perón regime of 1943–55. Although one can produce the names of dictators by the tens, it is difficult to find good political theorists on the Latin-American scene. There are many willing to turn governments out, but few who can explain why.

One type of revolution is one in which national independence results. In a second type, a president may be forced out of office by a political rival who has many good person-to-person relations but who pays no attention to stipulations of the constitution. This type, often accompanied by armed conflict, is the most common in Latin America. Since the turn of the century, there have been some ninety of this kind.

A third type—the one that people are always talking about—is the social revolution that recasts the entire social order. Mexico and Cuba are said to have experienced this kind, the former beginning in 1911, and the latter since 1959. It might be suggested, nevertheless, that each of these countries is underwritten today, one indirectly, the other directly, by Great Powers, without which help each would be hard put. One might insist, too, that there has been no real social revolution.

If there is anything common, typical, in all this, it is that a Latin-American revolution is a change in government brought about by other than constitutional means. The pattern for the usual one is so well structured that the same things occur: a *junta* is organized secretly, including certain military commanders, agents will be made ready in foreign countries, attacks on the government will be given wide publicity—if possible—including charges of graft, corruption, and collusion with foreigners. Recent events in Santo Domingo and elsewhere illustrate this point. In all this, personalism is the order of the day, and in this the pattern resembles very much the revolutions of the Near East of today and of yore.

To say that the troubles of the Spaniard or the Latin American are attributable to the poverty of his land is to perpetuate a myth. To complain that Latin Americans are prisoners of their own geography is to perpetuate destructive self-pity. In spite of the aridity of certain zones and the imposing jungle and mountain barriers, so many foreigners have been able to grow rich in these areas that we now hear the cry of exploitation and imperialism.

The future

Conventional histories and historians have approached the problem of Hispania through an imaginary creation, Spain, which for the purpose of analysis of modern Hispanic character did not exist until the Hispano-Christian began to reap his harvest of life with Semitic peoples, a life of some eight hundred years' ripening, and had cultivated the art of dominion over other peoples by integration with the person. By the same token, Latin America has been interpreted through its institutions, most of which are French or North American in inspiration, while the actual nature of these nations is to be found in the culture pattern. Although the constitutions and the laws of our sister republics resemble ours, and though these nations are nominally democracies, the real determining factor in any attempted evaluation should be sought in the way of life of the people. How do they interact?

The future of the Spanish-speaking people does not look bright, as far as collective existence is concerned. Until there is general mutual forbearance and, as Ortega y Gasset says, more *convivencia* events will take care of the future, and Latin Americans will continue to be victims, not authors, of their collective life. As long as mystiques rather than principles prevail, these nations will toss themselves from dictator to hero to president and back, while on the international scene, they must join a bloc or perish, such is their economic dependence and political capriciousness. The *revolución*, so widely advocated by some Latin Americans and by American apologists for Marxism, would create social unrest, to say the least, and destroy private investment and eventually bring about both domestic and foreign decapitalization. Then the tortilla would be burned on both sides!

Real development requires incentive, talent, and an environment that will produce capital. It means that unless the Western nations invigorate and direct development through exploitation, the Communist Bloc will do it with the whip.

The case of Cuba shows what is in store for a country that chooses the whip. Although this little island had one of the highest per capita incomes of Latin America, the Marxists screamed from the very beginning of the Castro take-over that the exploitation of the capitalists had made Cuba a hovel of misery and poverty. Then they proceeded to preach class hatred, they annulled the right to hold property and made the State the owner of all; they destroyed reputations with insults and calumny, they attacked the Western exploiters but praised the Russians and all others of the Communist Bloc. Under the guise of agrarian reform, they confiscated most of the land of Cuba. Interestingly, many Americans have been taken in by the Castro regime, and even some Protestant ministers still defend his cause.

Yes, the future is dark. But challenging dark futures is the substance of Western civilization. The situation is touch-and-go in many of the nations south of the border.

In Mexico there is a measure of stability and a higher standard of living than was the case a few decades ago. It is the opinion of this writer that these improved conditions are due, not to the *revolución* so much as to a reversal of the *revolución* since 1940 — since the presidential campaign between Almazán and Avila Camacho. Although the latter had to win as candidate of the Revolutionary party, the former produced the handwriting on the wall. American capital and American tourist dollars have built a stronger economy. Although the income from tourism now amounts to virtually the total national budget, a poor distribution of wealth still prevails.

Argentina continues to suffer the destruction of the Perón revolution and the flight of foreign capital. President Illia, always under check by the traditional Hispanic force, the army, had to walk a tightrope between *peronistas* and generals, between the Leftist admirers of Evita and Argentine business. There is lacking, as elsewhere in Latin America, a considerable segment with convictions and principles.

Chile, with somewhat stronger democratic tendencies, lay on the brink of Marxist triumph until the 1964 victory of Frei. With a lower per capita income than that of Cuba before Castro and a large sharecropper population, it is now up to the Christian Socialists under Frei's direction.

Brazil's President Goulart seemed determined, at all costs, to be Leftist. As the vice-president of the ill-fated Janio Quadros, he had journeyed to Communist China, and his own capricious Left-leaning administration finally brought vast public demonstrations and the army intervention of 1964. With a rather prosperous South and a poverty-stricken Northeast, a life expectancy of less than forty years, Brazil's half-illiterate population, mostly rural, does not appear to have the *convivencia* that makes a self-sufficient community in the twentieth century.

Paraguay, Nicaragua, and the Dominican Republic are held in check by dictatorial forces or juntas—an old Spanish custom.

Colombians sit on a volcano, as one of their university presidents recently told the writer, in fear that the relative balance of hatred between liberals and conservatives, which has been the cause of some 300,000 deaths since 1948, will erupt into real violence or will be the excuse for a take-over by a Leftist combination. Even the Catholic Church in Colombia is now making a play for the support of the underdog to overthrow the *Oligarquía*. The writer heard three sermons while in Colombia, supporting Leftist revolution and advocating an examination of the principles of Marxism.

The great wealth of Venezuela has not reached the population-at-large, not because of American exploitation and greed, but because of the Hispanic moral pattern of Venezuelans. That nation has a long history of *revueltas* and *dictaduras*, student strikes, and politics by riot. Rómulo Betancourt walked a tightrope for his entire term, the first to be completed in Venezuelan history, and for his successor there is still a Left-of-Left group that could bring chaos in a hurry. Here again, Venezuelans are not interested enough in Venezuela. They, too, are spectators and victims.

Of the countries of Central America, Costa Rica exhibits the results of early deviation from the Hispanic policy of using native labor under the *encomienda*. Because there were few Indians in the area, the colonials of that region began to work their own small farms. Although few of its citizens go to high school and college, only about 15 per cent are illiterate, and military coups and riots are practically unknown. With one of the highest population increase rates in the world (4.0 per cent), Costa Rica, with its low production, will continue to depend on big imports.

Guatemala, Honduras, Nicaragua, and El Salvador are typical bits of the more unfortunate American Hispania, with nearly 70 per cent of the population illiterate, a life expectancy of about forty-five years, and extreme political instability. Guatemala has averaged about one revolt a year for the past twenty, and El Salvador recently had three overnight changes in the national administration during a year. In all of these countries, there is complete economic dependence on the United States.

Communities are no longer supported by the products of the neighborhood. Cooperation and interdependence over wider areas go with higher standards of material comfort, and the impact of industrial society on feudal society is nowhere more evident than where East meets West, south of the border.

But in the Hispania of the 1960's some two-thirds of the people are still only indirectly touched by the problems of international affairs and the ideological conflicts. They are not concerned with the surpluses of world markets, and while a few keep in touch, most live in a climate of immediacy, which seems to be the rubric of Latin society.

The population explosion and the tendency to overpopulate urban centers has complicated any move toward expanding frontiers of exploitation of resources, and change is pitifully slow. It would seem that the gains in production have been more than counteracted by tremendous gains in population and ever more dependence on the national government. Tad Szulc (*New York Times*, January 11, 1961), reported that the five-year trend toward declining production and income had quickened, although in absolute figures the area had produced more goods than ever. He went on to say that there was actually less food per inhabitant than in 1938.

Insecure governments make attempts to please all political sectors or economic groups, first one then another, creating a wage-price spiral whose reaction is an austerity program, which in turn causes further political troubles and more government insecurity. In large populations of uninformed, these are good grounds for demagogues and dictators.

As Pedro Laín Entralgo has stated ("Spain as a Problem — Yet Again," *Texas Quarterly*, 1961):

> The guiding norm of modern Western Life can be summed up, I think, under these three: 1] The effective sharing of life between those who do not hold the same political and religious view (the spectacle of a nation in which there is genuine public freedom and truly representative democracy expresses very well what I mean by effective); 2] the establishment of a state concerned with the achievement and regulation of the general welfare and based upon the existence of a civic morality, that morality by which a man feels inwardly bound to fulfill his duties as a citizen; 3] A general and healthy regard for the secular achievements of the human intelligence and consequently for science and technics.

The difficulties of the Hispanic people in the present world stem from the fact that conditions of interaction and *convivencia* haven't changed to agree with these Western principles. The Hispanic attitude toward these rules has made ever more evident the problem of Hispania.

The remedy must include the sharing of a common life, the respect for civic morality that promotes and achieves objectively the good for all citizens, and a respect for science and technology, again secular achievements of the human intelligence that are forged in the competition of mutual respect. All of this means anthropocentric rather than egocentric; intermediacy rather than immediacy; action rather passion. What should be the posture and attitude of the United States in the light of this knowledge and understanding of our Latin-American neighbors?

In the first place, it would seem, we should recognize on the basis of our own experience, that political freedom is not a *summum bonum.* As Reinhold Niebuhr maintains (*Columbia University Forum,* Summer 1961), order and justice come first, and democracy is the culmination of a long *convivencia.* Free institutions presuppose a force of respect and responsibility within the behavior pattern of the community. Furthermore, as Niebuhr says, if democracy derives political authority from the "consent of the governed," the governed must have at least minimal competence in judging the performance of their governors and in recognizing their own place in the political organization.

We should recognize, secondly, that Latin Americans will probably continue to fall prey to dictatorships and despotism which represent the failure of the community to achieve order.

Thirdly, we must realize that communism, proposed by some as a solution, is a fantastic religiopolitical system, completely dogmatic and hate-inspired. It would destine one class, the proletariat, to become the masters of the whole historic process.

The United States should reject completely the Marxist-inspired allegation that it is our policy to recognize dictators. We have recognized governments which, in the Hispanic pattern, have been able to maintain order. It would seem, in short, that the attitude of the United States toward its very personable neighbors south of the border should conform to our own *modus vivendi,* which, in an Anglo-Saxon way has been built on a system of competitive interaction and the exploitation of materials and resources within a spirit of fair play and a climate of intermediacy. The key, then, to effective inter-American relations, as far as we are concerned, may be exploitation in the original meaning of the term: an unfolding.

And there is much evidence of the benefits of North American exploitation on the Latin-American scene, notably in Puerto Rico, Mexico, Venezuela, and Cuba. Under adverse conditions, but with the guidance of a dedicated leader, the inhabitants of Puerto Rico now have one of the most equitable distributions of wealth in the world, and an excellent life expectancy. Puerto Rico has been exploited economically, educationally, and politically by the United States. The implication is plain: material aid should always be accompanied by conditions and direction that emanate from the community of the giver. Rather than give what we have, we should give what we are.

The Catholic Church
and the conversion of Mexican
Indians

The beginning of evangelism

In spite of the general belief that the Spaniards were a ruthless lot of fortune seekers intent on material gain alone, an examination of the writings of the period of the conquest reveals the fact that there were other motives in the colonization of America. Noteworthy was the zeal displayed by the clergy, with the backing of the political and military leaders—and even as their agents—for the ecclesiastical penetration of New Spain.

Swayed by a crusading spirit brought about by hundreds of years of struggle with the Mohammedan, the Church took a leading part in the acculturation of the American Indian. In an atmosphere of religious fanaticism, Cortés and other captains of conquest became agents of the Faith while the clergy became instruments of the State, both insisting on the conversion as well as the submission of the natives.

With Isabel la Católica as a symbol of uncompromising orthodoxy, the Spaniard was little given to ratiocination in matters religious and his approach was direct and authoritarian, but he was probably much more concerned with the spiritual future of the Amerindian than either the French or English were to be in the following century. The best evidence of this is the very large stock of material published during the sixteenth and seventeenth centuries in Mexico City alone, much of which was directed toward the conversion of the Indians. (See author's *Spanish Literature in Mexican Languages as a Source for the Study of Spanish Pronunciation*, 1934, for a bibliography of this material.)

The Spanish writings in Indian languages or concerning Indian languages were of two types for the most part: grammars and dictionaries of some native language or religious works in the Indian language. The grammars, usually termed *artes*, were designed to help subsequent priests learn to talk to the natives and to hear their confession. The dictionaries, always called *vocabularios*, have, in the case of several of the tongues never been excelled. The writers, usually members of one of the religious orders, tried to fit these new forms of speech into the unwieldy molds of the classical grammars, but nevertheless compiled important observations and thousands of words that have been the bases for later studies.

The religious writings of the Spanish friars were translations of the formulas of the Catholic Christianity of the period and portray in detail the thorough application of the doctrine to the process of Hispanic acculturation.

From the time that Charles V received news of the discovery of Tenochtitlán he considered himself duty bound to take charge of these newly found infidels. He imparted the need to those closest to him at Ghent, among whom we find Juan de Tecto (Van Tacht), Juan de Aora (Aar), and Pedro de Gante (Van den Moere). And these three, who were to give to the first efforts a Flemish flavor, were followed by twelve Franciscans, later to be called *los doce apóstoles*. The head of the group, Martín de Valencia, with four others remained in Mexico City, while others were sent to the cities of Texcoco, Tlaxcala, and Huejotzingo. These centers were subsequently to be characterized by their Franciscan activities, and much of the original writing was done by members of this order.

The Dominican Order was ready to send twelve men to New Spain with the twelve Franciscans, but they were ordered to Hispaniola instead. A number of the group finally arrived in Mexico in 1526. Due to certain difficulties with Cortés the first mission was a failure, but from 1534 the Dominicans took an active part in the conversion of the people of the territory, especially in Oaxaca and Yucatán.

The third great religious order, that of St. Augustine, established itself in New Spain in 1535. Its main field of action seems to have been south and west of the city, notably in Michoacán. By 1572 it had forty-six monasteries. Jesuit priests did not appear until 1572, but were immediately active in furthering education in the new land.

From the time of the arrival of the famous twelve, the Church grew in the number of clergy, the natives were drawn away from their pagan religions, idols were destroyed, and some of the children were gathered into schools. Learned fathers like Pedro de Gante and Toribio de Benavente baptized thousands.

Besides the ecclesiastic divisions within the orders themselves, there were administrative divisions of the Church proper, such as the bishoprics of México, Michoacán, Tlaxcala, and Oaxaca, to which were later added Guatemala and Nueva Galicia. It was at this level that the State dominated, for the high officials of these administrative divisions were designated by the Crown.

The task of evangelization was aided somewhat by the structural similarity of the Aztec religion and the Catholicism of the period: each had a system of priests, burdensome pomp and ceremony, and baptism. It might also be argued that the character of the Mexican was favorable to eventual evangelization. Gerónimo de Mendieta, *Historia eclesiástica indiana* (1870), p. 438, speaks of the meekness of the race in physical terms: "The cause of their natural meekness is lack of bile and an abundance of phlegm, and because of this they suffer a great deal with our Spaniards, since we are choleric."

The educational efforts of the priests were seconded by the viceroys, and several schools were founded, notable among them that of Santa Cruz at the monastery of Santiago Tlatelolco, inaugurated in 1536 under the viceroy Antonio de Mendoza. The teachers for these schools normally came from the *frailes menores*, and it is known that they taught Latin as well as Spanish.

A letter from Pedro de Gante to Philip II in 1558 gives an idea of educational efforts in the early days.

> Captain Cortés commanded that from all the land within thirty leagues of where we were, all the sons of the nobility should come to Mexico, to San Francisco,

to learn the law of God and to teach it; also to learn the Christian Doctrine. And so it happened that directly about one thousand came together, and we had them closed up in our house day and night, and we didn't permit them any conversation with their parents, but only with those who served them and brought them things to eat. All of this so that they would forget their bloody idolatry and excessive sacrifices, in which the Devil took advantage of innumerable quantities of souls; for certain, there had been an incredible sacrifice of fifty thousand souls.

During the morning the brothers had them get together and pray and sing the Minor office of Our Lady, from first to ninth, and then they heard Mass, and then they went to read and write, and others to learn to sing the Divine Office in order to officiate. The more clever ones learned the Doctrine in order to preach it in the towns and villages—QUOTED BY Mariano Cuevas, *Historia de la Iglesia en México* (1921) II, 200.

The problem of language

Perhaps chief among the obstacles to a rapid shift to Christianity was the fact that the Spaniards were coming into a land of many strange languages. Cortés had been fortunate in having his interpreters, Marina and Aguilar, but for the immediate task of conversion the first friars had to resort to gestures. Juan de Torquemada, *Monarquía indiana* (1723), III, ch. 12, reports: "It was mutely and by signs, pointing to the sky and saying that that was where the only God that they should believe in was, and then turning the eyes to the ground, pointing to Hell."

According to Mendieta many of the clergy were taught the Indian languages by the very children whom they were instructing.

This method (gestures) brought very little fruit, because the Indians didn't understand what was said in Latin, nor did they cease their idolatry, nor could the friars reprimand them or teach them how to get rid of it, because they didn't know their language. This kept them quite sad and disconsolate back in the beginning, and they didn't know what to do, for although they

wanted and tried to learn the language, there was no one
to teach it to them. And meanwhile, the Indians, with
all the reverence that they had for them, did not dare
say a word. In this need, as in all others, they turned to
the source of goodness and compassion, the Lord our
God, increasing prayer and adding fast and suffrages,
invoking the intercession of the sacred Virgin Mother of
God and the Holy Angels, whose devout worshippers
they were . . . and God put it into their hearts that they
should become children with the very children who were
their pupils, in order to participate in their language.
So leaving their dignity, they began to play with them
with sticks and stones during their leisure moments to
take away the obstacle of communication. And they always carried pen and ink in their hands, so when they
heard an Indian say a word, they wrote it down, along
with the meaning. Then in the afternoon the brothers
would get together and compare their records and try
to match the Indian words with most appropriate Spanish. And it happened that what it seemed they had
heard today, tomorrow turned out to be something else
(pp. 219–20).

Regardless of the accuracy of Mendieta's statements concerning the methods employed by the early friars for learning Mexican, the fact remains that many of them began to
take an interest in the language of Anahuac and Tlaxcala,
and later in other tongues of America. The missionaries
found it indispensable to master the languages in order to
transmit religious ideas to the natives. They also took pride
in composing their own *artes, vocabularios, doctrinas cris-
tianas,* and *confesionarios.*

Necessity was not the only reason for the appearance of
so many works on Indian languages during the sixteenth
and seventeenth centuries. These authors were imbued with
the spirit of the Renaissance, and furthermore they were
proud to be from a land that they usually referred to as
Castilla. Add to this the fact that printing was introduced to
Mexico as early as 1539, thus preserving for posterity literally hundreds of books.

The prototypes of Spanish literature in the Indian languages of America are in the Náhuatl or Aztec language.

Later there appeared writings in Huaxtecan, Otomí, Tarascan, Totonacan, Mayan, Mixtecan, Zapotecan, Quechua, Quiché, and many others. Within sixty years after the conquest of Mexico there were grammars, dictionaries, and religious books in all of these tongues and many more. Many of the books were already in extra editions.

The arrangement of the *artes* of the early writers is essentially that of the first grammar in any modern language, the *Gramática castellana* of Antonio de Nebrija, printed in Spain in 1492. The Spanish terms used in the *vocabularios* compiled were those that had been used by Nebrija with additions from the vocabulary of the author concerned. Borrowed terms from Spanish began to appear quite early in the columns of native words, especially in cases where there were no equivalents in the Indian language.

The adaptation of doctrine

The Spanish missionaries did not try to adapt the teaching of the catechism to the religions that they found in New Spain. For the most part, the priests were obliged to resort to Spanish words to picture religious concepts, as will be noted in the material following. This may have been partly due to the recognized similarity existing between the religion of Anáhuac, at least, and that of the Spaniards, for there was evidently a fear that the incorrect use of terms would bring back thoughts of the ancient pagan beliefs. However, we do find the word *Dios* often translated *Teotl* in *doctrinas* and *confesionarios* in Nahuatl.

In 1538, Charles V authorized the printing of a *doctrina* with these words: "And advise those who examine it to take care that the words don't hinder the Christian doctrine and religion through the meanings that the Indians gave them in their language."

A comparison of the *doctrinas* and *confesionarios* of the first fathers in New Spain with the works of the type published by Pedro de Alcalá in Spanish and Arabic, reveal that they are essentially the same in form and manner of presentation. It is interesting to note, however, that there is a tendency manifest quite early in the American religious works to apply the Christian doctrine, and confession based on it, to conditions particularly Mexican. In the quotations from the works of Molina, Sahagún, Baptista, and others, this is evident, especially in the questions on the Ten Commandments.

Although the first Spanish priests were undoubtedly in great earnest in presenting lists of sins of which the Indians might confess, they were nevertheless asking for confession of sins that were naturally of another civilization, and it must be supposed that the natives may not have even heard of certain situations concerning which European clergymen questioned them.

The feeling that the promiscuous questioning of the natives concerning their sins might suggest possibilities was expressed by Manuel Pérez, an Augustinian friar, whose *Arte de la lengua* Mexicana was published in 1713. In discussing the *Sacramento de la penitencia* and its application among the Indians, he said: "Whether the Confessor should ask the Indian about his sins through the Commandments? The reason is because by asking too much, the Indian may open his eyes to some things he doesn't know. If he isn't asked, he may leave out many sins, and sometimes he says nothing about them because he isn't asked." This priest suggested that the confessor ask the native to confess the sins that he could call to mind, and that the confessor follow this with a few general questions on the Commandments. He also recommended that the questions be varied according to the status of the person confessing.

If the early priests followed all of the questions listed by Molina, Juan de Baptista, León, Feria, and others, the natives were asked for information concerning their most intimate relationships. However, it is undoubtedly true that many of these questions were given in the books written by these men for the benefit of other clergymen who might be learning the native tongues.

Molina's writings constitute not only one of the most extensive groups on American Indian languages, but after nearly four hundred years, his dictionary is still consulted as an authority on the Mexican language. In the prologue to the *Arte* of 1571, p. 2, Molina states that he had labored diligently with this tongue:

> Since my tender age until now I have never ceased to labor . . . in order to console in some way these same ministers and to encourage their pious and charitable intention—and not without lots of work—I have tried to write many things in the Mexican language: that is, two dictionaries, a Christian Doctrine, and other works that are already printed, with many others that are about to be printed, and that are very useful to this Church.

The importance of Molina's first work, the *Doctrina xpiana breue traduzida en lengua Mexicana,* is attested by the following excerpt from the first page of the book as printed in the *Nueva colección de documentos para la historia de Mexico* (1888), II, 34–61:

> Here begins a teaching that is called Christian Doctrine, which all the children and young people, children of the natives of this New Spain, are to learn. It deals with the things that are very necessary to learn and to know and to present as a task to Christians in order that they may be saved, and so that they will know what to reply when somewhere they are asked something about Christianity. And in order that this Doctrine may reach all places, and be known by all, it must be put into the other languages, that is, in that of Michoacán and in that of the Otomíes, etc. And Bishop don fray Juan de Zumárraga commands those who teach everywhere and who show how to read and write, to teach this Doctrine first, so that they will know it by heart before they undertake learning the rest.

The *doctrina,* which first appeared in 1546, presents an exposition of the main formulas of Catholic Christianity *en la lengua y en romance* (in the [native] language and in Romance [Spanish]). The Persignum Crucis, the Credo, the Pater Noster, the Salve Regina, the Ten Commandments, etc., are given first in Náhuatl and then in Spanish. Later works of this nature usually present the material in opposite columns.

The first edition of Molina's great dictionary appeared in Mexico City in 1555 with the title *Aqui comiença un vocabulario enla lengua castellana y mexicana.* Copies of the

book have become quite rare. The one in the possession of
the Library of the Museum of the American Indian contains
an interesting manuscript vocabulary of the Matlaltzincan
language. In the prologue Molina explains, in terms similar
to those of Andrés de Olmos, certain difficulties that had be-
set him in the composition of the work.

> Certain difficulties which I have met have been the cause
> of my not getting at the work before. The first and
> principal is that I didn't suck this language with my
> milk, nor is it native to me. Rather I learned it by a
> little use and exercise, and this can't uncover all the
> secrets that there are in the language.
>
> In the name of the Holy Trinity, Father, Son and Holy
> Ghost, and of the always virgin Holy Mary our Lady.
> Here begins a confessionary, which the Reverend Fray
> Alonso de Molina, of the Order of San Francisco com-
> posed and arranged, translated into the language of the
> Náhuas by the author himself.

In 1565 Molina's *Confessionario breue* came from the
press, and was destined to be the model for many other productions of the type. Náhuatl and Spanish questions on the
Commandments, Sacraments, etc., are arranged in parallel
columns with the intention of providing confessors with a
means of questioning Indians in the regions where only
Náhuatl was spoken. Among the questions on the Commandments are to be found the following:

> » Did you ever call on the Devil or did anyone call on
> him before you and you didn't stop him?
> » Did you ask a Sorcerer to cast spells for you, or did
> you ask him to make what you had asked for come true?
> » Did you believe in dreams?
> » Did you ever believe or consider a bad omen the owl
> when he hoots or the hoot owl when it screeches or when
> it makes a noise with its claws or a certain beetle that
> you saw somewhere?
> » Were you baptized twice or did you receive con-
> firmation twice, or did you marry in two or three places,
> and by chance are all those whom you married before
> the Holy Mother Church still alive?
> » And in the house of our Lord, are you perchance
> restless, or do you sit there joking with others, telling

stories or talking with some? Did you covet anyone or
do you sit there smiling at the women?

FOR WOMEN:

» Do you perchance work on Sundays and holidays?
Do you weave, sew, wash clothes, etc.?
» Did you bathe with men in the hot baths or did you
commit some sin there?
» Perhaps you didn't go to Mass because you didn't
have anything to wear and were ashamed?
» Have you taken a potion to abort the creature, or did
you kill your child by purposely giving him something to
suck so that he hurt his mouth and couldn't nurse any
more? Or, while sleeping, did you kill him by throwing
yourself on him? Or, perhaps because you took those
potions (with which you tried to abort the creature)
did a sickness overcome you?
» Did you drink some brew which would keep you from
having more children?
» And you who are a woman doctor, have you learned
medicine and the art of curing well? Or do you pretend
that you are a doctor, and you don't know the medicines,
herbs and roots that you gave the patient for which
reason his sickness grew, or the patient you wanted to
cure ceased to exist?
» Did you paint yourself, adoring yourself and putting
something on your face so that they would covet
you?

FOR FOREMEN:

» On Sundays and Feast Days do you take the proper
precautions and see to it that the workers get together
and attend Mass to hear the sermons?
» By chance did you command the workers to work the
land or build houses or go to the woods?
» Did you mistreat anybody? Did you hit him with a
stick? Did you break his arm; did you break his head;
did you pull his hair or did you hit him in the head with
something, or did you kick him or butt him or did you
crush his skull?

FOR MEN:

» Did you covet some woman, or did you lie with her?
» With how many women have you had intercourse?

» Did you kiss some woman, or did you hug her, or did you grab her teats, or romp with her?

» When you sleep, and you dream that you have intercourse with some woman, and after you have awakened and you remember your dream, are you pleased with it? Because if you take pleasure from the dirty delight of which you dreamed, you are committing mortal sin, and if you are sad and contrite over it, it will not be considered a sin, since you were sleeping.

» Did you make any married woman pregnant, and does her husband think now that that child is his?

In the *Confessionario mayor* (1565), in addition to enlarging on the material in connection with the Ten Commandments, Molina includes questions on the Church Commandments, Works of Mercy, etc. The questions on the Seventh Commandment reveal an interesting application of confession in America.

» And you who are a dealer, and move about in the market places, by chance did you not properly regulate the intentions of your dealings and trade?

» And you who sell *cacao*, did you mix the good *cacao* with the bad, so that it would be used and sold, deceiving the people? Did you put ashes on the green *cacao*, or did you mix it with white earth so that it would look good; or do you put *tzoualli* dough in the hull of said *cacao*, or ground avocado seed, thus falsifying the *cacao*? And the small cocoa beans, do you roast them, to make them look large and fat?

» And you who sell avocados, do you deceive the poor Otomíes, perchance, or the little boys, giving them damaged and bad avocados, and the ones that are about to ripen, do you rub them and ripen them with your fingers, thus deceiving your fellow-man?

» And you who sell beads, and who sell calendars, paper, scissors, knives, combs, and all this, did you deceive or trick anybody?

» And you who sell tamales, perhaps you didn't put very much dough in them, and you put lots of beans inside, or you wrapped them in many corn husks, so they would look big.

» And you who run warm baths, did you establish the bath that you have with authority of justice, and perhaps do men and women go around together (when they bathe)? Maybe something evil was committed there and you didn't hinder it? And perhaps not only the sick bathed in your bath, but also the healthy and those who didn't need to.

The eighth production of Fray Alonso was a *confessionario breue* very similar to that of 1565. A series of admonitions is followed by questions on the Ten Commandments. The word *Dios* is often translated by the Mexican *teotl*. This translation is common throughout the writings of Molina and other early writers. Even compounds, such as *teotlatolli* and *Teoamoxtli* are used quite often in referring to the Scriptures. The following excerpt from the *amonestación* preceding the questions may be of interest: "Now listen, my dear son. You have come to tell me your sins; your blackness, your filthiness, your stench and corruption. You must remember that you are a sinner and that your heart feels and you truly understand that you have offended God our Lord in many things. And because of your sins He is very angry with you; and if you don't confess them, He will throw you into Hell, where you will suffer forever, and where the demons will punish you and torment and afflict you, and you will never leave there."

The application of confession in New Spain is pictured to some extent by the alphabetically ordered index of the *Confesionario mayor* (1578) of Alonso de Molina, some of which follows:

> » Fasts which the natives must observe, under penalty of mortal sin.
> » Search for your sins: it is necessary that the penitent one do this so that he may confess them.
> » Meat: when the natives must abstain, under penalty of mortal sin.
> » Deceptions of various sorts that the natives have in buying and selling.
> » Feast days to be observed, which the Church requires of the natives, under penalty of mortal sin.
> » Governors, mayors, councilmen and other persons who are chosen by the counting of votes, if by chance the penitent, because of his occupation or because of

passion gave his vote to the one who was unworthy for
said office, failing to elect the appropriate one: said
elector should confess this, because he sinned mortally.

» Tears and sentiment, which the penitent should have
when he confesses.

» Places, territories and towns, where the penitent may
have been; he should bring them to memory in order to
remember the sins that he committed in them, and to
confess them.

Certainly the most important writer of this group of early
Americanists, from the standpoint of the recording of history, rites, and customs of the Mexicans, is Bernardino de
Sahagún (1499–1590), a native of the province of León.
While studying at the University of Salamanca, Fray Ber-
nadino joined the Franciscan Order, and came to América
in 1529. It is known that he spent some time in the Valley
of Puebla and that he taught for many years in the Colegio
de la Santa Cruz at Tlatelolco.

The capital work of Sahagún is the *Historia general de
las cosas de Nueva España*, written between 1547 and 1569.
He divided the book into twelve parts, each containing
many chapters. Although it was first written in Náhuatl, it
was later translated into Spanish, and in 1577 Philip II asked
that it be sent to Spain. A copy was delivered to the Council
of the Indies, but at least one remained in Mexico. Suffice
it to say that the *Historia general* is the best known source
of information on the customs and rites of the ancient Mexicans, and several editions and translations have been made.
Interestingly enough, it is in this work that we first read of
chewing gum and tomatoes. The former Sahagún describes
gum as a substance chewed by the women of the street to
keep their teeth white!

Aside from a *Vocabulario trilingue* and many lesser works,
Sahagún's production included an interesting *Psalmodia
Christiana*, whose purpose was explained by the author in
the prologue:

Among other things in which these Indians of New
Spain were very curious was the worship of their gods,
which were many, and they honored them in different
ways; also the praises with which they honored them day

and night, in the temples and chapels, singing hymns and making choruses and dances in their presence. When they did this, they composed in different ways for different fiestas and they made different steps for the dance. And they sang different songs in praise of these false gods whose feast they were celebrating. Since then one has been working, now that they are baptized, to make them leave those old songs with which they praised their false gods and have them sing only praises to God and His Saints, and this during the day, also on religious holidays and Sundays and the Saints' days of His churches. For this reason they have been given songs of God and of his Saints, so that they will leave the other old songs, and they have received them.

One device that was employed for teaching Christianity was the dialogue. Juan de Gaona (1507–60) wrote a book of this sort under the title, *Colloquois de la Paz y Tranquilidad Christiana,* in which the material was presented as a conversation between a father and a student. The long title of the first chapter is indicative of the nature of the text: "How too much appetite and desire for temporal things makes spiritual things insipid and tasteless. And how the Devil begins with small things in order to deceive and defeat men in greater things."

Another Franciscan, Juan Baptista (1555–1615), wrote a list of allocutions and bits of advice under the title of *Huehuetlahtolli* (old men talk), in which parents and civil authorities speak on the occasion of weddings, births, death, municipal affairs, etc.

» Talk of a father to his son advising him to be good.
» Reply of the son to his father.
» Talk that a mother gives her daughter, advising her.
» Talk of a father to a son who is getting married.
» Talk of a husband to his wife.
» Reply of the wife.
» Talk to the councilmen of Tlaxcala on how to govern their city. It may be applied to any city.
» Talk on how a doctor should treat and console the patient.

Typical is the following advice given by a mother to her daughter:

» Well, my dear daughter, don't be lazy, nor careless, but rather diligent, and clean, and keep your house in order.

» Serve and bring water to your husband, and take care to make the bread well.

» And the things of your home. Put them where they belong, each in its place, and not just anywhere.

» Wherever you go, my daughter, go with restraint, and modesty, not hurriedly, nor laughing, nor looking out of the corner of your eye, and don't look at those who come facing you.

In order to take care of the concept of Devil, the Spaniards suggested that *Tlacatecolotl* (owl man) be used. The owl was an omen of bad luck. Angels became sky men, *Ilhuicactlacatl*. As late as a hundred years after the Conquest, the confessionaries were still asking the Indians questions about idols and beliefs of the old Aztec religion, and by 1746 there is evidence that the confessors thought best not to ask detailed questions of the natives: "they might open their eyes."

Thus were the formulas of the Catholic faith perpetuated in another race in America, and the hundreds of books and manuscripts produced by members of the four religious orders contributed greatly to the acculturation of millions who have become an important part of the Hispanic world.

The Spanish language in America

Introduction

Contrary to popular opinion, Latin is not dead. It is spoken as a first language by millions of people in some thirty countries and is gaining ground by the moment. True, it has changed somewhat.

The speech of Roman soldiers, merchants, and colonists, the popular Latin of another day, was taken bodily to Iberia, to Gaul, to Dacia, and to many other regions. As it grew and developed it was eventually called by several other names — Spanish, Portuguese, French, Italian, Romanian, etc. — and although lexical elements of Germanic, Arabic, and other sources have made their way into these stocks of popular Latin, they have had to adapt themselves to its structure.

In terms of the number of speakers, Spanish is the largest manifestation of spoken Latin. Those who now think and express themselves in Castilian, or Spanish, number about 160,000,000, and they live in some twenty countries. Moreover, one section of this language community, Latin America, is the fastest growing area of the world. It is estimated that by A.D. 2000 Spanish will be the language of nearly 500,000,000 people. Under normal conditions of development only Chinese and English will be spoken by more, although Russian and Hindi will be close behind.

Castilian Latin became prominent because of the hegemony of north central Spain in the process of reconquest of the Iberian Peninsula from the Moors. It grew and took form under conditions of coexistence with Semitic peoples, and its predominance among the other forms of spoken

Latin is not due to intrinsic values, but rather to extralinguistic factors: political and military power and organization, Church-State relations, literary ascendancy, and a high birthrate!

The Spanish of Latin America, like most colonial speech, tends to be conservative in its structural changes compared to that of the mother country. This could also be said of American English and Canadian French. In addition, American Spanish reflects certain regional traits of the Peninsula, notably the Southwest. In other words, the Spanish—or Castilian—of America seems to be Andalusian Castilian of the sixteenth and seventeenth centuries.

This essay is an attempt to describe briefly the structural character of American Spanish and to tell something of its semantic development, keeping in mind that it is a simplex of expression and a part of the Hispanic behavior pattern, which was wrought in coexistence with Near Eastern peoples. With its considerable element of American Indian vocabulary, it can be said that East meets West, south of the border in yet another way.

Finally, it is the purpose of this section to delineate the main characteristics of the Spanish of each of the countries in Latin America. Aside from slight deviations from the general Hispanic pattern of pronunciation and syntax, there are different applications of terms from country to country and Indian words are widely used, especially for domestic items in several regions—the first Spaniards came over without their women.

As an illustration of regional differences, the following table shows the popular words for little boy, bus, and blond in certain countries.

	little boy	bus	blond
Mexico	chamaco	camión	huero
Guatemala	patojo	camioneta	canche
El Salvador	cipote	camioneta	chele
Colombia	pelado	autobús	mono
Costa Rica	güila	chiva	macho
Argentina	pibe	colectivo	rubio
Cuba	chico	guagua	rubio

Most of these words are actually Spanish (of Latin origin) but several are from the Indian language of the area. The fact that there are differences of this sort should be expected in a general culture that contains so many national boundaries.

It is useless to attempt to designate the Spanish of this or that country as more correct, more beautiful, or superior. Speech is perpetuated in its structural features by children, who have no interest in such things. Adults have difficulty in changing the habits of a community except in the written form or in oratorical expression, where devices for effective delivery become a form of art, or even a science. In spite of this, many Spanish-speaking people still believe that academies make languages and that the principles of usage emanate from normative criteria. There is also a strong feeling in the Hispanic world that foreign words (*barbarismos*) should be kept out of the language.

The Spanish Simplex

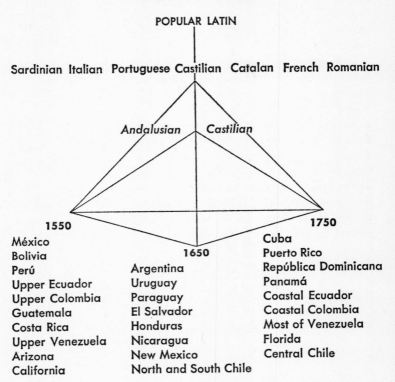

POPULAR LATIN

Sardinian Italian Portuguese Castilian Catalan French Romanian

Andalusian   *Castilian*

1550   **1750**

México		Cuba
Bolivia	**1650**	Puerto Rico
Perú	Argentina	República Dominicana
Upper Ecuador	Uruguay	Panamá
Upper Colombia	Paraguay	Coastal Ecuador
Guatemala	El Salvador	Coastal Colombia
Costa Rica	Honduras	Most of Venezuela
Upper Venezuela	Nicaragua	Florida
Arizona	New Mexico	Central Chile
California	North and South Chile	

This chart represents in rather simplified form, the Latin origin of Spanish as spoken in America, its peninsular development from north to south, and the American results of successive changes in its Andalusian form. Since Spain's principal ports were in the south, as was the seat of Colonial operations, most early settlers came from that area.

Shown also is the fact that Spanish, or Castilian, is a simplex, not a complex, in that its dialectal manifestations are mutually intelligible. The speech of Italy is a complex. The time factor on the Latin-American scene is noted. Accessible regions tend to represent, especially in pronunciation and syntax, the latest developments during the long Colonial period.

Symbols used to represent the principal phones of American Spanish

Occlusives	Fricatives	Affricates	Nasals	Laterals	Flaps, Trills
[p] [b]	[ɸ] [β]		[m]		
	[f] [v]				
	[θ] [d̪]				
[t] [d]	[s] [z]				
	[ş] [ẓ] [ɍ̌] [ɍ̌]	[tʃ] [ts]			
	[c̜] [j] [š] [ž]	[č] [ŷ]	[n]	[l]	[r] [rr]
	[x] [g] [gw]		[ñ]	[ʎ]	
[k] [g]			[ŋ]		
	[h] [ɦ]				[R]

Historical Considerations

The fundamental traits of American Spanish are to be found in Castilla, but only the changes that took place in the Andalusian dialect seem to have become established in America. Thus it is that the unvoicing of the voiced inter-vocalic sibilants, which made them coincide with voiceless ones that already existed, as well as the loss of aspirated *h* and the confusion of / b / and / v /, all had their origin in Old Castile, extended themselves to the south and finally to America. On the other hand, in Sevilla and the southern part of Andalusia, the apico-alveolar / s / of Spanish was lost and its place taken by the sibilant represented ortho-graphically by ç. This tendency became the American one, since most of the early settlers came from the south. Thus to a southerner, *casa* became the same as *caza*. These are pronounced today in southern Spain and in Latin America (except Antioquia, Colombia) as [kasa]. In northern and central Spain there is still a distinction: [kaṣa] and [kaθa], the hooked ṣ standing for the apico-alveolar articulation, the θ for an interdental, similar to the voiceless *th* of English.

Several other developments in southern Spain were taken to America by successive waves of *pobladores*. American Spanish is therefore Andalusian-Castilian, and many of the differences in pronunciation in America date back to periods of crystallization of tendencies in the various areas of America, the mountainous regions generally preserving the early characteristics and the coastal sections accepting the later changes.

Much substantiation has recently been given to the the-ory of Andalusian hegemony in the settlement of America by the research of Peter Boyd-Bowman. His four-volume work, *Indice geobiográfico de pobladores,* (Volume I was published in 1965 by the Instituto Caro y Cuervo, Bogotá, Colombia) catalogs carefully the Peninsular origins of some 40,000 Spaniards who came to America between 1492 and 1650, using the records that Spain has kept all these years in the Archivo de Indias, Sevilla. Boyd-Bowman's work also tells where these people went in America, and he has been able to show much other interesting statistical information related to sections of the period covered, and pertaining to age, sex, and station of those involved. This is undoubtedly the most thorough check on the European origins of any colonial people. At times during the more than 150 years concerned, nearly 70 per cent of the settlers were from Andalusia. As the years went by, more came from farther north, until by the eighteenth century—and on to the present—Spanish immigrants have been mostly northerners. The culture pattern, including the language, was already set, however.

It might be said that many of the *andalucismos* that are now a part of American Spanish and were imported in the sixteenth and seventeenth centuries, are aspects of a general trend in articulation that one might term *linguaplana* or tongue flat. The apico-alviolar / s / was lost when it no longer seemed worthwhile to raise the tongue to the upper gums; the [š] became gradually a simple aspiration, to be confused with the / h /, still aspirated in the South. Later, the [s] syllable final lost its grooved quality, becoming first a lisped sound, and finally only an aspiration. The articulation of / ʎ /, a palatal lateral, was weakened to that of the / j /, thus erasing another phonemic distinction; / l / and / r / were likewise confused when the complete vibration of the second of these was not realized. Finally, the / n / final became velar as a sign of open transition.

In the evaluation of all these changes, one can distinguish features that have become constants from those that are sporadic in occurrence. The constants are of complementary distribution and are linguistic norms, so to speak. They will be heard in the speech of each individual under the circumstances expected. The sporadic variants are not always present and are not expected by the listener. On the other hand, when he does hear them, he is not shocked as he might be by a foreign pronunciation. In the speech of El Salvador, for instance, all people always pronounce / b /, / d /, / g / as occlusives after any consonant, and they always pronounce / n / as a velar in open juncture, but the articulation of prevocalic / s / vacillates between [s] and

[θ] among speakers of that country and the / s / syllable final vacillates between [s] and [h]. The constants are truly dialectal and the sporadic idiolectal, although the very feature of vacillation may be dialectal.

In the history of Spanish—and dialectology is a part of this history—some of the sporadic traits have come to be constants and have even come to be considered national characteristics.

Two of the characteristics of Latin-American Spanish seem to go back to the time of the conquest and settlement. The first of these, the articulation of / b /, / d /, / g / as occlusives after any consonant or after the semivowels, where the Spanish of Spain has fricatives, is still to be heard in Colombia, El Salvador, Honduras, and Nicaragua, where they are constants rather than free variants. In certain other countries, notably Costa Rica, Guatemala, Bolivia, and Ecuador, the same traits occur as free variants. Thus in El Salvador, for instance, *las barbas* is [lah bárbas] rather than [laz βárβas] and *el buey volvió* is [el bwej bolbjó] rather than [el βwej βolβjó] as it would be in Spain, Mexico, or Lima, for example. A Colombian would tend to say [ai gálgoz derrázgos orguʎósos] rather than [ai gálgoz derrázgos orguʎósos].

The second old American trait of pronunciation is the so-called *seseo,* or the articulation of what had been two separate phonemes in Old Spanish as one, with the consequent loss of one, but contrary to popular opinion, it was not the / θ / of Spain that was lost in America, but rather the real Spanish / ş / of a pair / s / and / ş /. The / θ / did not exist as [θ] at the time of Columbus nor for over a hundred years later, but rather as [s], which had been [ts] in the remote Middle Ages. So the American-Spanish sibilant [s] is actually the ancestor of / θ /, and the *seseo* is really a *ceceo.* The Spanish [ş], is still heard in Spain, was leveled to [s] in southern Spain and America.

Moreover, it is of interest that the idiolectal and dialectal variants of this sibilant of America probably reflect the evolution toward [θ], a change that did not reach America in force because it was slow in realization and because American Spanish had reached a stage of crystallization before it was the standard in Spain. One hears in Mexico, Ecuador, Peru, Bolivia, and generally in the highland areas, a very delicate apico-dental / s /, while in many vast regions, the / s / is dorso-alveolar, with the point of the tongue on the lower teeth. And although the acoustic effect is not too different, it shows a diffusion that indicates less tension in grooving—a step toward a lisped sound. This lisped / s / is heard in southern Spain, in Sevilla Province, and in extensive areas of Andalusia, and is so lax in the grooving that acoustically it resembles [θ]. In America it is heard among thousands of people in El Salvador, Honduras, Nicaragua, Venezuela, Coastal Colombia, north of Buenos Aires in Argentina, and in the lowlands of Bolivia.

Highland Ecuador exhibits another sibilant oddity that may reflect former conditions of Spanish pronunciation. The / s / of that region is voiced before a vowel in a following word. *Las aguas* is [laz ágwas].

Testimony seems to indicate that early in the sixteenth century a modality of articulation, *linguaplana*, gradually gained ascendancy in the Sevilla area and spread during the next two centuries to most of Andalusia and a large part of Extremadura. It would be pure speculation to say that this was a part of a substratum force of Arabic or *Mozarabe* origins, but there is ample evidence that the Moorish and other Semitic elements of the Spanish population had great difficulty in pronouncing the [ṣ] of Castilian, usually rendering it as [š] or as [s]. At any rate, the first manifestation of this mode of speech was the loss of [ṣ] and its leveling to [s]. One could say that the tongue dropped from behind the upper gums to the teeth. The next step in this same category was the lessening of the grooving tension, and finally the simple aspiration of the sibilant at the end of a syllable. The process consumed perhaps one hundred and fifty to two hundred years.

Tongue flat articulation must have changed the [š] (*dixe, faxa, México*) to [h] or [x] by the same process of dropping the tongue to a flat position, the articulation becoming velar or laryngeal. Indications are that this change took place between 1550 and 1650. It therefore became American as well as Peninsular. It would seem that southern Spain was still

pronouncing the / h / from Latin / f / when this change
took place, and hence made its / š / [h] rather than [x].
Northern Spain developed a real gutteral [x], and in America again the areas that were in constant contact with southern Spain's ports (Cuba, Puerto Rico, Venezuela, Panama,
and Central America) have the "latest from Sevilla." Other
regions of America developed a guttural or a palatal as time
went on.

Yet another manifestation of *linguaplana* seems to be the
leveling of [ʎ] to [j], which began apparently in the middle
of the seventeenth century and for some reason was associated with urban centers, first of southern Spain and
Latin America and finally of even northern and central
Spain, where it is gaining ground today. Nevertheless, large
areas of America still distinguish / ʎ / and / j /, *valla* from
vaya, *halla* from *haya*: Bolivia; Peru, except Lima and the
northern coast; Paraguay; Ecuador, except the coast; and
Bogotá, Colombia. In this change, as in the / s / and / x /,
there is a dropping of the tongue point or blade. The manner
of distinction in Ecuador and in Paraguay is not that of the
traditional / ʎ / and / j /. Ecuador tends to distinguish [ž]
from [j] and Paraguay, [ʎ] from [ŷ].

One of the latest results of the flat-tongue vogue is the
lax articulation of the / r / that leads to its confusion with
/ l /; the phonetic results at times resemble [r] and at times
[l]. Often it is difficult to distinguish. This tendency shows
itself at the end of a syllable—*mar, puerta, izquierdo* [mal],
[pwélta], [iskjéldo] or [ihkjéldo] or *alto, clavel* [árto],
[krabér]—and is especially noted in the region of Sevilla, in
Puerto Rico, Panama, Cuba, and Venezuela.

Although there doesn't seem to be evidence in the Colonial period of the change, one of the most extended characteristics of American Spanish today is the velar / n/ [ŋ]
as a sign of open transition. *Enamora* is [enamóra] but *en
amor* is [eŋ amór] in many regions of America, and in southern Spain. English-speakers and Germans who hear this
allophone for the first time think immediately of *ng*, since
the phone of *sing* is similar. In a language that does not
have much open juncture, this feature and the now-popular
fricative or sibilant final / r / may be signs of a changing

structure. Although [ŋ] is the manifestation of / n / before [k, g, x] in all Spanish, it is to be heard as an allophone of open juncture in southern Mexico, all of Central America, coastal Colombia, most of Venezuela, Cuba, Puerto Rico, Dominican Republic, Peru, Ecuador, Bolivia.

Perhaps the only outstanding feature of American Spanish that is not traceable to Andalusia is the assibilation of / rr / and / r / final and postconsonantal. This tendency has been called Bogotá *r*, Guatemalan *r*, Costa Rican *r*, etc., but, as a matter of fact, it is found in vast areas of America. In many places, it becomes unvoiced and is actually confused by outsiders with / s /: *la ropa*, as pronounced by many people of Guatemala [řřópa], sounds to a Spaniard like *sopa* [ṣópa]. Both articulations are actually alveolar fricatives. The final / r / in this same pattern often sounds like [s] or [rs], *decir* [desíř] (women tend to use the sibilant style more than men) in New Mexico, Guatemala, Costa Rica, eastern Colombia, Ecuador, Bolivia, Chile, western and northern Argentina, and Paraguay.

Mexico

Among speakers of Spanish, a Mexican is recognized by his intonation and by his tendency to lengthen the articulation of his / s /, and in general his preference for the consonant over the vowel. The difference between Mexican intonation and the normal might be shown by the following device:

Represented are the four steps that are possible in the normal intonation pattern of Spanish; also the stressed and unstressed syllables. The so-called Mexican tendency is to strike a point between the normal cadence and the emphatic, giving the utterance a minor key effect. Not all Mexicans do this, nor does anyone do it on all occasions. It is a trend.

The / s / of Mexico is one of tense grooving and tends to be prolonged, often at the expense of the preceding vowel. There is a strong tendency to eliminate the vowel in such phrases as *bloques para apuntes* [blóks pára apúnts] or *choques y accidentes de coches* [čoks i aksiđénts đe kočs], although it must be admitted that this is a simplification of the tendency.

The *jota* / x / of Mexico is generally postpalatal, although in the north it becomes prepalatal before the front vowels. In the entire country / ʎ / and / j / have been leveled, and in the north the intervocalic / j / is so weak that it is often lost: *silla* and *capilla* become [sía], [kapía].

Among the syntactic traits of Mexican Spanish, one can cite the use of *tú* as the familiar form of address, and as in all of Latin America, its plural is *ustedes*. *Vosotros* is not used, except in affected oratory. In the states of Chiapas and Tabasco, *vos* is used as the familiar form, as in Guatemala.

Mexicans are very fond of the diminutive, and of the possibilities, *-ito* and *-ico*, where there is a / t / in the preceding syllable, they prefer *-ito*, and the augmentative *-ote* seems to be more popular than in some countries.

Typical adjectives of the Mexican scene are *mero* and *puro*. The first of these is so popular that it means not only "mere" but "very," "real," "just," "same," and other things. Among adverbs of unusual application, *hasta* deserves attention. It may mean not only "until" but "not until." *Hasta las cuatro viene* would mean "He does not come—or he won't come—until four." And then there is *ahorita,* often pronounced [oríta], which may mean "right now" or "pretty soon" or "just a while ago" or simply "now," while *ahora* has lost face to the extent that it means "today": *el periódico de ahora.*

Mexican Spanish is also known for its large Aztec or Náhuatl vocabulary, much of which has entered the cultural streams of the entire world: *chocolate, cacao, coyote, chicle, tomate, petate, metate, mecate, ocelote, jacal, milpa, elote, ejote,* and hundreds of others, most of which are associated with the domestic scene.

Guatemala

The *guatemaltecos* are called *chapines* among Central Americans, and although the Aztec word *quetzal* refers to their monetary unit and the name of the country itself is Aztec in origin, the Indian languages that are still spoken by hundreds of thousands in that country are of the Maya family and not related even distantly to Aztec.

The Spanish of Guatemala is characterized by a strong assibilated / rr / [řř] and by [ř] for / r / except in intervocalic position. The *jota* tends to be [h] rather than [ç], velar / n / marks open transition and the intervocalic / j / is so weak that in certain situations it is not heard. As a result there is a tendency toward ultracorrection, and while *bella* may sound like [béa], *vea* often turns out to be [béya]. Guatemalans generally pronounce their / s / with clarity.

A fairly universal feature of the Spanish of Guatemala is the *voseo*, or use of *vos* as the subject form of familiar address. The verb used with this is plural and the pronoun objects and possessives are always singular. *Cuando te vayas, llévate tu perro contigo,* as one might say in Spain or in Mexico, would be *cuando te vayás, llevate tu perro con vos.*

Little boys are *patojos* in Guatemala, and if a young lady is cute enough she may be a *patoja* until she is thirty or more. Blonds are *canches,* so an attractive blond could be a *patoja canche.* The *chóferes* of Mexico become *motoristas* and the reply to *gracias* tends to be *propio* or *suyo.* Much of the Aztec vocabulary of Mexico is used also in Guatemala.

El Salvador, Honduras, and Nicaragua

Perhaps more than any other group of independent countries, these three form a linguistic unity in most respects. They represent in phonology a middle point between the highland conservatism and the lowland later trends. They call each other *guanacos, catrachos,* and *nicas* respectively and are always talking of Central American union, which has been approached more than ten times.

The phonological phenomenon of recent discovery—although it is probably archaic—in these republics, is the occlusive pronunciation of / b /, / d /, / g / under certain circumstances where they would normally be fricative: *desde el verde jardín* [déhde el bérde hardíŋ]; *las barbas del rey de bastos* [lah bárbah del rrej de βáhtos]; *Margarita ha dicho algo de las gangas* [Margaríta aďičo algo ďe lah gaŋgah]. Where standard Spanish would have fricatives after other consonants, except / m /, in the case of / b /; / l / and / n /, in the case of / d /; and / n / in the case of / g /, these countries—and most of Colombia—have occlusives.

It is in this region of Central America that one hears a lisped / s / that approaches [θ] among many residents, and especially in the working classes. The / ʎ / and / j / are leveled, and, as in northern Mexico, the intervocalic is a semivowel or disappears. The *jota* is [h] in all speakers, and there is a strong tendency to aspirate final / s /.

Ultracorrection is rampant in the area, and one hears [awktomóβil], [piksína], [conseksjón] for *automóvil, piscina, concepción,* and even [ekspór] (English "sport").

The Salvador-Honduras-Nicaragua region is rich in forms of combinative analogy, especially noun formation on the basis of other nouns. The suffixes *-ada, -ida,* and *-ón* are of extensive application: *babosada, pendejada, lambida, atolada, paisanada, perrada; barbón, narizón, pistón quemazón, andalón;* and the longer diminutive form *-ecito* that might be used in Mexico or Spain is simply *-ito: llavita, lucita, crucita, piedrita.* The place where things grow or are to be found is indicated by the suffix *-al: cañal, guacal, platanal, cafetal, piñal, pinal.*

Along with the other Central American countries, except Panama, this region uses the *vos* for familiar address, and in the way described for Guatemala: *Vení y decíme, son ustedes, vos y tu padre, ladrones.* One says in El Salvador, *entre más como, más flaco me pongo; voy donde el médico* (the more I eat, the skinnier I get; I'm going to the doctor's). Many indigenous words are used in everyday conversation, most of them from the Pipil, a sublanguage of Náhuatl. A blond is a *chele,* a boy is a *cipote, pushco* is dirty, and *peche* is slender, and then there is the usual stock of Aztec terms that were imported after the conquest of Mexico.

Interesting applications of Spanish terms through a process of semantic substitution are exemplified by *gurrión* (sparrow) for hummingbird, *norte* (north) for any wind, *porte* (bearing) for size, *taburete* (stool) for chair, *seno* (bosom) for armpit, and *recto* for straight ahead. The great *plaga* (plague) of Anglicisms is in evidence, as everywhere, but unique are *hand* [haŋ] for foul in basketball and *pichel* for pitcher.

Costa Rica

Most of the *Ticos* live high in the mountains, and most are of Spanish origin. Only a few Indians are to be found in Costa Rica, and the Negro elements are on the Caribbean slope and coast. Although some Spanish speakers call them *costarriqueños*, most Ticos prefer *costarricenses*.

Due to currents of settlement, the pronunciation of Spanish in Costa Rica resembles that of Guatemala more than that of neighboring Nicaragua, Honduras, and El Salvador —the last three are quite homogeneous in their pronunciation pattern. Like Guatemala, Costa Rica is noted for its assibilated /rr/, along with assibilated /r/ syllable final. It also shares with Guatemala a fairly conservative articulation of /s/ syllable final. In common with all Central American and Caribbean countries, the /n/ is [ŋ] when final, as a sign of open juncture: [eŋ amór] but [enamorár], and intervocalic /j/ weakens to the point of elimination through vocalization.

As a part of the syntactic structure of the dialect, *vos* and related forms operate where *tú* would prevail in Spain or Mexico today, and lexically, Costa Rica shows less Aztec influence than Guatemala, El Salvador, or Honduras.

Panama

The Spanish of Panama, recently depicted rather thoroughly by Stanley Robe (*The Spanish of Rural Panama*), might be termed trade-route Spanish, in that it has the phonological character of the parts of America that were in constant communication with Spain and yet were removed from the courtly influences of the viceregal centers. It resembles strongly the Spanish of Cuba, Puerto Rico and Venezuela and the northern coast of Colombia.

Along with other Caribbean residents, the Panamanians tend to aspirate their / s / at the end of a syllable, or to eliminate it entirely; *Estos son los dos pescados* is apt to be expressed as [éhtoh soŋ loh ɗoh pehkáoh]. The late Andalusian confusion of / r / and / l / is nowhere in more evidence.

It is to be noted that the Mexican tendencies that have carried over to much of Central America do not reach Panama in strength. Rather the Isthmus leans toward the Caribbean. While a Mexican would refer to a Spaniard as a gachupín if he wanted to show any disrespect, a Panamanian would call him a *ñopo*. The non-Latin elements in the popular speech may be Afro-Cuban or indigenous to the territory —or English!

Colombia

With three high mountain ranges and several important ports, Colombia might serve as an example of the growth of American Spanish from Peninsular models. The relative inaccessibility of its high sierras and valleys makes it possible to find at least five distinct linguistic zones in this former viceroyalty of Nueva Granada. The dialects therefore represent stages in the historical development of southern Peninsular Spanish; in general, the most inaccessible are the earliest and the most accessible represent the latest in Andalusian vogues before independence.

Strange as it may seen, Colombian Spanish has two traits in common with that of El Salvador, Honduras, and Nicaragua: the *jota* (/ x /) is [h] in all regions, and the / b /, / d /, / g / are occlusive after any consonant: *pardo, barba, algo, desde, las vacas*, all have occlusives where a Spaniard or a Mexican would use fricatives.

The five main varieties of Colombian Spanish—there are others—are Bogotá, Tolima, Nariño (*pastuso*), Antioquia, *costeño*. The Spanish of Bogotá has the conservative distinction of / ʎ / and / j / and like Costa Rica and Guatemala, tends to assibilate the / rr / as well as the / r / final.

Pastuso Spanish is in many ways Ecuadorean and, like the Spanish of Highland Mexico, slights the vowel in favor of the consonant, tends to pronounce the / d / of *-ado*, and uses an apico-dental / s /, strong and well defined.

Antioquia's Spanish is unique in America in one way. The / s / is apico-alveolar [ş], like that of Spain, and although no distinction is made between *casa* and *caza*, one Colombian ambassador to Spain, an *antioqueño*, always gave the impression of talking like a Spaniard. The second distinguishing feature of this region's Spanish is the / j / of such tenseness that it even becomes affricate intervocalically: [máŷo, kaβáŷo].

Coastal Colombian Spanish has the features of Cuban Spanish: the aspirated / s / at the end of a syllable, velar / n / in open transition, the confusion of / l / and / r / in some sections, the articulation of an alveolar / č / that is no more than [tj].

The designation Tolima has been suggested for the fifth area. Actually much more territory is indicated, but this type of Spanish, while having the general traits of all Colombian Castilian, does not assibilate the / rr /, does not use the apico-alveolar / s /, does not distinguish / ʎ / and / j /, and does not have late *costeño* characteristics.

Along with all American regions of Spanish speech, the / h / of Latin / f / origin is still aspirated as a rural trait. Notably prominent in Colombia, too, is the bilabial / f / [ɸ].

Colombia is unusually formal in most sections as far as direct address is concerned. Many speakers use *usted* almost exclusively—even to cats and dogs. Not only is this the case within the family, but many relatives speak to each other as *su merced*. The *voseo* prevails in Antioquia, in Santander, and in the *valle*, while Bogotá generally, and the coast always, employ the *tuteo*.

As a part of its formality, Colombia has a reputation for a wealth of vocabulary, especially in its urban Spanish, and the hyperbole, the metaphor, and the euphemism have a prominent part in oratorical and written expression. Nevertheless, as everywhere, there are *provincialismos*, and to the horror of many, English is gaining ground daily.

Typical of Colombia are the idiomatic expressions *siga*
and ¡*a la orden*! The first is said to invite one to enter and
the other to ask, "What can I do for you?" Black coffee,
especially the demi tasse, is a *tinto* and to invite one to par-
take, one says: ¿*Le provoca un tinto*? This same sentence to
a Spaniard might mean, "Does red wine make you fight?"
Instead of sending regards with *saludos*, Colombians use
saludes (healths).

Instead of the Mexican *chamaco*, the Argentine *pibe*, and
the Guatemalan *patojo*, the Colombians have *pelados*, and
little boys of the street, of whom there are unfortunately
too many, are known as *chinos*, and as in Central America,
the sidewalks on which they are apt to be found, are *an-
denes*, literally "platforms."

Venezuela

The land of oil and cattle, and many long-termed
dictators, money comes in *bolívares* in honor of the liberator
who was born there, the ranches are *hatos*, the buses are
guaguas ("waa-waas" or babies), the blonds are *catires*.

The speech pattern of Venezuela is for the most part that
of the Caribbean, and therefore late Andalusian. One "eats"
his final / s /; / l / and / r / are confused at syllable end; / n /
is [ŋ] as a sign of finality and, as in El Salvador, Honduras,
and Nicaragua, many people pronounce the / s / as [θ].

As far as address is concerned, most of Venezuela is *tuteo*
territory, but sections near the Colombian frontier are *vos*
areas. The vocabulary of Venezuelan Spanish is rich in Indian words, mostly from the Caribbean languages, Arawak
and Caribe. *Curiara* (canoe), *catire* (blond), *vaquiro* (pig)
are examples.

Ecuador

In a country where thousands speak Quechua (Inca)
in preference to Spanish and where many are bilingual, the
Spanish language of the upper inter-Andean region is very
conservative in its phonological evolution. Ecuadorians,
(except those of the coast) still distinguish / ʎ / and / j / as

[ž] and [j], still pronounce / s / with deliberate tenseness, and, like many Mexicans, slight the vowel in favor of the consonant. Because Quechua is so widely spoken, and because this language has a simple three-vowel system, the Spanish of the Highlands tends to heighten / o / to / u / and / e / to / i /. One of the best portrayals of this in the written language is the novel of Jorge Icaza, *Huasipungo*. Unique in Latin America is the final / s / before a vowel as [z]: [las ágwas].

The *voseo* is in contest with the *tuteo* in Ecuador (use of *vos*, "ye," instead of *tú, te,* "thee, thou" in familiar speech).

Peru

About 11,000,000 *peruanos*, or, as their neighbors may say, *peruleros* or *cholos*, occupy the territory of the Central Inca Empire of preconquest days. Their money is counted in *soles* and their babies are *guaguas*. Along with Ecuador and Bolivia, Peru belongs to heavily populated Andean Spanish America, and besides having many Quechua-speaking inhabitants, the region boasts a clear Spanish that gives evidence of sixteenth-century origin and viceregal nurture.

Except for Lima and the northern coast, Peru still distinguishes the / ʎ / and / j /, and the general impression of Peruvian Spanish is similar to that of Mexico, Bolivia, and Ecuador.

Nearly all of Peru uses the *tú* form of familiar address and, as one might expect, hundreds of Quechua words have entered the Spanish of everyday life. In fact, several *quechismos* have become universal terms: *pampa, cóndor, puma, puna, quinina, llama, alpaca, gaucho, chinita* (sweetheart), *poncho,* and many others.

Chile

Linguistically, Chile can be divided into three sections; the north and the south resemble each other more than either resembles the middle. The heavily populated central valley partakes of many of the traits of late Andalusian, through the port of Valparaíso and the city of Santiago.

Final / s / is dropped or aspirated, / l / and / r / are confused and / ʎ / and / j / are not distinguished. North and south do not share either of these levelings with the central valley; moreover, they tend to give more tension to the / s /. There are two features that seem to be found in all Chilean Spanish. The / č / is alveolar rather than palatal, and the / x / has a palatal element of semiconsonantal nature. Thus one pronounces *La gente de chile* as [la xjénte ďe tşíle].

In Chile the *voseo-tuteo* contrast has apparently become a social one. Members of a middle-class family may *tutear* while their gardner uses the *voseo* in his own family. The *voseo* of Chile uses the form *ái* instead of *ás* in the last syllable of the present indicative of the first conjugation.

In Chile buses are *colectivos*, babies are *guaguas*, beans are *porotos*—and so are little boys.

Argentina

The Spanish of this vast territory is of two main types, according to the direction from which the settlers came. The west and northwest was settled from Peru and Chile early in the seventeenth century or in the 1590's. The Buenos Aires area and the humid Pampa were settled first about 1535, but definitely from 1580. Between these dates the original inhabitants were in what is now Paraguay, having been driven up the river by Indians. As we might expect, the interior of the country shows more conservative features than the *porteño* area. Uruguay is a part of the *porteño* region linguistically.

In parts of the northwest, the / s / is quite clearly articulated and in two sections there is a distinction made between / ʎ / and / j /. The porteño is noted for his / j / with strong [ž] articulation, while the interior, like Costa Rica, Guatemala and Bogotá, has the assibilated / rr /. The similarity is reflected in the way that people of Buenos Aires tease those of the interior, accusing them of making / rr / like / j /. Actually, the first is alveolar and the second is palatal.

Both Argentina and Uruguay are *voseo* territories, and the style has been recorded extensively in the gaucho poetry. As a cattle region, the pampas have a lexicon that is rich in terminology of the *estancia* and of horses. To such an extent is this true that metaphors are often of this origin. English (of England) and French are contributors, and one hears of *five o'clock tea a todas horas*, and the frequency of *chau* for good-bye attests the influence of Italian, the original language of more than half the inhabitants of Argentina.

Residents of Argentina are called *che* in some quarters, since they use the expression to attract attention, but those of the interior are called, especially by Chileans, *cuyanos*. If the *bife* (steak) is *macanudo* (great), you are in Argentina.

Cuba, Dominican Republic, and Puerto Rico

The Spanish of Cuba could be termed trade-route Spanish, since it shows rather typically the American evolution of Andalusian trends of the seventeenth and eighteenth centuries, trends that don't seem to be present in the more inaccessible hinterland. Add to this the Afro-Cuban influences that date from slave days and the strong American-English loans in the twentieth century, and we have perhaps the least conservative Castilian.

Cubans tend to aspirate their syllable final / s / or drop it altogether and the tendency is as marked or more so in Puerto Rico and Santo Domingo. In all three / l / and / r / are confused, most in Puerto Rico, and in all, the final / n / is [ŋ]. In contrast to Mexico, Ecuador, Bolivia, and Peru, where the vowel may be slighted, the Caribbean regions tend to slight the consonant in favor of the vowel. In Puerto Rico, and to a certain extent in the other two, / č / is [tj]. In Puerto Rico—much less in the other two—/ rr / is [R] in about half the population and is apparently gaining. It will be recalled that this development into an alveolar *r* occurred in French and in some Portuguese dialects. Cuba, Puerto Rico, and the Dominican Republic are *tuteo* countries, although there are some vestiges of *voseo* in Camagüey, Cuba.

In vocabulary, English has made great inroads. Even the verb "to type" may be *taipear*. Castro's propaganda press tells of *despachos* of the press association and people learn to *atender clases* in rooms without much *furnis* (furniture).

Spanish in the United States

Among the foreign languages taught in the schools of the United States, Spanish holds first place except at the university level, where it is a close second to French. Not only is the language taught extensively, but it is spoken natively by perhaps three million people who are American citizens.

The nuclei of Spanish speech in the United States show various origins and the oldest group is that of New Mexico and southern Colorado, where the settlers have maintained a linguistic continuity since shortly after 1600, and where many of the structural characteristics resemble those of Central America more than those of Mexico. Many New Mexicans are still bilingual, especially those of the small towns, but Spanish is losing ground to English, especially in vocabulary.

New Mexicans are recognized among Spanish-speakers by their tendency to vocalize intervocalic / j / or to leave it out entirely: *capilla* [kapía], *ella* [ea]. They have a tendency to assibilate / rr / and to pronounce / x / [h], and like *salvadoreños*, they aspirate many of their final / s /. Historically, they represent a later period than that of central Mexican speech.

Arizona, California, and Texas, if they resemble any other settlement, are reflections of an earlier type of Andalusian Spanish imported bodily from Mexico in more recent times. In a sense they are Spanish of 1850–1950 from Mexico, while New Mexico represents 1600–50 from Spain.

In the Spanish of the border, except New Mexico, the / x / is [x] or [ç] and the / s / is not aspirated to the extent it is in New Mexico and / rr / tends to be [rr] rather than [r̃r̃].

Florida has a settlement that dates back to about 1886 at Tampa, and within this group one can distinguish the northern Spain origin of many speakers as well as the Cuban trend of the young people. All this population grew around the cigar industry, and under the influence of Havana in recent decades it has become a *costeño* type. As one might expect, the lexicon is replete with English or corruptions of

English.

New York City represents another large contingent of speakers of Spanish, and this language is the second one heard as one walks the streets of the great metropolis. The speakers of New York come from several countries, but the dominant group linguistically is the Puerto Rican. The children of Spanish-speakers of New York tend to abandon that language in favor of English, as Sephardic Jews have tended to do in this country in recent years. Spanish, already deficient in technical, scientific, and business terminology, is daily infiltrated by English. It would seem that, unless there are many replenishments, Spanish will leave the Gotham scene by the end of the century.

Trends in Latin-American Spanish

There seem to be two rather opposing forces that operate in the evolution of American Spanish (this is probably also true of colonial French and colonial English): one that seems to be characterized by a structural conservatism (in the grammar and phonology); the other an inventiveness and picturesqueness of expression in the realm of semantics that compensates for the poverty of devices of function and inflection.

Three very important books by Charles Kany, of the University of California, (*American Spanish Syntax*, 1945; *American Spanish Semantics*, 1960; and *American Spanish Euphemisms*, 1960), describe these aspects of the Castilian of the Western Hemisphere as well as any documents that are available to those interested. Kany has divided the analysis of syntactic phenomena on the basis of parts of speech and incidentally records regional variants that have become typical of the sections indicated. The semantic study is arranged on the basis of types of change, from substitution, through nomination and metaphors to analogy and permutations. The picture of euphemistic usage is arranged by situations that engender euphemistic expression: superstition, death, financial status, delicacy, decency, etc. In these compilations it is evident that the Latin American of Spanish speech tends to overuse, on a regional basis, certain syntactic devices, orders or units, and moreover he will apply these inflections or suffixes to more stems or basic semantemes than a Spaniard might.

Because the vocabulary of many of the uneducated settlers was limited and the Andalusian sailors introduced maritime terms there sprang up an extensive vocabulary of mistaken identity and of jocose designation. In the same population, the educated had and still have the inclination to express themselves in a flowery hyperbolic and euphemistic style. An examination of newspapers from all the large cities of Latin America shows this universal trend and makes it difficult to distinguish the journalistic style of Chile from that of Mexico, or the newspapers of El Salvador from those of Ecuador.

There is a general tendency among Spanish Americans to differentiate gender of nouns that refer to occupation or status of people, and to create feminine forms where they may not have existed in older standard Spanish. Not only *presidenta, ministra, dependienta* but *liberala, sujeta, abogada, arquitecta*, and even *tipa* have been heard.While standard usage calls for *los niños se lavan la cara*, there is a trend toward *los niños se lavan sus caras*. Whether this is a vestige of former ways or whether it is English influence is a question.

In the realm of the adjective, it should be noted that *cien* in preference to *ciento* is the rule in all Latin America when no noun follows: *cien por cien; le voy a dar los cien*. In Central America and somewhat in Colombia, the word *primera* is apocopated preceding a noun: *la primer noche*. Adjectives are generally used adverbially: *corre muy rápido; toca el piano muy lindo; ése lo hace muy feo*. Frequently the adverb *medio* is made to agree with the adjective it may modify: *media muerta; medias locas; medios dormidos*.

There are two interesting extensions of adjective or adverb forms that operate on a regional basis. In Mexico and to some extent in Central America, the word *mero* has gone far beyond its original meaning of "mere" or "sheer," and is applied both adjectively and adverbially to indicate situations of precision or closeness: *En la mera esquina, el mero jefe, ya mero*, and many other expressions of the sort are common in Mexico. The other word that has been extended, chiefly in the southern countries, is *recién*, which in Spain is limited to adverbial usage in such combinations as *los recién casados* or *recién llegado*, but which in Argentina, for instance, may mean "recently," "soon," "just," and other extensions of the original idea.

In several sections of South America, *no más* has the sense of "just" or "why" or "right" in idiomatic English: *Acaba de llegar, no más; pase, no más; allí, no más*. The correlative expressions of comparison, "the more . . . the more," etc., as in Andalusia, are expressed in urban centers as *mientras más . . . más*, while in many areas, especially rural, *entre más . . . más* is more common. Very rare in America is the standard Spanish *cuanto más . . . tanto más*.

Charles Kany's *American Spanish Euphemisms* describes in amusing detail the Hispanic-American euphemistic tendencies: ways of softening the harsh, of disguising the indecent, of expressing with circumspection the indelicate, or of embellishing the vulgar. This penchant, combined with the hyperbolic, gives Spanish-American journalistic writing a baroque style. The following rather literal translation of an item from the *Tiempo* of Bogotá, Colombia, December 11, 1960, is typical:

> The agent of police, distinguished with the badge 07777, who performed vigilance in that sector had to intervene in the case, and as he intimated capture of the antisocials, the latter set upon him with intention of attacking. One of them with a knife in the right hand. The agent, seeing the imminent peril to his personal integrity, found himself in the imperious necessity of making use of his revolver of official designation, discharging at the antisocial a bullet and causing him death in an immediate manner. The raising of the cadaver was undertaken by the judge of turn of the permanent (court) of the North, who started the original investigation.

This flowery style, being quite poetic, makes ours seem prosaic by comparison.

With respect to the second-person pronouns and the corresponding verbs, pronouns, and possessives, there is considerable divergence between usage in Spain (except in Andalusia) and Latin America. In all of Spanish America the plural for both familiar and polite address is *ustedes* with the third-person plural of the verb and third-person object pronouns and possessives. This corresponds to Andalusian usage generally. The polite form singular, *usted* is universal in Spanish, although in sections of Colombia and Ecuador, *su merced* is used, even within the family. The familiar singular in all of Spain and in most of Latin America is *tú*, but the plural of this is *vosotros* with second-person plural forms in Spain, except Andalusia, while the American plural is *ustedes*.

The situation not generally known is, as mentioned above, that the familiar singular in Argentina, Uruguay, Paraguay and Guatemala, El Salvador, Honduras, Nicaragua and Costa Rica, as well as in parts of Colombia, Venezuela, Ecuador, Peru, and as a social mark in Chile, is *vos*, used with a shorter form of the second-person plural verb, with singular object pronouns and possessives but with *vos* as the object of prepositions. The imperative is a direct derivative of the Latin imperative but shortened. Instead of *tú hablas, comes, vives*, one says *vos hablás, comés, vivís*; and instead of *siéntate, sentate*, the latter a corruption of *sentad-te*. The verb *ir* is replaced by *andar* in the imperative: *andate. Vení; decíme; ¿qué hacés? Llevate tu libro con vos.*

The American-Spanish usage with regard to object pronouns conforms generally to an older Spanish pattern. *Lo* is direct object for both persons and things masculine, *la* is the feminine direct, and *le* is indirect for both genders; plurals have / s /. Nevertheless, there is a strong tendency to use the singular indirect for the plural, even in journalistic writing: *al intimidarle captura a los antisociales*. Contrariwise, rural elements often add a verb-suggested / n / to the reflexive pronoun *se* to indicate plural: *siéntensen*.

As far as tenses are concerned, the preterit is much more popular in Hispanic America than the present perfect for an act completed in the past. Madrid in recent decades has tended toward the present perfect.

The verb *haber* used impersonally tends to form a plural except in the present indicative finite: *habían dos hombres*;

¿Cuántos habrán? The same thing happens to *hacer* to indicate elapsed time: *hacen tres meses.* Notable confusions of adverb and verb occur in Central America, among other places. *Dentrar* is a popular verb, even among educated speakers, and in the same region, many say *abajar* rather than *bajar* and *avenir* rather than *venir.*

As Charles Kany (*American Spanish Semantics*) has indicated, in the lexicon of the Spanish of Latin America are many genuinely Spanish—yea Latin—items that were popular in Spain at another time or that were of a more dialectal character at the time of the settlement of America. Where a Spaniard would say *ascensor,* an American would say *elevador;* for *atar* he would say *amarrar;* for *bandeja, charola;* for *billete, boleto* or *tiquete;* for *echar, botar;* for *enfadado, enojado* or *bravo;* for *guisante, arveja* or *chícharo;* for *ligero, liviano;* for *rápido, ligero;* for *puerco* or *cerdo, chancho, marrano, cochino, cuchi, tunco.* A hundred of these could be listed.

Due to new situations on the American scene, combined with a certain lack of knowledge and training among the Spanish *pobladores,* semantic substitutions were made on a large scale. As has been indicated, seafaring terms were applied to things and actions far from the coast, and one still embarks on the *flota* of Bogotá when he boards a bus, and *flete* is by rail usually.

One of the most interesting substitutions is that having to do with the seasons. In the torrid zone, where there are actually no seasons of heat and cold, the Spaniards began to call the wet periods *invierno* (winter) and the dry, *verano* (summer), even though there might be several of each. If there is a flood, one may say, "We had a bad winter last week." The answer to the question, *¿Qué tal el invierno?* (How was the winter?) may be *¡copioso!* (copious).

Within the realm of what Kany calls nomination, we find slang expressions for well-known or even highly appreciated objects and a whole series of nicknames for Spaniards and other nationalities. North Americans are referred to as *gringos* in Mexico and the western part of South America. In the River Plate region, *gringo* means Italian. We are also referred to as *yanquis, machos* (males), and very politely, *nuestros primos* (our cousins), the latter in Mexico.

Two powerful trends in Latin America at the moment are the analogical tendencies to form new nouns by adding suffixes to old ones to create nuances of violent action, large group, daintiness, grotesqueness, or contents. The suffixes *-ada, -azo, -ón, -ito* seem to be more popular than ever and are applied where they might not have been years ago. In Bogotá, one speaks of taking a *septimazo*, usually [sekti-máso], when he walks down Carrera Séptima, one of the main streets. In Guatemala City, *sextear* is to stroll down Sexta Avenida. English may enter the picture as in *voy a tomar una nadada* (I'm going to take a swim) or *le dieron una gran almorzada* (they threw a big lunch for him). The termination *-ito* has extended itself to adverbs: *ahorita, lueguito*; and to greetings: *adiosito, chaucito*, the latter from Italian inspiration by way of Argentina.

The second trend, also in the realm of analogy, is of a correlative type and shows a great deal of English influence. In an attempt to imitate North American social reporting, advertising, academic and technical procedure, there are hundreds of semantic loans, as well as the more obvious direct borrowings. A shower for the bride-to-be becomes *aguacero* or *chubasco*, according to local usage. *Alto costo* and *alta calidad* attest the influence of American advertising. "Round trip," "to play a role," "is being," "to kick the bucket," may be translated literally, creating Anglicisms that finally sound Spanish. *Educación* takes the place of *pedagogía*; *argumento*, of *discusión*; *atender*, of *asistir*; *audiencia*, of *concurrencia*; *acta*, of *ley*; *complexión*, of *tez*; *parada*, of *desfile*, etc.

Direct borrowings show up especially in sports, in business and commerce, in foods and drinks of the quick-order variety, and in entertainment: *basquetbol, fútbol, boxeo, béisbol, batear* (to bat), *fildear* (to field), *pichar* (to pitch), *noquear* (to knock out); *lobista, piquetar, comité, mitin, líder, control, agenda; lonche, lonchería, sandwich, jaibol* (highball), *coctel, ponche, bar; swing, twist, chance, flirteo, impacto*.

Under a general heading of what Spanish Americans would call *tabú*, the Spanish-speaking person avoids matters having to do with the devil, animals of bad omen, evil eye. By means of *indirectas*, he evades getting to the point when it is a question of stupidity, money, debts, robbery, arrest, jails, police. And such things as sex, underwear, the bosom, excrement, the belly, etc., are either highly glossed or are expressed in very vulgar terms. The prostitute, the procurer, homosexuals, pregnancy, masturbation, giving birth, are all expressed euphemistically in the conversation of every day.

Extremes are reached in an attempt to avoid using a word that may be crude in some sections. To keep from saying *huevo* (egg), one has even resorted to *el hijo de la esposa del gallo* (the son of the wife of the rooster), and in Cuba due to the vulgar meaning of *papaya*, this fruit has to be spoken of as *fruta bomba*—this extends to the Spanish of Florida. In Puerto Rico it is called *lechosa* (full of milk).

It should be noted in this connection that Spanish swearing is sex-based and that in exclamations the name of the Deity is not considered sacrilegious, in fact there is a certain religious fervor implied when one says *Dios mío. Jesús* is used a great deal by women, and is no stronger than "heavens to Betsy." *Por los clavos de Cristo* (by the nails of Christ) might be shouted out by a very proper Spanish lady. To swear in Spanish is to conjure all sorts of fantastic sex relations and to call one's mother bad names. This latter is the *colmo* and will start a fight immediately. To such an extent is *madre* used in curses that if one says the word in a loud voice, everybody within hearing looks to see what trouble is going to start. The word *puta* (whore) is the favorite in some countries, and a person might even be called *hijo de veinte putas*, a rather difficult plight! In Mexico, the word of this sort that men employ constantly is *chingado*, the past participle of the verb meaning to copulate, especially among animals. Another verb of this same sort, universal in the Spanish world, is *jodido*. People are called *cabrón* (he goat), but the implication is cuckold, they are called *pendejo*, presumably from the Latin *pendiculum*, and it means "fool" in many countries today. From the vulgar word *carajo* come a host of euphemisms: *caracoles, caramba, canastos, caray*. There are many gestures that symbolize these vulgarisms, and many times athletes have been ejected from games for using such gestures to the whole audience!

The dominant foreign influence in Spanish today is English, but there have been periods when Spanish had a great deal of influence on English. The two major periods of Spanish loans to English have been the sixteenth and seventeenth centuries, and the nineteenth and twentieth centuries.

In the era of contests on the Spanish Main and while America was being settled by Spanish and English, our language took many words from Spanish: alligator, Negro, cannibal, doubloon, corvette, cockroach, vanilla, creole, siesta, sombrero, mulatto, and others. From the Southwest, and within the past one hundred years, several fairly common terms have been added to English: corral, lasso, lariat, cinch, stampede, hacienda, ranch, mustang, vamoose, canyon. Interestingly enough, English has always been quite ready to accept these new devices for indicating nuance or flavor, but Spanish still tends to reject officially the English *barbarismos*, in spite of the fact that it needs them to be able to refer to concepts and things that are imported from the United States or England.

Excursions to Mexico

The Tourists

These are by way of confessions of a tour conductor, a leader of twenty excursions of schoolteachers to Mexico between 1926 and 1956. The impact of Hispanic culture on American women—and vice versa—could be a subject for much writing and great speculation about the efficacy of this type of Peace Corps. But, for the present, let us consider some of the elements of the person-to-person coexistence.

The groups varied in size from the number that could comfortably travel in one station wagon to ninety-five adventuresome females of the Roaring Twenties who filled three special Pullmans. The purpose of the tours varied from simple sight-seeing to serious study. During the first ten years I was assistant tour conductor in charge of the operations and arrangements of a nationally advertised summer-study group for teachers of Spanish. Involved was the task of accompanying them from the border, with stops at Monterrey, Saltillo, and San Luis Potosí, to the National University of Mexico. On weekends the teachers were taken by caravans of taxis or by train to points of interest in central Mexico, and several times a week they were escorted to the theater to see three-act plays.

From 1936 to 1956 I took groups of teachers and students from the Rochester, New York, area by car or by a caravan of cars, often referred to as the Canfield Car Caravan. These trips covered some eight thousand miles and provided for visits to Monterrey, Mexico City, Puebla, Fortín de las Flores, Cuernavaca, Taxco, Acapulco, Oaxaca, Guadalajara, and, on occasion, Mazatlán, Guanajuato, San Luis Potosí, or Saltillo.

Experiences of the conductor included all sorts of negotiations with Mexican citizens, from government officials to laborers, and incidentally provided a close look at the American woman abroad for the summer. We wore stiff straw hats and carried canes, we bargained for taxis—for everything. We teased waitresses, climbed pyramids, boated through the canals of Xochimilco, carried thirty-five-pound sacks of one thousand pesos from the bank to the hotel to pay the bill for the group, drank tequila, and sang barbershop harmony in public places. We played jai alai during earthquakes.

Experiences of Coexistence

Several evenings a week it was my duty to take the ladies to the theater, having read the play before and given them a summary in English. This trip was often made on foot, while Mexican youths called out to the teachers such things as: "Huera" (Blondie, the color of a bad egg), "Desoscuras protestantes" (undark Protestants), or, as on one occasion, "Good-bye, chicken." On the theater excursions we usually arrived at our reserved seats about curtain time. Usually the theater was empty, but gradually the orchestra would arrive and finally the audience, *poco a poco*. To while away the time, we often indulged in a little vocal harmony, but hisses from those Mexicans who were there reminded us that this was not done. The fact that the play was forty minutes late in starting didn't bother those of Hispanic pattern.

On the occasion of our first play, we heard someone mumbling the lines of the comedy just ahead of the actors. Investigation at first produced no results; he was hidden! At times, it seemed that he spoke louder than the actors. When it was evident that this was the traditional prompter reading the play aloud from his shell in front of the stage, we became even more interested in this manifestation of the person-to-person culture. One evening in Puebla, we were accompanied to the theater by a local reporter who didn't like the way in which the prompter seemed to out-shout the actors. As customary, our newspaper friend hissed loudly; others joined, either in accord or to silence him. We almost had a riot that night, because each time the prompter was shushed, he spoke louder.

The big episode of our train ride to Veracruz in 1926 was the participation of General Gómez, prominent presidential candidate, in our songfest, and the subsequent invitation by him to some of the girls of the group. He came into our car to listen to our rendition of *Adiós mi chaparrita, Adelita, Cielito Lindo*, etc. and asked if he might join us. After a few songs, he said that he would like to meet about three of the girls. As a consequence, three of our party were invited to his home in Veracruz.

As the twenty-two-year-old leader of the party, I was asked by the twenty-five to thirty-year-old women whether they should go. My reply was stock for such occasions: "Use your own judgment." They did, and went. It later developed that the general had given them some of his select wine, then without warning had produced a ring and offered it to the woman from St. Louis. She said, "I'll have to think it over, General Gómez." She did. In the fall, General Gómez was shot and killed as he led a revolt with Serrano against the national government.

One day in Pachuca, as we were eating our first meat course after the soup, the town poet came in. After tapping his forehead a few times, he composed a rhyme about each of the ladies present. Soon the village *mariachis* arrived, followed by numerous beggars asking alms for the love of God; each received a few *centavos*. Finally we paid for our meals, which cost an average of seventeen cents in United States currency.

In Morelia, arrangements having been made by an agent of the federal government of Mexico, our group of teachers was asked to parade up the street to the hotel. The schools were even dismissed so the students could watch the parade. As it reached the Hotel Valencia, word came from the secretary of the governor that he would like to receive the group at his office immediately. After an exchange of speeches between the Basque secretary and the Americans, the party put itself in the hands of Jesús Valencia y Moreno, the proprietor of the hotel.

The water pressure of Morelia wasn't quite enough to reach the second floor of the Gran Hotel Valencia, and early each morning don Jesús was to be found "struggling with the water," as he said. Since there was no running water in any of the rooms, nor in the bath, the girls had to sign up for a bath, and watch the *rey de los baños* prepare the bath in a tub that had been painted muddy brown to make the color of Morelia's water less evident.

A chapter could be written on what we euphemistically call rest rooms. There are those of the Chick Sales variety, and, at one place in Pátzcuaro, these were staggered one above the other so that the circumstances and episodes of the one on high were apparent to the one below through the back wall. Then, there were the alternate *damas y caballeros* in Oaxaca with special boxes for used paper; it was not to be thrown in the toilet! At a public one in Xochimilco a woman stood by the urinal to collect five *centavos* from the customer.

Not long before we left Morelia, the governor invited the group to a tea dance. The time stated on the invitation was five-thirty; the place, one of the large hotels in the city. Knowing something of Hispanic custom, we arrived about an hour after the announced time. There was a small committee of decorators present and a lot of confetti on the floor. Over the entrance was a large wreath which spelled out a welcome to the party. Our group sat around for some time; finally the orchestra began to arrive, piece by piece, then a few men. By eight o'clock, things were under way and were still going strong at one in the morning! In the meantime, the Basque secretary to the Governor had appeared with cognac, and several other northern Spaniards with their bagpipes.

Strikingly, most local arrangements were made by an agent of the federal government, and governors and mayors were given orders by the central government.

Then there was Oaxaca and the story of Gertrude and don Antonio. The group of American teachers, of which Gertrude was a member, was staying at the Hotel Francia.

Don Antonio was the proprietor. During the course of a three-weeks' stay, the two had become good friends, neither one serious in pursuing the friendship beyond the summer. Nevertheless, due to the fact that they had been seen together on several occasions, Oaxaca gossip had it that they were to be married that fall or early the following year. To such an extent did this informal communication prevail that shortly after the return of the group to the United States an item appeaared in the Oaxaca paper, as follows:

Engagements: We are informed that within a short time, since preparations are already being made, Mr. Antonio C., Proprietor of the Hotel Francia, will contract matrimony in this city with an American teacher, who formed a part of the excursion that visited this capital in the latter part of last June. We shall advise presently the date of the celebration of the nuptials to which we allude.

As don Antonio wrote Gertrude, he was in a dilemma, since a local family had even gone so far as to set aside a room in their home for his "fiancée." It was their understanding that in the United States it was not proper for the bride to stay in the groom's home before the wedding. The solution to this whole problem was one becoming the pattern of Oaxaca: Don Antonio received a letter from a "friend of the bride," testifying to her "tragic death in an automobile accident." This was followed by a mourning band on don Antonio's sleeve for a respectable period, a moment of silence at the Rotary Club's dinner, and, finally, a notice in the paper: "On a recent date, there died in Glendale, California, U. S. A., Miss Gertrude C., victim of a painful accident. The aforesaid señorita was engaged to marry Señor don Antonio C., a person quite well known in this city, who received by telegram the sad news, and for this reason his friends have presented to him their condolences." Good old Oaxaca, good old Hotel Francia!

Typical of the Andalusian-American architecture is the wide front door which leads to the patio through a *zaguán*— a vestibule wide enough for a car. There is no back door, and a block of buildings is solid masonry. Thus, at the Francia, the chickens and turkeys for tomorrow's dinner came in the front door today, right through the patio restaurant as don Antonio and his sister argued and bargained with the Indian vendors. One had a preview of events to come. It is interesting to observe the differences between Easterners and Westerners in such circumstances. Easterners are more upset gastronomically and psychologically than the Texan, for instance, and what really makes some wince is to have the dirty vendor come through the dining room with a basket of vegetables on the head, while don Antonio yells at the top of his voice for Josefina, the maid, who is on the first floor—which is really the second!

In 1935, there was the parade-reception for the governor, García Toledo, Bands of men from all the neighboring towns were out, directed by the political leaders of the great Revolutionary party—*the* party, mind you. One of these groups decided to pay a visit to the *señoritas profesoras norteamericanas* to tell them where it stood politically. Its leader advanced, after being assured of an appreciative audience at the door of the Francia, and made a long speech, helped by the mezcal that he had already consumed and by the mezcal-inspired shouts of his followers. He said the same things that Cubans are saying today: "We are against imperialism, especially North American imperialism. We are against fanaticism, especially Catholic. We are for land reform." After which the mezcal jug was passed. The leader turned out to be a teacher from one of the mountain villages of Oaxaca. Like many of the leaders of this type, he was anti-Catholic, although born one. He had been taught a large Marxist vocabulary and that Mexico's Indian past was its glory; he would tell you all of this in Spanish. The Indians who followed him knew virtually nothing of any past.

There was the time that the governor of Oaxaca sent a messenger to the Francia that he was giving a dance for the *señoritas profesoras norteamericanas* that very night. The catch was that the *señoritas profesoras* had already packed all their finery for an early morning departure—never to return! But, as they say in Spanish, one made heart out of guts, threw the house out the window, and all were ready at the announced time of eight. The governor and his staff of generals arrived between nine and ten, preceded by his own orchestra. He and his large staff sat at a special long table arranged by don Antonio, cognac was ordered, and the governor said, "Would you please introduce me to that blonde over there." After another glass of cognac, "The tall one on the right." Some of the *señoritas profesoras* never got to dance, but as the night wore on, and the other guests of the Francia tried to sleep, the two groups vied with each other in singing their native songs. Everyone was hoarse by morning, and it was morning before one retired to be awakened for the narrow-gauge trip to Puebla at 5:30 A.M.

Puebla, Mexico, with its colonial atmosphere, its gingerbread houses, its Hidden Convent of Santa Monica, its cathedral with onyx altars and pillars, its churches and more churches, its tile factories, its *portales,* all symbolizing the Hispanic penetration of the sixteenth century.

Puebla, with the hotel owner from Castile with deep-set eyes, prominent lids, and a beard, who said he had not had a drink of water in thirty years. One night a boy from the *Colegio de Jesús* climbed to the second-story balcony of the room of an American girl. Her screams caused him to drop to the pavement and her to be hoarse the next day. As the proprietor said, she had probably shown her teeth in the boy's presence. "Give them a finger, and they'll take the whole arm!" When the Hotel Colonial in Puebla opened it found itself besieged by a labor union and a red and black flag draped around the building—a personal appeal to the governor made the pickets vanish.

The problem of parking a car and knowing that it will be safe is a grave one in some places. The large cities of Latin America are infested with petty thieves (some not so petty), and where there are highways that Americans use, there is always the "wachucar-mister" boy. As one parks his auto, a boy rushes up and asks, "Wachucar?" Like many Mexican stories and songs, there is a double meaning. For when one returns to tip the boy for having his car watched, he finds that it has been washed!

The caravan of ten cars was nearing the town of Teotihuacán when one of the *choferes* near the front of the line signaled for a stop. Immediately, as was the custom, nearly all the other drivers got out and walked up to the car. Apparently, there was engine trouble and the chauffers were ready to conduct the customary clinic of the road. As we approached with the question, *¿Qué pasó?* the consulting "physicians" were already giving diagnoses and advice, which rather literally translated went as follows: "Our colleague, Joseph, suggests that the clutch may be skating." "Yes, but the motor doesn't put itself in march!" "Hand me that English key (monkey wrench) that's on the stirrup of that penultimate coach." Yet many of these men were practically illiterate!

As we rolled into the town of Hidalgo, looking for the only gas station indicated on the map, dusk was settling over the sierras to the west. Entering the modest one-pump establishment, I used the flippant Spanish expression for such occasions, "Throw me forty." The proprietor's face took on the expression common among Hispanic people under the stress of chagrin or disappointment: the corners of the mouth turned down, the shoulders lifted, the eyebrows raised slightly. He said, "I feel it much, but there is no gasoline—besides, the pump doesn't function. How is the oil?" Times have changed since then—nowadays gasoline is sold all over Mexico in modern, often spick-and-span stations.

Gringo Wedding

The National Defense Education Act provides for, among other things, summer institutes for further intensive training of foreign-language teachers. Level One institutes of French, Spanish, German, and other languages are scattered about the United States—some sixty-five altogether—while some fifteen more (Level Two) are established in Mexico, Germany, France, Puerto Rico, and even in the Soviet Union. Under contracts with the United States Office of Education, American universities and colleges conduct the institutes to give intensive experience in applied linguistics, methods of teaching, conversation, composition, the culture of the area concerned, etc. Participants are chosen by the contracting college and usually number from fifty to eighty for a given institute. They are paid a stipend of seventy-five dollars per week, plus fifteen dollars for each dependent, who, incidentally, do not accompany the participants.

Level Two summer institutes in Mexico numbered three in 1964, and the one at San Miguel de Allende, Guanajuato, sponsored by Bradley University and staffed by eight professors of Spanish, brought together fifty-two high-school teachers of Spanish for a seven-weeks session. Participants and professors lived in local *posadas* or private homes.

Among the high-school teachers was a charming lady from Colorado who had post-institute marriage plans, but who decided during the institute to have her future husband meet her in San Miguel for a Mexican wedding. Mexican law requires a civil marriage ceremony, whether there is a religious one or not, so the prospective bride made arrangements with the justice of the peace, the "marrying judge." As one of the professors, I offered the terraza and other facilities of our rented home for the wedding.

The groom arrived from Colorado in his camper, accompanied by his sister, two days before the scheduled wedding. The bride, who spoke Spanish well, went with the groom to get the license, which was finally issued by the same "marrying judge." However, for a while it looked as though the wedding might not materialize. The groom spoke no Spanish, neither did his sister, who had crossed the border with him. It seems that at Ciudad Juárez they procured the usual tourist cards, and in answer to the question ¿casado? (married?), they had said sí, which they did know. As a result, each was listed as married, and in the eyes of the Mexicans, to each other. When the judge examined their Mexican tourist permits, it looked like contemplated bigamy. "There can be no wedding," said the judge, "the man is already married, and his wife is with him." Since the bride spoke Spanish well and had become rather well acquainted with the official, she was able to convince him that, through a lack of understanding, a mistake had been made at the border. The resolution of the matter came about on a "personal" basis. As old friends, the judge accepted her sworn avowal that neither had been married and that the whole thing had been an error in communication. The elderly judge gave a broad, toothless smile and issued the license.

So all was readied for the al fresco wedding on the terrace of the little villa we had rented for the summer in San Miguel de Allende. The hour of one o'clock was selected to avoid the usual late afternoon rain, which, in fact, did come down in bucketsful about four. Matilde, our faithful cook, housekeeper, and counselor, had purchased and prepared several chickens and arranged flowers in the house and outside. Merced, the expert gardener of the property, had shaken the walnut tree and gathered up all the nuts so the ceremony would not be interrupted by falling objects. A microphone was installed among the branches of this tree and a tape recorder hidden in the bushes. The whole ceremony, including the coughing, ahems, and asides of principals and guests, was recorded for posterity.

The wedding ceremony, translated idiomatically, was as follows:

Judge: Matrimony is the only means of founding the family, of preserving the species, and of helping to overcome the imperfections of the individual in his striving for the perfection of mankind. Man is not sufficient unto himself, and mankind implies conjugal union. Married people should be sacred to each other, even more than they are to themselves.

The male, whose sexual attributes are primarily valor and strength, should give his wife protection, food, and guidance, always treating her as the most delicate and sensitive part of himself, and with the magnanimity, the generous kindness, that the strong should show the weak, especially when she surrenders herself to him and when she is judged by society.

The woman, whose gifts are abnegation, beauty, compassion, perspicacity, and tenderness, should give the husband obedience, pleasure, help, consolation, and advice, always acting with the abnegation that we owe to the person who supports and keeps us, and with the deference that will avoid irritable and brusque feelings.

Each should have respect, deference, fidelity, confidence, and tenderness for the other, and this should be a part of the conjugal home. And their task is to attenuate their own faults and errors. They should not maltreat each other nor wrong each other. It is cowardly to use force, and it should be their constant concern to set a good example so that their children will have a model of dignified, serene, moral conduct. Such conduct will compensate ultimately for the trials and tribulations of life and will produce a happy family, with children, the fruit of their affection, who become good responsible citizens.

Mr. F—— W—— R——, you have made application for marriage to J—— F—— J——. Do you take her as your wife?

F. W. R.: Sí.

Judge: Miss J—— F—— J——, you have made application for marriage to F—— W—— R——. Do you take him as your husband?

J. F. J.: Sí.

Judge: You have agreed to marry in the presence of all this company. Will you please sign the corresponding documents.

The luncheon preceded by *margaritas*, followed and consisted mostly of ham, chicken salad, and hot biscuits. However, since the bride's original estimate of thirty people turned out to be forty-five, several cans of tuna fish entered the picture before all finished eating. American friends of the couple gave a fiesta at one of the local *posadas* in the late afternoon. While the *mariachi* band played and the tequila flowed, the late afternoon rain came down in sheets.

Guatemalan interlude 1963

The Trip to Guatemala

The following observations on the fascinating mores of Hispanic communication and institutions were made during the summer of 1963 with the fine collaboration of Mary Walker Canfield, who for many years has shared with the writer the romance, rumba, and revolution of Hispania.

After a semester at the University of Illinois, where I was visiting professor of Spanish, we drove through Mexico to Guatemala to fulfill an obligation to Bradley University's NDEA Institute as *profesor de lingüística*. This second-level institute was held at the Instituto Guatemalteco Americano in Guatemala City, from June 20 to August 10. The participants were fifty American teachers of Spanish selected from many applicants from all over the country. Instruction was given by a staff of some ten professors, many of them native Spanish-speakers, in Hispanic culture, methods, stylistics, conversation, Indian languages of the area, Spanish American dialectology. Students and professors lived in the homes of *guatemaltecos*, and several trips and visits to points of interest were planned. Each participant wrote a paper about his contacts with the people of Guatemala and their way of life.

It would seem that several of the things that we noted on this visit tend to reinforce the original contention of this series of essays: that the real nature of nations and peoples is to be found in their ways of communication, and that the Hispanic pattern is one of the dramatic personal flourish in a climate of immediacy.

The two highway ports of entry to Guatemala from Mexico are El Carmen and Mesilla. The first is just beyond Tapachula, Chiapas, Mexico, which may be reached in the dry season by road from Tehuantepec, but in the rainy season one ships the car—and rides in it—by rail from Arriaga to Tapachula. The Mexican highway that makes connections with Mesilla, Guatemala, is paved all the way to the border and goes through some of the most spectacular scenery in Mexico between Tuxtla Gutiérrez and Comitán, including the high mountain city of San Cristóbal de las Casas.

At Ciudad Cuauhtémoc, Chiapas, Mexico, one passes three checkpoints of Mexican customs, one for vaccination certificates, one for tourist cards or passports, and the third for car registration. The permit of importation received at Laredo is surrendered; another will have to be taken out on the return. On both sides of the border, men associated with the respective officialdoms ask in hushed tones if there is any money to be changed. Rates are not bad!

A high fence marks the border. On the other side of this stand the guards of Guatemala. At the first stop the tourist card or passport is examined and stamped; at the next, several yards beyond, the auto registration is checked and a temporary importation permit is made out. At this same point customs officials examine the baggage, usually opening only the large suitcases. After attaching special Guatemala *Turista* license plates over the regular New York ones, they give the word to proceed, boasting that they have only two stops, while the Mexicans have three!

The section immediately beyond the border is a deep canyon which becomes deeper as the road continues southwestward. This sector of the Inter-American Highway is affectionately called *El Tapón* (the stopper) because of the frequent landslides during the rainy season that leave it *tapado* for hours or even days at a time. As we started through the *Tapón* we saw how many landslides there had been this season; the remaking of the road must have been a daily affair. Several bulldozers are always on hand. Although we did not have to stop once during this fifty-mile stretch of narrow dirt road, it was evident that one could have lots of trouble. In fact, friends who came through two days later were delayed twelve hours in the *Tapón* and didn't get through until after dark.

Beyond the *Tapón* the road is wider, but because it was built with improper drainage facilities on the inner side, it shows the results of heavy rains, and we had to drive with unusual care to avoid deep ruts, rocks, and mud. It was a game to keep the underpinning of the car (especially the transmission and the gas tank) untouched by objects on the road or by the road itself. One climbs as he goes through the canyon to an altitude of nearly ten thousand feet beyond Huehuetenango. Near San Cristobal one reaches the paved road, a good piece of engineering, and the last one hundred and fifty miles are covered in about three hours. An outsider's uncertainty over this road is increased by the lack of communication among responsible people in Guatemala about its condition. Apparently the tourist bureau gets its information from the daily papers, and the men stationed at the border seem to know only what the tourists tell them about the condition of the road.

Guatemalan Bureaucracy

As the permit for temporary importation of the car was only for thirty days, we were told that it would be necessary to go to the Ministerio de Hacienda (Treasury Department) in Guatemala City for a renewal before the expiration date. The process of securing this renewal affords one of the best examples of man-over-institution presented by Hispania on all sides. Although one man could have taken care of the whole renewal in two minutes, I was lucky to spend only five or six days in securing this precious *prórroga* of importation on a temporary basis.

First I went to the National Palace and was told where the Treasury Department was. It so happened that I arrived during the only two hours of the day that the office serves the public. A young lady clerk explained that I should get a sheet of ten-cent *papel sellado* (legal paper, lined and sealed) and on this I should write in the proper legal language a petition to the minister of the Treasury asking that I be given an extension of thirty days on my permit of importation of the car. Once that this was done, I should return and present it to another person in the same office, along with my passport. Investigation shows that the *papel sellado* is a source of millions in internal revenue. It is available everywhere, but especially in stationery stores, and each sheet bears two numbers. Stacks of it in the form of petitions grace the tables and files of government offices.

A day or so after getting these instructions, I returned with the request couched in flowery Spanish, baroque style, properly signed and flourished and took it and my passport to the designated man. He carefully read it, announced that it was actually acceptable, and that I should return two days later. I left the request and my passport with him. When I arrived two days later, I was sent not to the office of the first part but to another. The clerk there looked in a card file, could find nothing and sent me "back in there." I chose the fourth of several rooms and happened to see the girl who had served me in the first place. She had complimented me on my Spanish the first time and now became solicitous and asked me what she could do. I told her that the clerk in number one had sent me to number four. She began to look for my original petition and passport, going through many stacks of *papel sellado* on several desks and files. She finally found the letter and the passport—still untouched. As if the honor of Guatemala were at stake, she grabbed a form and began to type madly. After completing the form, she handed it and its carbon copies to a man who seemed to be floating around all four offices. He disappeared and was gone about forty minutes. Meanwhile the señorita ordered food and drink, as did other employees. A man came in to pay a gambling debt, and I made change for him. Most of the workers showed a singular restlessness, moving from desk to desk and from room to room, with very little work being done. In fact, the señorita must have felt this to be the case for she got out the office manual and read "do's" and "don'ts" to the men, obviously putting on a show for me.

The papers and passport were finally brought in by the man who had disappeared, and he directed me to the number one office. I shook hands with him and with two of the señoritas and went. The clerk there was really a gruff person. When he deigned to look up from his tasks, he grabbed my papers and from a large box of rubber stamps began to select several. He stamped copy after copy, signed, stamped again, peeled off carbon copies, and finally handed me one of these: "This is your copy." He then put all of the papers and my passport on top of a bookcase. "What about my passport?" I asked. "You may pick that up at the customs house in a couple of days—maybe Monday."

The customs house was some seventeen blocks from our residence, but I made the trip during the siesta period on the day that had been indicated and reported to the secretary. The latter examined my copy—the only thing between me and my passport and permit—as if he had never seen such a document before. After reading it carefully, he took me to an underling who was instructed to take care of my needs. The latter also read it carefully and finally said that he had not received its companions from the Treasury Department. "Vuelva Vd. mañana."

So I went back the next day and went through the same two men to be sent to a señorita who found my documents in a corner on a table. She signed, stamped, stamped some more, and then said in a sweet little voice, "You will need an internal revenue stamp of ten-cent value." The second man saved me a trip to another part of the city by finding one that he had left over from some other transaction. There was no change, but someone went out to a store to get some. I shook hands with all concerned and was about to leave when the señorita suddenly remembered that she had forgotten one stamp! I would not be able to get across the border without it, she said.

As indicated earlier, at the Guatemalan border my passport and my wife's and my daughter's tourists cards had been examined, stamped, etc. It was only two weeks later that another American tourist showed me a card which he had been given at the same point (Mesilla), stating that the recipient was to report to *Migración* within three days after arriving in Guatemala or be subject to a fine. No such card had been given to me nor to others of our group who had come by plane. I reported to *Migración, Sección de Ex-*

tranjería (Section of Foreigners) and was told that I would need a photo and that they would then fingerprint me and give me permission to stay in the country as much as ninety days—and that I was actually subject to a fine. Without said permission, I should not be able to leave the country and might be sent back to Guatemala City, some two hundred miles, to get it—that is if I could get through the *Tapón* in the first place!

Turismo Nacional, the tourist bureau of the country, had been very helpful upon the arrival of our group by plane, and it occurred to me that the director should know of the *Migración* situation so he could recommend rectification of lapses or change in procedure. The director, whom I had met, received me cordially and got the chief of *Migración* on the phone. He first said that he was sorry to have to bother the chief with a little problem: a man was in his office who had arrived in the country on June 18 (it was now July 1), had been seeing the sights of the western part of the country, including Quezaltenango, Atitlán, and other interesting places, and had not been able to get to the city nor to *Migración.* Would he please attend to him if he were sent to his office immediately? The conversation closed with repeated statements concerning the kindness of the chief, of apologies for molesting him, and of how *amable* he was. There was not the least hint of delinquency on the part of officials or lapses of any sort.

A quick trip to *Migración,* with a photo which we happened to have, got us fingerprinted and stamped so that we could stay in the country. As we were chatting with the very pleasant and attractive girl who did the fingerprinting, another employee, apparently the subdirector of *Extranjería,* called me by name and asked if I would be willing to see the chief himself about this matter. "If you tell him, maybe he will believe us." I talked to the chief of the section, and he very casually told me the reason some people had not been given cards at the border: they had run out of them, and besides it was hard to remember such things!

The process of changing traveler's checks at the Banco de Londres y Montreal is an exciting adventure—if you have a little time on your hands. Let's say you want to change three hundred dollars into *quetzales*, the national monetary unit. You first sign the checks in the indicated place, then you get out your passport and give this and the checks to the first handler, who fills out a short form while you fill out a long form: name, address, activity to which you dedicate yourself, nationality, country of origin of the money which you are offering, amount of the proffered currency (written out and in figures), type of foreign currency, rate of exchange, type of document or instrument, numbers of the traveler's checks in series, and name of company issuing them. You "so declare" and sign your name, but the fun has just begun!

The long form in duplicate and properly filled out is taken by the first handler to a higher official who examines each check and the other two supporting documents, signs in the necessary places, and finally returns the documents and checks to the first man. The first man then gives the customer a copy of the long form, slips one copy of the short form and all the checks into a tray on top of other odds and ends, gives another copy of the short form to a third man, the teller, who then pays the customer without requiring any identification. He always asks what denomination the customer desires. All of this is done with courtesy and with flourish; and, after the second or third time, with handshaking on all sides and wishes that all may go well with you, ¡*que le vaya bien*!

Guatemalan Buses

Guatemalan bus drivers are called *pilotos*—with reason. They seem to feel like aviators! Although the driving is not quite so wild as that of Mexico, and much less so than that of Colombia, the point of view of anyone behind the wheel seems to be extremely egocentric. Pedestrians are those who get in his way and impede his personal flourish. The buses (*camionetas* in Guatemala and El Salvador) pass each other in an attempt to get to the next corner first. One wonders how the rattletrap vehicles hold together long enough to complete their runs, as they trail smoke screens of cheap diesel fuel and bluff their way into the intersections. Nevertheless, they seem to get to the assigned destination and for five cents per ride!

As you pay your fare you are given a numbered receipt which says that you are to have it ready for the inspector when he boards the bus and that it should be destroyed when you alight. If an inspector gets on—they often do—he will tear off half of the ticket so that if by chance the *piloto* should get it, he could not sell it to another passenger. (Passengers have been known to give the receipts to the driver as they get off; he can resell them and pocket the difference.) One sees in some of these countries inspectors of the inspectors, guarantees of signatures, and guarantors of the guarantors, with seals, stamps, and flourishes.

Life and Death in Guatemala

Cars left on the street are subject to stripping, and, if valuables are left in sight, the car may be broken into even in broad daylight, in spite of the *vigilantes* and *policía preventiva*, the first of whom blow whistles at intervals all night long to show their presence in the neighborhood. To avoid difficulties, and to keep the car from being struck by *pilotos*, we had our station wagon in a parking stall, referred to as a box. We could remove it at any time from the lot where the boxes were located as we had a key to the outside doors to the lot, which were kept locked between 7:00 P.M. and 7:00 A.M. Interestingly enough, the box next to mine was vacant for a time because its renter was shot during the curfew imposed by the present military government a couple of months before our arrival. One story had it that he was German and didn't understand the regulations or the commands to halt on the night of his death. The *patrulla* got him as he circled the square in front of the National Palace. Another story said that he was racing around the square in defiance of authority. At any rate, the *patrulla* was exonerated.

Guatemala City has the only bowling alley in Central America: *Boliches Electrónicos Bel*, good new alleys with automatic pinsetters. When the alleys are crowded one sees again the triumph of Hispanic personalism over any system or institution. The way to get an alley is to become friendly with a group that is bowling and ask if you may follow it. If consent is given, you collect the amount due and assume that group's obligations and place.

Waiting in line, *haciendo cola*, is not popular in any of the Spanish-speaking countries, including Spain itself—the rush for a ticket window can be a madhouse. In spite of the unwillingness to be patient while waiting for service, there is a corresponding disinclination to give personal service and a strong proclivity to delegate duties to others. In making a simple purchase at a drug store, one is given a slip, he takes this to a cashier, pays the bill, then goes to a third person to get the package.

Like the habit of buying groceries in small quantities, and frequently, one buys stamps by the letter. Hence it is that the post office is filled with people who are presenting letters to be weighed one by one and then stamped one by one. Standard rates seem to be based on a five-gram starting point, and the rate increases by a rather complicated scale. An airmail letter to the United States is seven centavos for the first five grams but only nine centavos for ten grams. It is quite a shock to the employees to be asked for fifty seven-cent stamps. How could a person need so many stamps in advance? Immediacy is the attitude of the day.

Sunday is an interesting day in the central park. The military band plays in the morning, and in the afternoon the maids strut their stuff in their colorful costumes of colonial tradition. One afternoon we went to the park and sat among the maids and mothers with their children. Suddenly from one corner of the square a loud speaker blared forth as a Protestant minister began to preach to the multitude. He supplied hymns and prayer and could be heard for a couple of blocks. He had gotten through perhaps one sermon, one hymn, and not more than a couple of prayers when a Catholic opponent set up the same sort of equipment on the opposite corner and tried to outshout the *evangélico*. In order to get the attention of the crowd, he began to tell what the Virgin Mary did not do: She didn't paint her face, nor did She make her hair stand on end as modern girls do! She wore it long—clear down to her waist. She didn't make beauty spots on her face as a charm. The effect was to amuse the people who were listening.

Interestingly enough, neither the Protestant Church nor the Catholic seem to be too much concerned with the betterment of social conditions. They are saving souls!

Our room was over the garage and had a common outside entrance with the doctor's room. Any visitor or vendor coming to see one or the other of us either rang the bell beside this door or used the knocker shaped like a hand—or both. We were awakened one morning, about 3:30, by a neighbor banging on the door to summon the doctor. (Earlier in our stay, he had been called in the night to care for the lady next door, who was having internal bleeding and was "in a very grave condition.") There seemed to be more voices outside than usual, when we awoke for the day around six o'clock, and, upon looking out of the window, we saw many cars parked in front. People, singly, in pairs, and in groups, were going in and out of the house, including several priests. We suspected that the sick woman had died, and at breakfast the doctor confirmed it.

All morning neighbors, friends, and relatives flocked to the house. Floral pieces began to arrive: sprays, wreaths, and crosses, mostly in combinations of yellows, pale blue, and white, and most of the pieces had a black bow. By early afternoon, the number of people increased, and many stopped to chat after making a sympathy call. The callers were all elegantly dressed. Cars were parked on both sides of the street, the entire length of the block. Neighbors on the other side of the street stood in doorways watching, so it did not seem discourteous for us to watch from our upstairs window. About 3:45 P.M. it became evident, as more people and priests arrived, that the funeral was about to take place. A few minutes later, a shiny, black, modern funeral coach pulled up at the door and double-parked. At the same time, some twenty or thirty women, all dressed in black with black-lace mantillas on their heads, left the house and the sidewalk in front of it to cross the street and stand watching. Presently, six men emerged from the doorway with a coffin, but, instead of putting it in the hearse, they carried it up the street toward the church, led by the hearse. The men fell into step and proceeded quite rhythmically. The relatives and other mourners, all dressed in black, followed the pall-bearers. In the meantime, several men had been hurriedly bringing out quantities of flowers and piling them in luggage racks on cars and station wagons. They, then, joined the procession; fortunately, the church was only in the next block. Many of the friends and neighbors of the deceased woman did not go to the church or to the cemetery, but lingered to visit a few minutes with each other before driving away or walking home. Within fifteen minutes, the traffic jam was over (for the buses, trucks, and other traffic had continued to move, as they were able, right through the entire time, even during the funeral march to the church). All evidence of the funeral had disappeared, and children were skipping home from school, laughing and chattering, as usual. Dead at 4:00 A.M., buried at 4:00 P.M. on the same day!

Street scenes and noises

We were told by a native *guatemalteco* that the three things the capital is famous for are church bells, firecrackers, and telling jokes (or, playing practical jokes). I can't speak for the latter, but certainly we heard plenty of the former two. They are almost synchronized, early in the morning. Separately, each of the six Americans living in the house, the first morning there, was positive that a revolution had broken out! The explosions came in rapid succession, followed by a brief pause, then bells, and another series of loud pops, sounding strangely like machine-gun fire. In our sleepy condition, we were gripped momentarily with fright. On one occasion, one of the national liberation holidays, so many packages of firecrackers were lighted almost simultaneously that a dense cloud of blue smoke was left suspended up and down our street for several blocks, for ten or fifteen minutes.

Day begins rather early on our street, and the parade that commences at daybreak (5:30 A.M.) continues to be interesting and slows down only after dark with the sharp whistle of the *vigilante,* who punctuates the quiet of the night with his personalized blasts. It's hard to determine whether the spasmodic whistle blowing is to warn would-be robbers or to let the neighborhood know that he is on the job.

The first sounds of the day are the church bells, which start as a single tocsin, followed a minute later by another, and then a constant ringing for a minute or two. This sequence goes on for an hour or so. Since the nearest alarm clock of this type is the next block and our room is on the street, there is no avoiding this effective awakening!

Only minutes after the first bells, the first bus of the day comes roaring down the street, and since there are few passengers and little traffic at this hour, the *piloto* makes a beautiful race down the deserted thoroughfare. However, it isn't long before the order of the day is set in motion: trucks loaded with gravel, wood, hardware, etc. are on their way to construction jobs. On top of the loads sit or lie men whose duties include loading and unloading, and many of these fellows are still asleep. Paper boys, calling in a loud voice *Prensa libre* or *Impacto*, recite in oratorical tones exciting bits of the latest news, including the fact that the lottery results are part of the edition. Along with the bells, the buses with their motor-gunning and gear-shifting, the newsboys, and the trucks, one distinguishes the unmistakable clanking of milk bottles, as the first of several milkmen comes down the street with his pushcart.

One morning we watched this milkman across the street. At one house his customer met him at the door with a pitcher (no bottles are left outside doors) and asked for only half a bottle. Since all is in quarts, he poured out what he estimated to be a half of the bottle. After she had closed her door, he reached for an empty (but not necessarily clean) pint bottle on the lower shelf of his cart. He emptied the remainder of the quart into it, put the red cap from the first bottle on it, and knocked at the next door, greeting the lady who answered the door in her flowery kimono with a freshly capped pint of milk. On one occasion, during the milk run, we heard a terrific crash of a bus followed by the breaking of glass. Investigation showed the bus stopped at the next corner and a small crowd gathering. Subsequently, while walking past the scene, it became evident that two of our early-morning noisemakers had met. Small rivulets of milk were running down the gutters and shattered milk bottles were scattered all the way across the intersection. A woman was busy sweeping broken glass from her sidewalk; bus, milkman, and cart had all gone.

Now the school children come in bunches, laughing and talking, the girls in their neat uniforms, sometimes escorting their younger brothers and sisters. In our neighborhood, the uniform of the girls is white cotton blouse with the collar piped in dark blue and with dark blue buttons, pleated dark blue suspender skirts, white sweaters, white anklets and black pointed flats. Many, especially those of the ten to fourteen year group have exaggerated hairdos. Boys of a similar age pass on their way to school, too, but there is no communication or apparent notice of each other. Later on come the businessmen, housewives, maids, all bent on their errands—and the lumbering buses every three minutes.

One should mention, too, the sanitation brigade. Early every morning there is a small procession of street cleaners emanating from headquarters about three blocks away. The parade of these neatly uniformed little men breaks up at each intersection as certain ones "peel off" to go to their assigned streets. The same group of about fifteen appears in a solemn parade about 4:00 P.M., pushing their little carts laden with brooms, mops, dustpan, and raincoat neatly folded over the handle of the cart. They march in formation, next to the curb, back to their headquarters.

Another division of the sanitary workers—not in uniforms—drives bright yellow, two-wheeled carts pulled by mules; the vehicles are shaped like small covered wagons. These men collect what the little blue-uniformed men in the pith helmets have swept into neat little piles along the curb. The combination is responsible for Guatemala City's reputation as the cleanest city in Latin America.

Indian women, descendants of the ancient Mayas, in their colorful *huipiles*, skirts, and *servilletas*, sometimes with a baby tied to their backs, come dogtrotting down the street, stopping here and there at the closed doors of the houses. They set down the heavily laden baskets which they have carried on their heads and offer to sell the fruit or vegetables to the maid who answers the knock on the door.

There is an occasional knife-sharpener with his whetstone cart, who announces his presence with a high shrill two-toned whistle, stopping often at the tailor shop across the street. Then there is the occasional broom and brush vendor, who seems to make few sales. Always and ever are the cumbersome, noisy buses charging by, taking advantage of the fact that our street, being an avenue (north-south), has the right of way and is one-way.

Strolling down a side street near our home one day, we noticed a tiny hole-in-the-wall shop. We stood at the door, looking in, attracted by the multitude of objects in such a small space. Nearly all of them were religious pictures in delicate lacy gold frames, miniatures, or figures, varying from small Virgins and crucifixes to large ones and life-size prone figures of an infant Christ. One wall was entirely shelves, filled with paperbacked books, probably on religious subjects. A rather timid, dark-eyed young woman, who was attending shop, invited us in, and the three of us filled the shop! We noticed some of the figures were painted, others all white. She explained that these figures were imported from Japan and were painted in the shop. She let us examine some watercolor paintings, one of which was a real beauty: a sharply-done Indian woman, a baby on her back, was kneeling in prayer before some burning candles, around which was an aura. Indistinct forms of other Indians were in the background, contrasting with the sharply-depicted central figure, Indian Madonna. The other two paintings by the same artist, a street scene in a village and a bit of the highway overlooking Lake Atitlan, were very mediocre. All three were priced at five dollars.

Our attention was drawn to the young woman, herself, and to the work she was engaged in when we interrupted her. She was cutting round shapes out of white paper. I inquired if they were petals for flowers, and she answered, "Yes . . . for the church . . . for a wedding," and her eyes began to shine in such a way that I asked, "Yours?" She nodded shyly but happily accepted my congratulations and wishes for happiness with obvious pleasure. It was then that

I noticed a pile of the finished flowers, and she verified my deductions that the petals were dipped in melted paraffin, and when still warm were molded in the shape of roses, pressing the petals together, with a stem! Such a painstaking labor of love in a country where gorgeous, fresh flowers are so abundant and inexpensive!

Sojourn in Panajachel

One day we were driving smoothly and comfortably along the splendid new highway toward our destination, the little Mayan village of Panajachel on the shore of that gem of lakes, Lake Atitlan. The entire drive from the capital had been through fascinating countryside, from the experimental agricultural projects, lush pine forests, and tiny Indian villages to the beautifully hand-planted farms, in terraces, marching up and down the steep mountainsides. The meticulousness and beauty shown in the raised rows left us filled with admiration at the patient artistic skill shown by these so-called backward people in carrying on the farming from which they derived their living and life—in the same crude fashion of their ancestors, nothing mechanized!

Suddenly, small and brief glimpses of the blue, blue lake appeared through the trees, and then it burst forth before our eyes with its full impact. The color, which changes with the mood of the weather, was a deep blue, heightened by the brilliant sunshine of the morning. The tall, dark volcanoes, seemingly emerging from the blue depths, stood serenely watching over all. We learned in Panajachel that the lake is so extremely deep and full of the crosscurrents of unknown, underground rivers that any unfortunate soul who should accidentally (or otherwise!) fall from a boat and drown would be lost forever. The drowned bodies never rise!

In a few moments, we were unloading in front of Casa Contenta, the unforgettable inn on the shore of the lake. Fourteen years before it had been a wonderful delight—tile-roofed, pastel-colored stucco cottages, nestled in a garden paradise of tropical flowers at the foot of a hill so steep that one had to look almost straight up to see the top of it. The cottages are grouped around several courts, each court in charge of a *mozo* whose duties include guarding the cottages, cleaning them, changing linen, keeping them in fresh flowers, and even turning down the beds in the evening. In the years since our first visit nothing had changed at Casa Contenta, except, perhaps, some of the faces. The flowers were unbelievably beautiful—all the usual tropical flowers and shrubs, but especially hibiscus and begonias, all kinds and all colors. Our little *mozo*—no more than five feet two or three inches tall—carried our bags in, showed us the cottage like a true host, and checked on all the supplies. He offered to build us a fire in the fireplace in the evening, if we wished it. In the sitting room of our suite we were delighted with a tall vase of Madonna lilies on a low coffee table. We had no more time to tarry here, just enough to freshen up and hang up a few things before getting to the dock for our launch trip across the lake to the Indian village of San Pedro, where a big fiesta was in progress in honor of San Pedro Day.

At first glance, we felt that very little had changed over the generations in this Tzutuhil-Maya village, but, after climbing the steep, cobblestoned hill to the square, we realized that certain progress had reached even this remote spot, accessible only by boat. There was a *feria* in full swing, and hundreds of Indians from the nearby towns had come to join in. On the crude but effective ferris wheel, giggling young Indians girls, who had their legs modestly tucked in with their colorful shawls, were swung up overhead as they ate pink cotton candy. The plaza was a seething, swarming mass of Indians in their best bib and tucker and in a gala mood. The girls and women, in their most brilliant handwoven blouses and dark blue skirts, had new, shiny wide ribbons braided in their plaits, usually making the braids several inches longer than the hair, with huge double bows at the ends and often at the top of the braid also. Some were wearing the colorful bands wrapped several times around the braids that were encircling the head, giving the effect of brilliant red halos. We saw the church and the hastily erected bullring, where later that day the bullfights would not end in the usual kill. On the way back to

the Casa Contenta for lunch, the expected afternoon rain
was gathering to the south of the lake in the mountains and
heading our way. Although the rain itself didn't reach us,
the wind was whipping up whitecaps and the launches
shipped a little water before gaining the opposite shore.

When we reached our casita at the inn our little *mozo*
had picked and artistically arranged about a dozen hibiscus
blossoms on our coffee table. They were choice giant blossoms in a variety of colors, and he let us know that this was
done only for us and our intimate friends.

Our dinner was accompanied by the usual marimba music, and the waitresses were elegant in their "formal" dress
—a sheer cotton blouse, worn tucked in at the front and
hanging free at the back; the finely pleated skirt of blue
cotton (figured or striped)—as they glided in and out
among the tables with the food. Our places were set with
brightly colored native-woven napkins, brown with white
figures for lunch, green at night, and purple in the morning; at each place was a carved wooden plate on which the
china plates for the various courses were set. That night, as
on every Saturday night, the marimba band (six marim-
bistas plus drums and a string bass) played for dancing
after the dinner hour.

The next morning we were all packed and ready for a
seven o'clock breakfast, and before eight we were on our
way to Chichicastenango. Our bags were left in our rooms,
but we were to check out on our return after noon, since
another crowd was expected soon after. The drive to
"Chichi" took about one and one-half hours for the twenty-
five miles. All of the trip is over high mountains and about
half of it on a winding dirt road with hairpin turns and at
times only one-way. The horn gets plenty of use. Actually
we didn't meet many cars going but on the way back the
road was filled with visitors en route to Chichicastenango's
big Sunday market, and a bit of jockeying was necessary to
pass on the narrow cliff-hanging thoroughfare.

At "Chichi" we found the usual picturesque, colorful,
milling crowd of indigenous Americans and United States
Americans, each curious about the other. As one recalls the
scene of hundreds of Indians of the community buying and

selling, the mind's eye sees brilliant reds, predominantly, but also bright blues, yellows, and greens—the distinctive clothes of region and caste. With time and with thousands of tourists, the merchants have become blasé and in many instances don't care to bargain anymore. One man seemed to be more interested in selling small hanks of dyed wool and cotton at ten cents each than in bargaining over a blouse and skirt, which would have brought some ten dollars. The language of the market is Quiché, but many of the sellers speak Spanish, and an occasional one speaks some English.

Baroque Journalism

An examination of the newspapers of Latin America has shown a very definite trend toward a flowery, poetic style of writing, which, along with ornate oratorical methods, constitutes important manifestations of the personalized, subjective communication systems—therefore culture —of the Hispanic people. Although the first page of the Guatemalan dailies is a translation of English dispatches from the big news agencies and press services, the city news and the society page are typical of the Spanish-speaking world with their hyperboles and their euphemisms.

The following examples of baroque expression were picked at random and are presented in a semiliteral translation to preserve the flavor of the original.

Humble Vendor of Ice Cream
Dies Plastered by a Truck

The Pilot Rolled Him on Trying
to Pass Another Vehicle

Beneath the wheels of a heavy truck perished yesterday Mr. Mario Salomé García, a humble vendor of ice cream, who every day was located in front of the building of the Central School of Commerical Sciences, in order to distribute his product among the student body of that plant.

It was 17:05 hours when the truck, license plate C-40753, driven by Mr. Francisco Javier Soto Chiu, was passing along Tenth Avenue, in front of the School of Commerce, but in passing another vehicle it ran over

Mr. García, who was getting ready to return to the building of Sharp Ice Cream.

Upon the impact of the violent blow, the ice cream cart turned over on the sidewalk, while its unfortunate conductor was struck by the rear wheels of the truck, which passed over his entire body.

The death of Mr. García, 52 years of age, was instantaneous, since his cranium remained completely broken, as well as various fractures in the legs and possibly in the ribs.

The body remained before public view for nearly an hour, as a consequence of the absence of the coroner, who was late in arriving to issue the report according to law.

Many curious ones grouped around the cadaver, which produced the bottling of traffic in that sector.

The pilot, Soto Chiu, was conducted to the first precinct of the National Police, from where he will be consigned to the tribunals of justice—

El Imparcial, July 13, 1963.

Social Life

The elegant Mrs. Victoria V. de Chávez, a lady who is highly esteemed in this society, will be with long tablecloths tomorrow, commemorating her onomastic date. We greet her, wishing that she spend it very happy and that she have many more, surrounded by her loved ones.

In Matrimony. The esteemed young people, Mr. Enrique Sánchez and Miss Elsa Piedad Vásquez, who will fix their residence in New York, united their destinies by means of the sacred matrimonial bonds. We congratulate them, wishing that they be immensely happy in the future.

Sugar Anniversary. Six years of happy entwinement were being celebrated in the warmth of the home by the esteemed couple, Mr. Rodolfo Ramírez and Mrs. Blanca de Ramírez, whom it is pleasing to us to congratulate, hoping that they will always be happy and that they will complete the hundredth anniversary of their union—*El Imparcial, July 15, 1963.*

Fifteen Springs. Today at 11:30 there was celebrated in the Church of San Agustín a mass of Thanksgiving motivated by the fact that the gentle Miss Alma Lucrecia Rosales has completed fifteen years. To attend to ceremony, one was invited by elegant folders by her father, Dr. Fabio A. Rosales M., whom we congratulate for this precious treasure, wishing Alma Lucrecia the realization of her rose-colored dreams.

He would have had a Birthday. One year more of his youthful existence would have been completed tomor-

row by Gustavito Villacorta Cifuentes, who in life had
been a modest person, owner of a brilliant intelligence,
a loving son and a loyal friend. For this reason his in-
consolable parents, lawyer Carlos Villacorta and Mrs.
Mirtala Cifuentes de Villacorta, brothers and sisters and
the rest of the family, have extended invitations to a
requiem Mass which will be offered in the Miraculous
Medallion, the day after tomorrow, beginning at 9
o'clock—*La Hora, July 20, 1963.*

The People of Guatemala

The population of Guatemala, like Ecuador, Peru,
Bolivia, and, to a certain extent, Mexico, is made up of several societies—some might call them castes. One speaks of
the *indios*, the *ladinos*, and the *latinos*. Although they are all
Guatemalan citizens, they represent historically three stages
of Hispanic evolution in the New World: the *indios*, the
early Colonial period of conversion and indoctrination; the
ladinos, the newly independent Guatemala of the nineteenth
century, still on the fringes of the modern world; the *latino*
is the twentieth-century sophisticate who is conversant with
international questions and considerably *agringado*. The
indio and the *ladino* are apparently still struggling to reach
the higher rungs of the ladder. Regionally, the *indio* oc-
cupies the western highlands, the *ladino*, the lowlands and
the eastern part of the Republic. The *latino*, as one might
expect, lives in the large cities, on large estates, or abroad.
One can become a *ladino* by changing clothes, a *latino* by
education or by having the right parents.

The surprise to many outsiders is that these groups are
not aligned politically according to their castes, for among
the common denominators of Hispanic communications systems is a lack of real political conviction on the basis of
tenets or precepts or issues—the alignment seems to be on a
person-to-person basis. Of the 400,000 people in the city of
Guatemala only some 15,000 seem to "really count." These
families know each other quite well and are *au courant* of
national affairs. Most of the others "don't know the score,"
and outside the capital only handfuls of people here and
there know what the issues of Guatemalan affairs are. *Oh
Hispania invertebrada!*

Capsule comments on Hispanic culture

The following comments on Hispanic culture are taken from "It's an Old Spanish Custom," a daily radio series presented by the author over station WBBF, Rochester, New York, in 1962–64.

AMERICA

One of the most popular misconceptions about America among Americans is that we are the only Americans and that Latin Americans are all South Americans. The word *americano*, American, is used by Spaniards for anyone who lives in this hemisphere, North or South. When one says to a Spaniard: *soy americano*, I'm an American, he may ask: *¿De qué país?* From what country? and when one replies: *Estados Unidos*, the United States, he may exclaim: ¡Ah, yanqui! We are actually *norteamericanos*, North Americans, and the people south of the boarder are *hispanoamericanos*, Hispanic Americans.

CASTELLANO

Another of the popular misconceptions among North Americans, especially among Anglo-North Americans, is that the Spanish Americans do not speak Castilian. One often hears their language referred to as Mexican or Puerto Rican, as the case may be, or as a mixture of dialects of some sort. Actually, the Spanish of America is as much Spanish as our language is English. And Spanish is Castilian, because it is the form of Latin that developed in the Province of Castilla in northern Spain. *Hablo castellano*, say many Latin Americans. This may be translated, I speak Spanish, or, I speak Castilian. The same translation would be proper for *Hablo español*.

TELEPHONE

While American telephone conversations are introduced by "hello," and the British ask "are you there?" the Spanish-speaking countries have a variety of ways of opening the conversation. For instance, the Mexican says *bueno*, which means "good," and interestingly enough the man says *bueno* gruffly, while the woman says it with an expectant tone, *¿bueno?* In Spain, one says *diga*, that is, "speak," or "OK, tell me!" In certain of the South American countries, the speaker simply tries to pronounce the English word hello, and it comes out *aló*, and in others, notably Argentina, the word used is a translation of our word hello: *hola*. So, it's *bueno*, *aló*, *hola*, or *diga* to open a Spanish telephone conversation. It's an old Spanish custom.

MAÑANA

We often refer to Spanish America as the "land of *mañana*." The implication is that things are put off until tomorrow. There may be another reason for the comparison. The word *mañana* means not only "tomorrow" but also "morning." So "tomorrow morning" is *mañana por la mañana*, "tomorrow during the morning." Not only this, but *mañana* may also mean "the future"; in this case it is *el mañana* instead of *la mañana*. *Mañana por la mañana hablará del mañana*, "Tomorrow morning he will talk of the future."

PASADO MAÑANA

Since life in the Hispanic countries is somewhat less institutionalized and hurried than in the United States, much more time is spent in discussion of the personal—in small talk about likes and dislikes, impressions of others. One's personal life becomes more important, and the outer world less so. Time is of this outer world. Hence it is that the so-called spirit of *mañana* is not actually a protest against punctuality. It is more a protest of the person against the rigors of group obligation. When you come right down to it, ours is the "land of *mañana*," a march toward tomorrow. Theirs is a dance for today!

FOOD WITH A SPANISH ACCENT

We Americans have many misconceptions regarding foreign foods. One of the most common is the belief that all Spanish-speaking people eat hot, peppery food, and we think in terms of *chile, tamales*, and *enchiladas*. These things are not Spanish but Aztec foods. They were eaten by the Indians long before the Spaniards ever came to America, and their consumption is limited today to Mexico and parts of Central America. *Chile* is an Aztec term meaning "pepper"—the real hot kind. Here in the United States, principally Texas, a concoction of beans and meat with a fairly generous seasoning of *chile* goes by this latter name or chile con carne. When Americans ordered this dish in Mexico, the waiter had to have a border Mexican explain in Spanish what chile con carne was. Interestingly enough, the word *Chile*, referring to the Republic of Chile is from another Indian language and means "chilly" or "cold." So we have the hot pepper of chile con carne and the chilly antarctic breezes of Chile in South America.

FOOD FOR THOUGHT

Many of the food products that are now common all over the world had their origins in Latin America and were first taken to Europe by the Spaniards in the sixteenth century. In Mexico, the Spaniards found what they called *chocolate* from the Aztec *xocolatl*; a fruit called *tómatl* by the Aztecs became *tomate* in Spanish. You may call it "tomayto," "tomahto," "tomaeto." The so-called Irish potato originally came from the Andean region and had been cultivated by the Quechua or Inca Indians for centuries. We call this vegetable either *patata* or *papa* in Spanish. Regardless of how you slice them, *tomates, patatas, chocolate*, it's an old Spanish custom.

MORE FOOD FOR THOUGHT
Although chickens of all sorts came to America from Europe, our main holiday meat dish, the turkey, came from Latin America. The Aztecs domesticated them and called them *huaxólotl*, an attempt to imitate the sound made by the gobbler. Mexicans of today say *guajolote*, while in Central America they are *chompipes*, and *piscos* in Colombia. In Spain and in most countries, thē Latin derivative *pavo* is a common word for turkey. Our ancestors thought they came from Turkey, hence our word for the bird. *Guajolotes* in Mexico, *pavos* in Spain, turkeys to you!

FRUIT FOR THOUGHT
Many of our tropical fruits have come to us from south of the border and the names through Spanish. For instance, what we call an avocado is actually *aguacate* and is from the Aztec Indian language of Mexico. *Ahuácatl* is the Aztec way of saying it. To a Spanish-speaking person, our word sounds like *abogado*, a lawyer. To them, we are slicing up lawyers for the salad. As a matter of fact, in the East, this fruit is called alligator pear. And even alligator is Spanish—the big lizard, *el lagarto*.

ARMS ON THE TABLE
The Hispanic style of eating, which differs considerably from that of the United States, is based on an angle approach, the chair some distance back from the table, the arms resting on the table. The fork is taken in the left hand, where it remains during much of the meal. The knife is used with admirable dexterity in the right hand. With a graceful wrist motion, the food is raised some six inches from the plate, where it is met by the open mouth, the head having been lowered somewhat to make contact. Bites are prepared, fruit peeled, and other difficult tasks performed without releasing the tools.

SOCKS

One time a Mexican came across the border to buy some clothing at a store in Texas. He spoke no English, and the proprietor of the store spoke no Spanish. The Mexican said: *Yo quisiera un par de calcetines,* "I want a pair of socks." The man didn't understand him, so he pulled down this, that, and the other thing from the shelves—shirts, underwear, overalls, etc., finally he came to socks. The Mexican said: *Eso sí que es,* which means "Now you're talking!" The clerk said, "Why didn't you spell it in the first place— S-O-C-K-S?"

BÉISBOL

The matter of baseball brings us into contact with Spanish. Nowadays, it's not only a very popular sport in the Caribbean, and in Mexico and northern South America, but some of our best big leaguers are of Hispanic origin: Carrasquel, Miñoso, Clemente, Pascual, Ramos, Aparicio, Javier, and many others in the big leagues. When they play baseball in Spanish, the terminology is largely English, but with a Spanish pronunciation and Spanish endings. One says *batear,* to bat, and a home run is called a *jonrón,* and you might hear something like this: *bateó un jonrón a los left-field bleachers,* "he hit a home run in the left field bleachers." Baseball is spelled *béisbol;* football, *fútbol;* and basketball, *básquetbol.*

JAI ALAI

One of the most fascinating games in the world is jai alai, also called *pelota* or *frontón.* It is also the fastest game in the world in terms of the speed of the ball: as much as 150 miles per hour. It is played in a three-walled court, nearly 200 feet long and 40 feet wide. The walls are thick stone and the floor is concrete. The player wears a long, curved basket on his right hand, and must catch and throw the ball in this basket, all in one stroke. A miss gives a point to the other side, and the end-score is thirty points or *tantos.* While the fast players rush to cover this long court, the audience bets on the outcome. Bookies shout the odds as the game goes on. While the usual game is a doubles match, there is a singles elimination contest involving six men and called the *quiniela*. Bets are taken in this case on the possible winner-runner-up combination. (Frontenis is a similar game, played by women, with racquets—EDITOR.) The game came from the Basque country, and nearly all professional players are Basques, with such names as Iturbide, Ibarlucea, Gurruceaga, Berrondo.

SUN-SHADE

The bullring in all countries that have bullfights is divided into sun or shadow—*sol o sombra*. The preferred seats are on the shady side, and you pay twice as much to sit in the shade as you do to sit in the sun. In some places they even have a compromise section where the sun shines part of the fight, and where it is shady the rest—*sol y sombra*. Some of the best entertainment at a bullfight comes from the audience, and, while the beautiful clothes and costumes are to be seen on the shady side, the loud wisecracks come from where the sun shines. *Sol o sombra, sombra y sol.* ¡*Olé*!

NO QUEEN

By the way, did you know that the deck of playing cards probably came into Europe through Spain? The Arabs, you know. The Spanish deck still represents the old form of these cards. The suits or *palos* (sticks) are golds (coins), goblets, spades (swords), and clubs. Our word spade comes from the Spanish *espada*. The clubs in the Spanish deck are real clubs. The ace looks like a shillelagh. Aside from this, the king is numbered twelve, the jack is number ten, and there is no woman in the deck. Instead, number eleven is a horse and rider, called *caballo. Oros,* gold coins; *copas,* goblets; *espadas,* swords; *bastos,* clubs. The deck has, therefore, forty-eight cards at the most, and for many Spanish games, the eights and nines are not used, leaving forty.

Our present deck is a continental one, greatly modified by the French, with a pike in place of the sword, but still called a spade, and with three-leaf clovers in place of clubs, but still called clubs, with diamonds in place of goblets, and hearts in place of gold coins.

SEA TALK

Many of the early settlers of Latin America were Spanish sailors from Andalusia. As a result, hundred of Spanish words used in Latin America are maritime terms. In some countries the bus lines are referred to as *flotas*, floats or flotillas, and the drivers as *pilotos*. One may get on a bus by *embarcando*, embarking, and get off by *desembarcando*, disembarking. Even the word to turn around is a seafaring term—*virar*, veer. When one is dizzy, he is *mareado*, literally, seasick, and he may be a long way from the water. In Latin America, to tie is *amarrar*, which originally referred to making ships fast to the dock, and in much of tropical Latin America, to throw out, even though it be the president, is *botar*, to launch into the water.

TEA TALK

In the southern part of South America, there has been a strong English influence over the years. The English helped develop Argentina, and with their exploitation they brought the habit of afternoon tea. To such an extent did tea become popular that the Argentines even referred to the drink itself as five o'clock tea, or simply *faiv ocloc*. There is a restaurant in Buenos Aires that advertises *Five o'clock tea a todas horas*, Five o'clock tea at all hours! *Vamos a tomar el faiv ocloc*, Let's go take some five o'clock. It's an old Argentine custom.

MORNING TALK

Since Spanish has a tendency to be picturesque in expression, the exchange of greetings early in the morning is quite interesting. The most common is *buenos días*, good days, literally. The whole original phrase would be "May God give you good days." In some places, they simply say *buen día*, one day at a time. People also ask: ¿*Descansó*? "Did you rest?" But perhaps the most picturesque is: ¿*Qué tal amaneció*? or "How did you dawn?" According to Américo Castro (*The Structure of Spanish*

History), this is another Semitic concept couched in neo-Latin words.

SHORT TALK

Spanish-speaking people like nicknames. In fact, they have several grades: some that make fun of people, some that are affectionate, and others that are used for nations or nationalities. While we are called *gringos* in some places, they also have names for each other. In Mexico, Spaniards are called *gachupines*, probably a corruption of *capuchín* for the Capuchin monks; in Colombia, *chapetones*; in Cuba, *gallegos*, because most of the late arrivals came from Galicia; and in Chile, *godos* (Goths). Guatemalans are *chapines* to others, *salvadoreños* are *guanacos*, people from Honduras are *catrachos*. Costa Ricans are *ticos*, and Nicaraguans, *Nicas*.

SLANG TALK

Among other popular slang expressions in Spanish are those involving the names of fruits. The head may be a *melón*, *calabaza* (pumpkin), *coco* (coconut, *el piso alto* (the upper story) or *la chocolatera* (the chocolate pot). The heart is a *mango*, but this same juicy tropical fruit can stand for a pretty, attractive young lady. One recalls the election of a university queen in Guatemala, in which one of the candidates was referred to by her male supporters as *un verdadero señor mango*, a real mister mango. A real peach! One might advise: don't lose your coco and fall for one of these mangos! As a matter of fact, a person must be careful of which fruit he mentions where. *Papaya* is taboo in most of Cuba, since it is reserved for certain anatomical allusions.

MORE SLANG

Like English, Spanish has many slang expressions. They are usually in the area of euphemisms, or softened statements to make things seem not quite so bad as they really are. For instance, a long slim fellow, "a string bean," might be called *de largo viaje*, a long trip. To stab someone might be expressed as *medirle el aceite*, to measure his oil. The jail is often called *el pulguero*, the flea bag. And one of the favorite requests one hears in Spain is *dame un pitillo, pollo*, give me a little whistle, chicken, or, give me a cigarette, buddy. While *doblar la esquina*, to turn the corner, may be like our "to pass on," *soltar la sin hueso*, to let loose the boneless (the tongue), may mean to start talking.

DOG TALK

It is interesting to note that even the noises made by various animals apparently differ from country to country according to the language spoken where the animal lives. Thus a French dog says *graff, graff*, and English or American dogs say bowwow, and a Spanish dog says *guau, guau*. By the same token, an American cat mews, and a Spanish cat says *miau*. The sounds made by humans in calling animals also vary. We call dogs by whistling or using the word *here* with the dog's name. The Spanish method is to say *toma, toma*, take, take, as if they had something to offer. We call cats by saying "kitty, kitty, kitty," the *t* pronounced as a flapped *r*, and the British use "kitty, kitty, kitty," with *t* as such, but the Spanish-speaking person says *ps-ps-ps* or *mis-mis-mis*, or a variant thereof.

BLONDE TALK

Like many other commonly used terms, the word for blond varies from country to country in Latin America. They compare these rather rare creatures to all sorts of things. In Colombia they are called *monos*, monkeys; in Mexico, the word is *huero*, the color of a bad egg. In Guatemala the word is *canche*; in El Salvador, it is *chele*; in Venezuela, *catire*; while in Spain, *rubio*, a word understood by the educated everywhere. In Costa Rica, the word is *macho*, male, a reminder of the many big, blond American men who have been in the area. The blonde in Costa Rica, strangely, is a *macha*, literally a feminine male!

BUMPER TALK

Among other picturesque customs of Spanish-speaking countries is that of naming trucks and buses for girl friends of the drivers. Throughout Central and South America, one sees flashy signs painted or printed on the bumpers, both front and rear, indicating admiration for María, Dolores, Concha, Margarita, or Carmen. Along with this goes the tendency to use the bumpers for wisecracks about the charms of certain *señoritas,* and this is where the Spanish-speaking person has great imagination. *Mírame, chata.* ¡*Yo te hago más chata*! "Look at me, Flat-nose. You'll be even flatter when I hit you!"

ARE YOU PROVOKED?

Spanish is one language, the descendant of one Latin manifestation, Castilian; but there are dialectal differences among the twenty countries of Spanish speech. Just as a word that is used in England may have an entirely different meaning in the United States, so it is that a very polite invitation in Colombia for instance, may sound slightly ridiculous in Spain. A Colombian who invites you to have a cup of coffee with him will say: ¿*Le provoca un tinto*? Would "a dark one" tempt you? To a Spaniard, this would mean: "Does red wine make you want to fight?" By the same token, a Mexican refers to the shower bath as a *regadera,* while to a Spaniard the term means a watering can or sprinkler.

ELEVENS TALK

An interesting expression is that employed in several places in Latin America for what we might call a snack or a coffee break. They say *tomar las onces,* to take the elevens. One explanation is that this was first done at about eleven in the morning, since the midday meal tends to be scheduled at one or two. Another is that it is a euphemism for going to get a drink, and that the word *aguardiente,* brandy, has eleven letters. *Vamos a tomar las onces.* It's an old Spanish custom.

COCKTAIL

Did you know that some of our old soft-drink terms are from Spanish? Sarsaparilla and sassafras, for instance, are both of Spanish origin, along with the word or concept of the cocktail. This latter is apparently a translation of *cola de gallo*, which was used in the Yucatan peninsula back in the Colonial period for a drink of rum mixed with sugarcane syrup, which concoction was subsequently stirred with a root which resembled the tail of a rooster, hence, cocktail. And even the word sherry comes from *Xerez*, now *Jerez*, in southern Spain. The English evidently thought it was a plural, so they knocked off the final sibilant: sherris, sherry. Spanish *x* was pronounced as a palatal sibilant, similar to the sound represented by *sh* in English.

COCKROACH

Captain John Smith in one of his letters, published by the Hackluyt Society and also quoted by A. L. Mencken in *The American Language*, refers to an insect which was bothersome in some parts of the new American colonies, the cockroach. Apparently he had heard the word first from the Spanish as *cucaracha*. He thought he heard *cacarooch*, and so named the India bug, as he called it. Centuries later the rebel army of Pancho Villa started a satirical song known as *La cucaracha*, sung to this day by students of Spanish, if by no one else.

GRINGO

We are often referred to as *gringos* in Mexico and in most of Central and South America. The word was thought to have come from the song, "Green Grow the Rushes," sung by American troops in the 1846–48 invasion of Mexico. Investigation has shown that *gringo* was used for English and Scotch and other foreigners before the Mexicans had ever heard the song. The *Facundo*, written by the Argentine statesman Domingo Faustino Sarmiento before 1845, refers to Sir Walter Scott as a *gringo*. It is probably a corruption of *griego*, Greek. The language we speak is "Greek to them." Interestingly enough, the Italian is the *gringo* in modern Argentina.

COCA COLA

The trade name Coca Cola has two Spanish components: *coca* and *cola*. *Coca* really means cocaine, but the product has none, as far as is known. And *cola* is a tail; *coca cola,* cocaine tail. In Bogotá, Colombia, the young male teenagers are called *cocacolos,* the girls *cocanitas,* and in parts of Mexico, one may order a coke by first pointing to his *coco* and then to his *cola.*

METAPHORICALLY SPEAKING

Spanish is one of the most picturesque of languages in the use of the metaphor. They delight in speaking of one thing in terms of another. The common word for head is *cabeza,* but it is often referred to as *coco* (cocoanut), *calabaza* (squash or pumpkin), or *casco* (shell). Not only this, but a person who has curly hair may be called a *tirabuzón* (corkscrew) or *colocho* (woodshavings). A man who is becoming gray may be a *tecolote* (owl) in Mexico or Central America. So, take care of that *coco colocho,* especially if you are a *tecolote!*

COUNTDOWN IN THE CANEBRAKE

One of the Spanish place-names that is very much in the news, these days, is Cape Canaveral (now Cape Kennedy), Florida. As a matter of fact, both *Cañaveral* and *Florida* are Spanish words. The state derived its name from the words *Pascua florida,* meaning "flowery Easter." The name of the cape in Spanish, means "sugarcane field": *caña* is sugarcane; *veral* indicates the place where it grows. One might say that the stalks that the Spaniards planted to point heavenward have been replaced by the Atlas, Titan, and Mercury. And in the flowery land of yore, we now have a countdown in the canebrake.

KEY WEST AND AROUND THE HORN

Many original Spanish geographical terms have been misunderstood by English-speaking people. What was Cayo Hueso, Bone Key, became Key West because of the sound of *Hueso* (wesso). The *Cabo de Hornos* (Cape of Ovens), on the southern tip of South America, was thought to look and sound something like "horn," hence Cape Horn. Apparently the shape of the tip had more influence than the association with *Tierra del*

Fuego, Land of Fire.

NAME YOUR STATE

Many of our Western states, as well as some of the Southern ones, have Spanish names. For instance, California may be a corruption of two Latin words, *calida fornax*, hot furnace. Apparently the Spaniards first entered that region through the Imperial Valley. On the other hand, *California* appears in one of the romances of chivalry as a legendary island. Arizona is apparently a corruption of *árida zona*, arid zone, although there are those who believe it to refer to the Arizes, Indians of Northern Mexico; and Colorado simply means "red" in Spanish. Nevada means "covered with snow," and Oregon, one of the most interesting, could be "big ear," *orejón*. The Indians of that region, *los Orejones*, apparently had big ears! By permutation, the word also refers to a spur.

SEE YOU 'ROUND

Nowadays even English-speaking Americans say *hasta mañana* or *hasta la vista*, *hasta luego*, and so on. These are very common expressions in the Spanish language. The word *hasta* means "until," and, of course, *mañana* means "tomorrow." So, *hasta mañana* is literally until tomorrow. But they use the word *hasta*, as indicated, with other expressions, such as *la vista*, which means "the sight." *Hasta la vista* would then mean "until we see each other." This is very much like the German *auf wiedersehen* or the French *au revoir*. But the Spanish also use it with *luego* which means "then," *Hasta luego*, until then. *Hasta mañana, hasta la vista, hasta luego*. Any way you hear it, it's "so long," and it's an old Spanish custom!

FORTY WINKS, A SIXTH

In many regions where Spanish is spoken, one indulges in what one calls the *siesta*. The *siesta* usually comes after lunch and is a period set aside for a nap, or, at least it used to be. Nowadays, of course, most people are too busy to nap, so they just sit around and talk. Talking is important! It is to be noted that the word *siesta* comes from the Latin *sexta* which means "sixth," the sixth hour of the day. They used to start counting the hours at six o'clock in the morning, so by noon they were ready for a *siesta*. With the tendency toward procrastination which we find in some Spanish-speaking countries, the *siesta* now begins anywhere from one to three in the afternoon, but business hours run later than we're used to. The *siesta*, an afternoon nap, is still an old Spanish custom.

THE GIRLS BY ANY OTHER NAME

Have you noticed how many girls' names, in Spanish-speaking countries end in *o* and therefore seem to look like men's names? For instance, they have such names as *Consuelo* (Consolation), *Amparo* (Shelter), and *Socorro* (Help). The reason for this is that most women are named *María*, and they simply add one of the appellations of the Virgin Mary: *María del Consuelo, María del Amparo, María del Socorro*. Thus they are called by this second name. *Consuelo, Amparo, Socorro*, they are all Marías; it's an old Spanish custom.

WEIGHTS AND MEASURES

We often forget that we are one of the few nations that does not use the metric system. In Spain, and in most of Latin America, one weighs himself in *kilos*, he buys his milk and gasoline in *litros*, and he breaks the speed limit in *kilómetros por hora*. He may drive his car into a gas station and ask a man to "throw him forty," *écheme cuarenta*. The American tourist who drives his car over the Pan American Highway has to remember that the sign which reads "Speed limit 100" means that the speed limit is 62 miles per hour. *Kilos, litros, kilómetros*—as long as you stay in the metric system!

LUPE

Have you ever noticed how many of the people of Mexico have the name Lupe? Even men bear the name Lupe, which turns out to be a nickname for Guadelupe, the patron saint of not only Mexico but Latin America. The Virgin of Guadalupe was the symbol of Mexican nationality and independence from Spain. The word actually came from southern Spain and is made up of a combination of Arabic and Latin. *Wadi* was the Arabic word for river or valley, and *lupus* was "wolf" in Latin. The extent to which the Spaniards carried such terms to the far corners of the world in the sixteenth century is shown by Guadalcanal out in the Pacific, which also came from southern Spain and is Arabic. Guadalupe, Guadalcanal, and Guadalajara. East meets West, south of the border.

CHAU TO YOU, TOO

It would be rather safe to prophesy that within a few years we Americans will be using a new slang expression for good-bye. It will be *chau* (spelled *chau* in Spanish and *ciao* in Italian): ¡*Chau*! *chau*! The word came from Italy to Argentina, along with the heavy immigration of the early part of this century, and is probably a corruption of *schiavo* meaning "slave." Greetings from one slave to another, and back to the salt mines! From Argentina it is now spreading northward through Bolivia, Perú, and Ecuador to Panamá. It won't be long! *Chau* for now!

ENGLIS IS ESPOK

It is interesting to see how English affects the Spanish of our neighbors, Puerto Rico, Cuba, and Mexico. One hears *nicle*, *daime* (dime), *taira* (tire), *troka* (truck), and similar expressions, like *jot queques* (hot cakes), and one may find on a menu *waffles con maple*. But one of the best hybrids of Spanish-English crossing is the word used by Mexican laborers to mean "look out!" Normally, this would be ¡*cuidado, hombre*! but many will say ¡*wátchele*! from the English "watch" and the Spanish pronoun *le* (it): Watch it! ¡*Wátchele, hombre*!

EXCUSE PLIZ

There are several ways of saying "excuse me" or "pardon me" in Spanish, depending on the situation. For instance, if one passes in front of someone, he says *con permiso*, with your permission. He would also use this on taking leave of others. But if one steps on somebody's toe, he doesn't say *con permiso*, with your permission! He simply waits until the person says ¡*ay!* (ouch!) and then says *perdóneme* or *dispénseme*, the latter meaning literally "unthink it of me, please!" *Con permiso.* ¡*Ay, ay, ay!*

ONWARD AND UPWARD

Did you ever live where the first floor is the fourth, and where there may be two main floors between the ground floor and the first? In Spain and to some extent in Latin America, the street level is the *piso bajo*, the lower or ground floor; then comes main floor A (*piso principal A*); followed by main floor B (*piso principal B*); and then the *primer piso*. In a building without an elevator, it turns out to be quite a walk to the first floor!

HOUSE YOURSELF, MAN

The home and the family are important centers of Hispanic life, and the terms relating to marriage are derived from the word *casa*, house. To marry is *casarse con alguien*, to house yourself with someone. *Juan se casa con María*, John marries Mary. *Se casan*, they are housing themselves, or, they are getting married. *Están casados*, they are already housed. In other words, they are in a state of marriage. When the minister or priest marries a couple, he houses them: *los casa. Juan se casa con María, María se casa con Juan. El cura los casa.* It's an old Spanish custom.

HUH?

Most languages have very common and popular ways of saying "isn't that so?" or "huh?" Germans say *nicht wahr?* and the French, *n'est-ce pas?* "Isn't it true?"—Spanish says ¿*no es verdad?* or ¿*verdad?* and need the upside-down question mark preceding the question when written. For more popular circumstances, they say *no?* or *eh?* And one's Spanish dialect can often be spotted by his intonation in this word, *eh?* Those of the Caribbean say *ah?*; the Mexicans *eh?* with nasalization; the Spaniard *eh?* without nasalization. But some Colombians, in order to be on the safe side, say *sí, no?* Yes, no?

WATCH YOUR LANGUAGE

Although it is considered vulgar and even sacrilegious in English to refer to the Deity in exclamations, this is not true in many of the Mediterranean countries. When a Spaniard or Latin American says *Dios mío*, the force or intent is no stronger than goodness gracious or heavens to Betsy. The words *Cristo* and *Jesús* are used with semireligious fervor, especially by women, and might be compared to gosh or gee. As a matter of fact, the name Jesus (*Jesús*) is given to boys, and there is even a nickname for those so called: *Chus* or *Chucho*. We are often reminded of the Spanish professor who was embarrassed by the necessity of translating *Dios mío* in class and came up with, "Oh, scissors!"

HOW ARABIC

During the long Arabic occupation of Spain —from the eighth century to the fifteenth—there were many Semitic influences that were later to be noted there and in other European countries. Hundreds of Arabic words came into Spanish, and many of them later found their way into English by way of French. The check that you write for a jewel of so many carats, your alcohol, your algebra, your sugar, much of your spice and other things nice: *cheque, quilate, alcohol, algebra, azúcar*.

AT THE BARS

What is commonly called a *balcón*, a balcony, is not necessarily on the second floor. The most popular balcony is on the ground floor and consists of a barred window where the boy friend can talk to the girl friend on her own level. The act of talking through the bars is known as *mascando hierro*, chewing iron, and it has also been called playing the bear. From the point of view of the girl's father, the fellow looks like a bear pacing back and forth in his cage. And the boy friend has to *mascar hierro* until his intentions are recognized as serious, and he is admitted to the house.

HOW MUCH?

In the markets of all Spanish-speaking countries, bargaining is the order of the day. As a matter of fact, it is so much a part of the social and commercial scene that a vendor may be disappointed if he can't haggle for a while. *¿Cuánto es?* How much is it? *¿Cuánto vale?* How much is it worth? *¿A cómo se vende?* At what price is it sold? Both the buyer and the vendor use the diminutives and other softening devices to get the best of the other fellow. *¿Cuánto vale este huevito?* How much is this little egg worth? *Vale un pesito.* It costs only a little *peso.*

CASH

To pay cash is desirable, and to pay it on the barrelhead is even more so. The Spanish language has several grades of strictness indicated in the concept of each type of payment. *En efectivo* (in effective currency, so to speak) means "it is not on credit." *Al contado,* cash in hand, indicates that you can count it, while *al contado contante y sonante* means that you can not only count it, but you are counting it and you can hear it ring! So the grades are *en efectivo, al contado* and *al contado contante y sonante.* Strict cash on the barrel head!

ALL SET?

There is a very handy word in Spanish to give the idea of a set—a tea set, for instance—or a match, such as a tennis match, or a suite of furniture. This is the word for game, *juego. Un juego de te,* a tea set; *un juego de tenis,* a tennis match; *un juego de muebles,* a suite of furniture. As a matter of fact, they even form a verb phrase to mean "to match": the pants match the coat, *los pantalones hacen juego con el saco.* So we have a *juego de béisbol, juego de fútbol, juego de te* and *juegos* all over the house!

SEMANTICS

People get into all sorts of trouble by translating literally from one language to another. There are many false cognates and deceptive "equivalents." The word *anticipación* looks and sounds something like our anticipation but it simply means "in advance." On a bus you may see a sign: *pida usted su parada con anticipación,* signal your stop in advance. It doesn't mean that you indicate it with fond hopes of getting off. By the same token, *asistir* means "to attend," not to assist, and *atender* means "to help," to attend to. *Asisto a la clase,* I attend the class. *Atiende a la señora,* he waits on the lady.

INDIAN LORE

Among the many Indian words introduced into English from Spanish is *jaguar.* It came from northern Argentina and Paraguay and the Guaraní Indian language, and it refers to a low-slung, sleek and slinky animal and hence to an automobile of the same general characteristics. From another Indian language of South America, the Quechua or Inca, as we call it, we get the word *poncho,* usually pronounced by Americans "pancho." So the next time you put on your *poncho* and step into your Jaguar, think of South America!

TWO IN ONE

Perhaps the most interesting case of extensive bilingualism in the world is that of Paraguay. Nearly all people of this South American country speak both Spanish and in Indian language called Guaraní. Guaraní was spoken there before the Spaniards came in the sixteenth century. Later on, missions were started by the Jesuits, who were in turn driven out, the Indians reverting to type, to some extent. Today, a Paraguayan politician may start a speech in Spanish and finish in Guaraní—and nobody bats an eye. It is to be noted that Spanish is the prestige language, however, and is always used to supply communication needs at technological levels, unless, of course, the Paraguayan knows English.

THROW ME ANOTHER

Spanish turns out to be one of the most idiomatic of our modern languages because of the popular origins of a great deal of the culture. Proverbs and idioms of all types have an important role in the language. One of the most used of all words in idiomatic expressions is *echar*. It means literally "to throw." But you throw a letter when you mail it. You throw salt in your recipe, and you throw yourself to bed when you are tired. And most picturesque of all, when you go all out to entertain someone, you throw the house out the window, *echar la casa por la ventana*.

BACK ON THE RANCH
Along with the many Spanish words that have come into English from our Mexican Southwest are the words cinch and sombrero. Cinch is from the Spanish *cincha*, the strap that holds the saddle on the horse. It is tight and firm, secure, so it's a cinch! The sombrero is from the word meaning "shade." It's a "shader" and the man who sells *sombreros* is a *sombrerero*, a hatter. Captain John Smith referred to the Spanish-type hat of his day as "like a great cartwheel" (the first instance of this usage in English); the word has become the usual one for hat in Spanish, even for the very small ones women sometimes wear. Put on your sombrero; it's a cinch.

Then there is the hoosegow, from Spanish *juzgado* (a court of first instance, jail nearby), and many other terms used in the Southwest and in much of America. You may use a lariat, *la reata*, to *corral* somebody, and the ten-gallon hat may have gotten its name from the Spanish *galón*, a ribbon or braid, rather than from the reference to liquid capacity.

EARLY BIRD
One of the most interesting of the old Spanish customs is the *serenata*, or serenade. The *serenata* to the girl friend is usually given early in the morning, when all the family is home to appreciate it. Since the hour is predawn, they often refer to it as a *gallo*, or rooster. Along with automation and technology, it is now the custom to hire a whole orchestra to give the *gallo*, instead of the old situation of the dark-haired girl on the balcony and the boy with his red sash, playing the guitar down below.

Watch out for these *gallos* and *balcones*.

JUST WALKING AROUND

The late afternoon is the time for the *paseo* in most Spanish-speaking countries. This is the stroll, either around a public square, or plaza, or up and down a special street where traffic has been blocked off for the purpose. While the band plays, the boys walk clockwise, and the girls counterclockwise. So everybody gets a chance to look over everybody else. In Burgos, Spain, a certain street is dedicated to this; in Buenos Aires, it is Florida Avenue; in Bogotá, Seventh Avenue; and in Monterrey, Mexico, the public square. Small towns of the Hispanic world look forward to the *paseo*, an old Spanish custom.

WATCH YOUR R'S

It has been shown that one of the greatest difficulties the American who learns another language has is getting rid of his peculiar *r* and *l*. A device that often works in teaching the American to pronounce the *r* of Spanish is to have him say his own *tt* or *dd* within a word, rapidly: Betty, butter, muddy. Spanish *para ti* is almost the same as "pot o' tea" said rapidly. Even the double *rr* of Spanish is sometimes said in rapid speech: "Put it over there!" "Get it out of there!"

SPANISH DANCE

Some of the well-known types of popular music and dance steps of our time are of Hispanic origin. The famous *jotas* that one associates with a bullfight are from Spain. So are the *flamenco* and *fandango*. ¡Olé! The tango is from Argentina, and our recently revived popular "Three O'Clock in the Morning" was first played and sung in Argentina. Mexico has given us the ranch-type music, with its cowpuncher yells. The *congo, rumba, samba, huaracha, bossa nova,* and others of this ilk are actually Afro-Cuban or Brazilian and have much of West African in them.

IT'S PROVERBIAL

Among the many picturesque proverbs and sayings of the Spanish language are these two which have to do with warnings for the future. *Antes que te cases, mira lo que haces.* Before you marry, look to what you are doing. And then, *Si a Roma fueres, haz como vieres.* If you go to Rome, do as you see. As we say, "When in Rome, do as the Romans." You might add to these the advice, *a quien madruga, Dios le ayuda,* "God helps him who gets up early."

MORE PROVERBS

Spanish has a very picturesque way of giving advice through proverbs. There is one, for instance, that speaks of hunger as the best sauce: *la mejor salsa es el hambre.* Then there is the question of money: *poderoso caballero es don dinero,* Mr. Money is a powerful gentleman. To correspond to our "Rome was not built in a day," one says *No se ganó Zamora en una hora,* Zamora wasn't taken in an hour. As a matter of fact this Spanish town was besieged for seven years!

PROVERBS AGAIN

Two very interesting proverb admonitions of the Spanish language are related to the mouth. One says, *de la mano a la boca se pierde la sopa,* from the hand to the mouth the soup is lost, or "there's many a slip 'twixt the cup and the lip." The other warns that you should keep your mouth closed to stay out of trouble: *En boca cerrada no entran moscas,* flies do not enter a closed mouth.

AND AGAIN

One of the common proverbs of most languages is the one about the bird in the hand. While we say, "a bird in the hand is worth two in the bush," the Spanish, with more of a tendency to exaggerate, say *pájaro en mano vale cien volando,* a bird in the hand is worth a hundred flying. Then, there is the one about the jack of all trades. Spanish expresses this idea very simply: *Zapatero, a tus zapatos,* shoemaker, (stick) to your shoes! Don't try to do things for which you are not prepared!

IT'S ANOTHER PROVERB

The concept of looking out for yourself first is said in Spanish in a rather picturesque way: *Antes son mis dientes que mis parientes*, my teeth come before my relatives! Also quite picturesque is their idea that if clothes make the man, makeup makes the woman: *Compuesta no hay mujer fea*, there is no ugly woman with makeup on. From the vast storehouse of Spanish proverbs, here are a couple that resemble in intent some of our own: *Ninguno que beha vino llame borracho a su vecino*, let no one who drinks wine call his neighbor a drunk. The pot may be calling the kettle black. The second is: *lo que de prisa se hace, despacio se llora*. That which is done hastily is wept over slowly. Haste makes waste.

PROVERBIALLY SPEAKING

From this almost inexhaustible collection there come these samplings: *No te cases con mujer que te gane en el saber*, don't marry a woman who is ahead of you in knowledge. *Tío rico siempre tiene muchos sobrinos*, a rich uncle always has lots of nephews. The dollar makes 'em holler, one might say. Or, this other: *cuando está abierto el cajón, el más honrado es ladrón*, when the drawer is open, even the most honorable is a robber. We're all subject to temptation. Or, this one: *entre dos perros amigos eche un hueso, y verás enemigos*, throw a bone to two friendly dogs and you have two enemies.

JIPI

What we call a Panama hat does not come from Panama. It comes from Ecuador. The hat is made at a place called Jipijapa from the leaves of a special palm tree, and the hat itself is a *jipijapa* in Spanish. It is said that the weaving is done at a certain time of day when the humidity is just right. Although this is one of the principal industries of Ecuador, these *sombreros* are known in this country by the name of an important free port, Panama. *Un sombrero de jipijapa*, a Panama hat.

SEGÚN

One of the handiest words of Spanish is *según,* which means "it all depends." If one can't think of the proper answer to a question, he replies *según.* They tell of an American who had bought one of these little books, Spanish in eight days. He memorized the booklet and later had occasion to visit a Spanish-speaking country, where the natives talked to him in English. But as he thanked them for their fine attentions, he wished to exhibit his knowledge of Spanish, so he mustered up courage to say, with a strong American-English accent: "Muchas, grashas, señors, señoras, o señoritas, según el caso" (as the case may be). Just as the book had it!

COMRADE TALK

The Cuban crisis and Castro's propaganda messages have brought to our attention that members of his regime have begun to call each other *camarada,* comrade, in typical Communist fashion. Raúl Castro and *camarada* Jiménez made a trip to Moscow to arrange for armaments, says a recent edition of *La Revolución.* Although the word has not been used much until recently in Cuba, comrade is actually of Spanish origin. It comes from *cámara,* a chamber or bedroom, so a comrade turns out to be a roommate. From the Spanish *camarada* to the French *camerade* and the German *Kamerad,* used much during the First World War, we finally return to *camarada* Fidel Castro.

CHECK

The game of chess is undoubtedly of Arabic (or Eastern) origin, along with many other pastimes. Some of the terms of chess, which the Arabs introduced to Spain, have spread from there to other European languages. Checkmate is from *xaque mate,* the king is dead; in modern Spanish, *jaque mate.* In fact, the word *mate* means "kill" and *xaque* derives from the Persian *Shah.* The word check survives in other senses too. While the castles are called *torres* in Spanish, the pawns are *peones.* In fact, our word pawn is a corruption of the word *peon* from the Latin *pedonem,* one who walks instead of riding a horse. The knights are *caballos*, horses, as, in fact, the pieces are.

AY! AY! OUCH!

One of the most interesting things from nation to nation, and from culture to culture is the exclamation, or the way of saying Oh, or Ouch, or Hey, you, or Look out. Where we say Oh, the Spanish-speaking person would say *ah*, and where we say Ouch, he says *ay*, and this *ay* varies from person to person, from male to female, and from circumstance to circumstance. Where we use hey, Spanish speakers may hiss at the person whose attention they are trying to attract.

WHAT'S IN A PRONOUN?

The grammar of a language normally reflects the psychology of the people who speak it. For instance, in Spanish one does not ordinarily say, "I dropped it," but rather, "it dropped and I was involved"— *se me cayó* (it fell to me). One does not say "I forget" or "I forgot," but "it is forgotten and I am involved," *se me olvida*. This concept is rendered by the indirect object pronoun and the device is used a great deal in Spanish. A storekeeper may say, when asked if he has a particular product: *Se me acabó*, it finished itself on me. The language is Latin in origin, the concept is Eastern.

WHAT'S IN A NAME?

Spanish names are so complicated to English-speaking people that not long ago a man wrote a book to show librarians how to catalog books by Spanish and Latin-American authors. The reason for this is that it's an old Spanish custom to use not only the father's name but the mother's maiden name. First comes the given name then comes the father's name, and then the mother's maiden name. But one is not called by his mother's family name although it does come last. As an example, the well-known Spanish author Vicente Blasco Ibáñez, the writer of *Blood and Sand* and *The Four Horsemen of the Apocalypse*, Vicente to his intimate friends (Vincent): his father's family name was Blasco, so he is Mr. Blasco; his mother's family name was Ibáñez. He should be called either Mr. Blasco or Mr. Blasco Ibáñez, not Mr. Ibáñez. Vincente Blasco Ibáñez: baptism, papa, and mama—but all one person. It's an old Spanish custom.